SECRETS OF

Backyard
Bird-Feeding
SUCCESS

SECRETS OF

Backyard
Bird-Feeding
SUCCESS

Hundreds of Surefire Tips for
Attracting and Feeding Your Favorite Birds

DEBORAH L. MARTIN

with Arlene Koch

RODALE.

Direct and trade editions are being simultaneously published in August 2011.

Internet addresses and telephone numbers given in this book were accurate at the time it went to press.

Rodale books may be purchased for business or promotional use or for special sales. For information, please write to:

Special Markets Department, Rodale Inc., 733 Third Avenue, New York, NY 10017

Printed in the United States of America

Rodale Inc. makes every effort to use acid-free ♾, recycled paper ♻.

Bird illustration (page 13) © Denis Barbulat/Shutterstock; vintage bird frame (page 10) © Little Rambo/Shutterstock; illustrations (pages 62, 70, and 143) © Ralph Voltz

Photo credits appear on page 288.

Book design by Christopher Rhoads

Library of Congress Cataloging-in-Publication Data

Martin, Deborah L.
    Secrets of backyard bird-feeding success : hundreds of surefire tips for attracting and feeding your favorite birds / Deborah L. Martin with Arlene Koch.
        p.   cm.
    Includes bibliographical references and index.
    ISBN 978–1–60529–131–4 direct hardcover
    ISBN 978–1–60529–130–7 trade paperback
    1. Bird attracting.   2. Bird feeders.   I. Koch, Arlene.   II. Title.
    QL676.5.M3349   2011
    598.072'34–dc22   2011009424

Distributed to the trade by Macmillan

2   4   6   8   10   9   7   5   3   1   direct hardcover
2   4   6   8   10   9   7   5   3   1   trade paperback

We inspire and enable people to improve their lives and the world around them.
www.rodalebooks.com

For Bob, Sam, and Ben:
You are my wings.

contents

----

introduction ***Why Feed Birds?*** ix

one ***Plan a Menu Birds Will Love*** 1

two ***Seeds and Seed Mixes*** 17

three ***Suet, Peanut Butter, and More*** 45

four ***Nectar for Hummingbirds and Others*** 65

five ***Berries and Fruit to Bring in the Birds*** 81

six ***Creepy-Crawly Treats*** 99

seven ***Kitchen Castoffs and Home Cooking*** 111

eight ***Feeding Station Features*** 129

nine ***Bird Favorites for Your Garden*** 155

ten ***Birds at the Buffet*** 179

resources 286
photo credits 288
about the writers 289
bird-feeding friends who shared their thoughts 290
acknowledgments 291
index 292
USDA plant hardiness zones map 304

Female ruby-throated hummingbirds at a nectar feeder

Why Feed Birds?

On almost any day, at times when the house is quiet, I can hear the sounds of birds outside my windows. When the windows are open, I may awaken to the songs and calls of finches, chickadees, sparrows, cardinals, catbirds, and warblers—or to the raucous caws of crows. While working in my garden, I can hear the rustling of thrushes hunting for insects in dry leaves at the edge of the yard. If the songbirds go quiet, I know there's a reason—red-tailed hawks have a nest nearby, and I often hear their fierce screams. Elegant kestrels also drop by from time to time, putting a damper on the activity at my feeders, but giving me a chance to appreciate their beauty up close.

Birds pack the perches at feeders in winter, when natural foods are scarce.

I've also been awakened in the night by a disturbance among the birds that roost in the branches of the Douglas fir outside my bedroom window. I've stood in the chill from an open window in late winter to hear great horned owls calling in the darkness, and I've listened to the sounds of migrating birds, unseen as they travel high overhead through the dark sky.

After nearly 20 years in this house near Allentown, Pennsylvania, I still get a thrill from the sights and sounds of the dozens of wild bird species that appear just outside my windows. And, as much as my human neighbors and I do to invite the birds into "our" landscapes, I often feel that the birds are the real landlords who are graciously sharing their homes with us. This is despite the fact that we humans are not always the most courteous of neighbors to the wildlife around us. We operate noisy, polluting machines. We harbor well-fed pets that hunt wild birds for sport. And we cultivate vast areas of turf that offer birds neither food nor shelter.

From that perspective, it seems only fair to make some effort to repay the birds for the pleasures they've given me. By keeping a few feeders filled with sunflower and other favored seeds, by serving suet, and by providing fresh water, I can attract a few types of birds to visit my yard. By replacing some of the lawn with native trees and shrubs, I can create a habitat that invites those birds and many others to build nests and raise their young here. When I think about the enjoyment I get from watching the birds each and every day, these efforts seem a small price to pay.

Granted, it's easy enough to think of reasons to *not* feed the birds. Just for starters, keeping feeders filled costs money and takes time—two things that most people never seem to have enough of. If you factor in routine cleaning and maintenance of feeders and perhaps a birdbath or two, along with noisy birds, greedy squirrels, and messy shells, the balance sheet quickly can add up against this popular hobby.

Yet bird feeding is widely popular. In spite of the dollars-and-cents reasons against it, bird feeding attracts new participants each year. In the US Fish and Wildlife Service 1996 Survey of Fishing, Hunting,

"I grew up in suburban Philadelphia. We walked everywhere, because we didn't own a car. During our walks, my mother taught me to listen to and identify birds' songs. I then moved to New York for college and for 3 years I saw and heard only pigeons. When I married and moved to Bethlehem, we built a house in the woods. Once again, I began to observe and listen for the birds. My husband bought me Peterson's Field Guide for Eastern Birds *and tapes of birdcalls. I have many happy memories of sitting at my kitchen table looking at the plethora of birds who visit my backyard feeders, suet, and hummingbird feeders. During hikes with my family and dogs, we enjoy birds' vocalizations. Identification of a new bird is an exciting event for us."*

DEBBIE GOLDSTEIN, Bethlehem, Pennsylvania

and Wildlife-Associated Recreation, more than 52 million people reported that they offered food to wild birds at least part of the year. According to the survey, spending on food for birds exceeded $2.7 billion; expenditures on feeders, birdbaths, houses, and nest boxes were an additional $832 million. In 2006, the number of people feeding birds surpassed 53 million, according to US Fish and Wildlife statistics, and spending on food for birds topped $3.3 billion.

When asked why they feed birds, people give reasons ranging from their own pleasure and relaxation, to landscape enhancement and beautification, to a desire to help birds survive. People's reasons for bird feeding are diverse, but here are a few of the most common responses given when people describe why they feed birds.

Simplify winter bird feeding by choosing feeders that are easy to open and refill even with gloved hands. Use a bucket that holds a few pounds of seeds instead of lugging an unwieldy 25- or 50-pound bag.

Entertainment

Comedy, drama, intrigue, athleticism—turn your favorite chair away from the television and point it in the direction of a well-stocked feeding station. Watch the power struggles between birds vying for perch space at a feeder. Laugh at the antics of squirrels trying to circumvent barriers between them and a feeder filled with sunflower seed. Boo when a bullying jay drives other birds away from the food, then cheer when finches and chickadees feast at a tube feeder with perches too small for the jay to use. Who needs cable when there's so much going on right outside the window?

Education

Never have children been so separated from the natural world as they are now, and never has the natural world needed them more. In his 2005 book, *Last Child in the Woods*, author Richard Louv asks the question, "Where will future stewards of nature come from?" It's hard to imagine now, when most children recognize dozens of characters in television and video games but almost none of the native species of birds and trees in their own neighborhoods.

With a single bird feeder, a child may be

introduced to a few local bird species. These can be counted as part of a basic math lesson or, better yet, for the population science of national bird counts coordinated by the Audubon Society or the Cornell Lab of Ornithology. A child who engages at this level may then go on to build birdhouses (gaining measuring and carpentry skills) and provide nesting materials (learning about birds' reproductive behaviors and parenting strategies). A child who does not know what a bluebird looks like is unlikely to grow into an adult who understands the value of preserving habitat so that bluebirds continue to exist, even though that child may have learned in school about endangered species, such as tigers and elephants, on distant continents.

Relaxation

Counteract a frazzled hour sitting in heavy traffic with an equal portion of quiet contemplation watching birds at a feeder or a water source. The day's minor annoyances will quickly fade when you marvel at the ferocity of a male hummingbird defending "his" nectar feeder. Forget the person who cut you off on the highway or the long line at the market—the birds that are busily gathering food in your yard are working hard to feed their young and to consume the calories they need in order to survive, to reproduce, and in some cases, to migrate thousands of miles. Let your own troubles fly away as you watch the birds go about their lives.

Altruism

Although many people feed birds because they believe the birds will starve otherwise, this is rarely the case. Except during harsh winter weather when natural food sources are unavailable, it's unlikely that the feeders in your yard play a role in the survival of the birds that visit them. As you'll see in the chapters ahead, wild birds get nearly all their nourishment from natural sources. Even hummingbirds that seem to spend their days draining the sugar water from your nectar feeders are getting most of their sustenance from the small insects and spiders they eat.

In the milder seasons, our feeders and baths do help the birds in small ways. During migration, a full feeder and a source of fresh water can attract birds on the move to a safe "refueling" spot along their travel route. In early summer, adult birds engaged in the full-time care of hungry nestlings may find it easier to meet their own nutritional needs by visiting a nearby feeder, while they forage for insects for their young. Come winter, though, a feeder can mean the difference between life and death, when snow and ice combine with severe cold to limit birds' natural food supplies while increasing their need to consume calories.

Conservation

When our feelings of altruism inspire us to acts of conservation, we truly can increase in meaningful ways birds' ability to survive. The loss of useful habitat where birds can nest and raise their young is a much greater threat to many species than the loss of food sources alone. The most endangered species are those that need vast expanses of undisturbed forest for nesting. Human activity has all but eliminated such places from North America, particularly in the East. But even birds that can "make do" with smaller patches of wilderness are threatened by the loss of native plants, even in so-called natural areas. In *Bringing Nature Home*, entomologist Douglas Tallamy explains that the loss of native plants deprives birds of the insects (primarily in the form of caterpillars) that nearly every bird species relies upon to feed its young. When nonnative "introduced" plant species fill our landscapes and then escape cultivation and outcompete native plants in wild areas, the insects that fed on those native plants disappear and, gradually, so do the birds that ate the insects.

Effective conservation, then, takes place on multiple levels. In addition to providing seed, suet, and water in your yard, you can create habitat that includes shelter and nest sites, plants that produce seeds and fruit for birds, and native plants that serve as food for insects that become food for nestlings.

Reduce the size of lawn areas—decidedly uninviting places for most birds—and expand brushy edges where birds can find both food and cover from predators. If you and your neighbors each participate in this type of very local conservation, your neighborhood will become a place where many birds—including species that never show up at feeders—will find what they need to succeed.

Beyond that in your own yard and neighborhood, conservation can take the form of supporting organizations that help to secure bird habitats across the continent and around the world. (Contact information for some of these conservation agencies appears in

> *"Feeding birds has changed our lives. When we started learning about them by putting up bird feeders, we discovered a world we didn't previously know existed. We're now active in conservation issues and have made friends with new people across the country."*
>
> **RETT AND PRISCILLA OREN,** Venice, Florida

Resources at the back of this book.) You may also choose to support conservation by voting for elected officials who work for environmental stewardship. These "big picture" forms of conservation may not produce an immediate effect on the birds you see at your feeders each day, but such measures can go a long way toward ensuring that our future generations will enjoy a similar number and diversity of birds outside their windows.

Connecting with Nature

Growing evidence suggests that interacting with nature benefits us both physically and psychologically. Studies of young people with attention-deficit disorders indicate that

> *"Birds remind me of the simple beauty of nature, free of human thought, confusion, and complexity. While in the air, they seem to be free of gravity, as well.*
>
> *"I feel a deep sense of gratitude that birds choose to live around my home. It is amazing to me that wildlife of all kinds still finds ways to thrive on this planet. I really enjoy feeding birds regularly, especially in fall, winter, and early spring. It's a special feeling to know that I am a part of their life cycles. On a snowy and quiet winter morning, there is a sense of peace in watching them take turns flying to and from the feeder in the backyard."*
>
> **PETER MOSES,** Flourtown, Pennsylvania

spending time outdoors in natural settings increases their ability to concentrate and reduces their feelings of anxiety. Adults who work in offices with windows that provide a view of trees and green spaces generally perform better on tasks requiring concentration than do office workers who look out on pavement and concrete or who work in windowless settings.

Our bodies and our brains are hardwired for an existence—two or three generations past—based in agriculture and in outdoor, physical labor. Modern technology may put the world at our fingertips in many ways, but it also robs us of direct contact with nature that we crave without even realizing it.

Hanging and filling feeders and setting up birdbaths creates a reason for stepping out the door nearly every day and interacting with the natural world. Watching the activity of birds at a feeder gives us the chance to reconnect with nature and to disconnect, however briefly, from the constant barrage of information that comes at us from all sides. Try it for yourself, if you haven't already: Take 5 or 10 minutes each day to sit quietly and watch the birds, then see if you don't return to your daily tasks feeling refreshed and better able to focus on the things that need to be done. I suspect you'll also begin to find ways to spend a few more minutes each day watching the birds.

Feeding wild birds helps children connect with the natural world around them and gives them a sense of stewardship and responsibility for the environment.

Boost Your Bird-Feeding Success

Bird feeding is a simple activity with plenty of opportunities to learn while doing. In the chapters ahead, you'll find loads of tips from experienced birders and "regular" backyard bird feeders to help you make your own bird-feeding activities more rewarding. Throughout the book, contributing writer Arlene Koch shares insights gained from more than 35 years of bird-watching and feeding. Writer Sue Burton grew up watching birds with her family and brings her years of birding experiences to the bird profiles in Chapter 10. Many bird enthusiasts and friends shared terrific tips and experiences to enhance this book.

Chapter 1 discusses the kinds of foods preferred by different bird species. You'll find out why birds seek out particular types of food at certain times of the year, and how you can use that knowledge to increase the numbers and kinds of birds at your own feeders. Chapter 2 tells you what kinds of birdseed are best for sparrows and a host of other seed eaters. Chapter 3 focuses on suet and the types of birds—woodpeckers, nuthatches, chickadees, and others—that relish it. Chapter 4 gives details about nectar feeders and the hummingbirds and orioles that are their primary users (other species like them, too). In Chapter 5, you'll find out which berry- and other fruit-producing plants, shrubs, and trees to grow for birds, such as bluebirds and thrushes. Chapter 6 is all about the creepy-crawly creatures that nourish nearly all birds during some part of their lives. Chapter 7 deals with those foods

that both people and birds can eat, and includes simple recipes for treats you can whip up from ingredients in your kitchen. Chapter 8 discusses how to set up and maintain healthy feeding stations that attract a variety of birds, and how to safeguard your feeders against other wildlife. Chapter 9 covers bird-friendly plants in greater detail, and explains the multiple ways that plants can make your landscape more attractive (even to birds that don't show up at feeding stations). In Chapter 10, you'll find profiles, photos, and descriptions of more than 100 birds that visit feeders across North America, with lists of the foods and plants that are most attractive to each species.

Use this book to make the most of every feeder, every birdbath, and every part of your yard and garden to attract birds. It's easy to create conditions that welcome birds into your landscape—and by how much pleasure you'll get from feeding the birds and watching them go about their lives right outside your windows.

The journey from serving a few seeds to creating a landscape brimming with bird-friendly features begins with a single feeder.

one

Plan a Menu Birds Will Love

A bird's nutritional needs vary—along with the foods it eats—over its lifetime and across the changing seasons. Although each species of bird prefers certain foods and often has a specialized beak or other physical features that enable it to eat those particular foods, most birds eat a more varied diet than you might expect. The birds you see at your feeders might seem to take all their meals there, but they most assuredly get a lot of their nourishment elsewhere.

Goldfinches are reliable visitors at feeders filled with nyjer seed.

To make your yard more inviting to a greater number and variety of birds, it helps to recognize that birds need different foods at different times of the year. While a hopper-style feeder or tray feeder filled with sunflower seed will remain consistently popular throughout the year, offering a tray of calcium-rich grit or crushed eggshells during the breeding season will benefit a wide range of mating birds and will attract even those few that don't queue up for sunflower seed.

For example, cardinals are known seed eaters and are readily identified as such by their sturdy beaks, clearly meant to enable them to crack the shells of their favored foods. But young birds require a high-protein diet to provide the nutrients necessary for growth and development—so even seed-centric cardinals feed their nestlings a steady diet of insects.

Wild birds' diets adjust to the availability of natural foods at different times of the year, too. For example, sparrows may rely almost entirely upon the small seeds of grasses and weeds during winter, but summer finds them getting as much as half of their nourishment from insects. You don't have to have a PhD in ornithology to make sense of this—many birds feed on insects during summer because that's when insects are present. When cold weather takes bugs off the table, birds necessarily turn to other food sources, such as berries or seeds, or the birds migrate to places where insects remain abundant.

Like humans and other animals, birds adjust their diets in response to many factors. Migrating, breeding, raising young, finding abundant natural food in summer, or having to search for it in winter all require different amounts of energy and different strategies. Knowing which foods birds eat and when they eat them makes it much easier to maintain a successful bird feeding station.

Get to Know Your Neighbors

Whether you want to start feeding birds or want to feed more (or different) birds, it's useful to begin with an idea of what's possible in terms of the kinds of birds that will come to feeders in your area. Armed with that information, you can identify a few foods those birds prefer and decide on what kind of feeders and how many to put out.

Admittedly, most people go at this from the opposite direction: They buy a feeder, fill it with seed mix, and expect it to be instantly thronging with all the birds pictured on the label of the birdseed bag. Even when those expectations go unmet, this approach works adequately and often enough that it's still how vast numbers of people begin feeding the birds. Chances are good that a great many avid birders got their start in this very way.

Still, serving a meal without knowing who or how many your guests may be seems like a recipe for disappointment on both sides of the arrangement. If the food you offer is not appealing to the birds found where you live, your feeder may go untouched while its contents grow moist, moldy, and inedible. This can happen even with favored foods, because it can take a little time for birds to discover a new feeder. Starting small is a good idea and helps avoid spoiled, wasted seed.

By contrast, you might put up a new feeder and find that it quickly becomes crowded with unwelcome guests—pesky birds such as starlings and cowbirds, for example. While you can't control which birds find and visit your feeders, you *can* learn what attracts songbirds versus pest birds and then tailor your feeders and their contents in favor of the birds you want.

Why not reduce the frustration of the "serve it and see" approach and do what you can to offer desirable foods to desirable birds in ways that will increase the odds that they will become regular visitors to your feeders? Become acquainted with the birds that live in your area. In Chapter 10 you'll find a list of feeder birds that are widespread across North America and also lists of birds by region and time of year. Profiles of these birds detail their feeding habits and preferences, so you will know what to serve for each species as well as what it eats in the wild.

A good field guide, particularly one that's focused on the region where you live, will also prove useful in introducing you to your bird neighbors. Further guidance may be found at your local chapter of the Audubon Society, from knowledgeable staff at your nearest specialty bird-supply store, or from any number of online sources, including the National Audubon Society, the Cornell Laboratory of Ornithology, the National Wildlife Federation, and Internet retailers such as Duncraft and Wild Birds Unlimited. Contact information for all of these organizations may be found in Resources at the back of this book.

Be an Equal-Opportunity Bird Feeder

Everyone who feeds birds—whether they've been doing it for a long time or are just beginning—wants to attract the "good ones," meaning the pretty birds, the interesting birds, and of course the unexpected or rare birds. But experienced feeders and newcomers alike often are surprised to find that there are less desirable species of birds competing at their feeders with their favorites for space and seed. No matter how much you spend on high-quality seed and sturdy feeders, you're almost certain to attract house finches, brown-headed cowbirds, common grackles in the East, great-tailed grackles in the West, and red-winged blackbirds wherever you live in the country. When these species descend upon your feeders in large flocks, like they sometimes do, they can eat just about everything. When that happens, remember that they are wild creatures, following their natural instincts to flock at certain times of the year. Be patient and wait them out—they will disappear during breeding season and the summer months.

An occasional visit by a bird of prey, or raptor, is another unpleasant surprise for

Common residents of wooded and suburban habitats across North America, Cooper's hawks routinely dine on smaller birds. Despite their size, these agile flyers excel at diving into tangled brush in pursuit of their prey.

"If you're going to feed birds, then you need to be prepared to feed all the birds, not just the ones you want. And that includes the occasional visits by raptors, even though you may not want them there."

ROB NEITZ, Center Valley, Pennsylvania

which many bird lovers are unprepared. It can be upsetting to see a hawk or falcon swoop down upon a songbird or to find evidence of such an attack after the fact. And it's frustrating to realize that there are no songbirds at your feeders because there's a hawk perched on the utility pole at the corner of your yard. Smaller birds are "on the menu" for many raptors, and your bird feeders may unintentionally be serving a more diverse clientele than you realize. In addition to dining on smaller feeder birds, raptors also prey on rodents that are attracted by spilled seed at the base of a feeder. If mice or other small mammals are making nighttime visits to your yard to feast on seeds on the ground below feeders, you may also be hosting owls at your bird-feeding station. Each creature has its role to play in the natural order, and your feeder is simply the intersection where they meet. The birds in your backyard aren't "your" birds; they're just wild birds that are visiting there.

Where Native Plants Fit In

When it comes to choosing landscape plants to provide both beauty and bird food, it may seem reasonable to assume that any fruit-, seed-, or nectar-producing plant is as good as another. Based on that assumption, then, why not choose the most colorful cultivar or the one with showy double flowers, regardless of where it's from? After all, the native species may look all right, but the hybridized selection from Asia is a real showstopper when it blooms.

Although it's not completely understood, the relationship between a bird and the plants that are native within its species' natural range is complex and often codependent. Over centuries of coexistence, a bird species becomes innately predisposed to recognize the edible parts of the plants around it. Berries that ripen at a certain time of the year may actually drive migration, mating, or nesting, because the birds instinctively know when that particular food source will be available to supply the nutrition necessary for their activity. It's even possible, although not extensively studied, that those berries may provide exactly the right nutrients and balance of fats, proteins, and carbohydrates that the birds need at that season. At the same time, many of the plants that birds find most attractive have seed dispersal strategies that rely on those same birds.

Dinnertime Is All the Time

Like all living things, birds eat to sustain life. They have a high body temperature (101° to 110°F) and a high rate of metabolism, and they digest their food rapidly. Each day they have to eat a lot to store energy and body fat. Because they use up what they eat so rapidly, smaller birds eat more each day than do larger birds, and different birds process their food in different ways. Some birds store food in a crop, which is an enlargement of the esophagus, for digestion at a later time. But many of the birds that visit backyard feeders, including most of the songbirds that you want to attract, have no crop and therefore have to eat constantly. Insect eaters, birds like swallows and warblers, eat almost continuously all day and therefore have no need for a crop. Although these aren't species that normally would come to a feeding area, they will fly around a well-planned and well-planted backyard habitat that naturally offers them a good supply of insects.

Wherever you live, all birds eat voraciously in the morning to bolster and then sustain their metabolism after a long night of roosting or migrating. They all also eat voraciously in the late afternoon, either before roosting for the night or lifting off to migrate through the night skies during the migration seasons of spring and fall. Some birds are night, or nocturnal, migrants; others are daytime, or diurnal, migrants. Either way, flying long distances requires a lot more energy and food than a bird normally needs on a daily basis most other times of the year. Depending on the species or on an individual bird, some may also eat a lot in midmorning and again in midafternoon. There are always some birds that act differently than the normal expected behavior. One nuthatch may come in constantly to feed at the sunflower seeds or the suet in your feeders during the day, while another one of the same species will only visit occasionally. Some birds may ignore backyard food offerings most of the day and then suddenly decide to gorge themselves at what would be considered an odd feeding time. Northern cardinals of the East are famous for only showing up at feeders late in the day. But that doesn't mean that they haven't been eating all day; they have, but just not at your feeders. On the other hand, some sparrows, jays, or titmice may come in to eat so often that it seems like they never leave.

Who Eats What?

It may seem contradictory, but when it comes to diet, most birds are both specialists and generalists. Many species have physical or behavioral characteristics—a unique beak or the ability to cling to a tree trunk—that enable them to eat a particular food or type of food. But nearly all birds eat insects when they're available, and many will take advantage of other seasonal foods,

seed eaters

Chickadee

Cardinals, chickadees, titmice, towhees, grosbeaks, nuthatches, large and small finches, sparrows, jays, many others

- Some have sturdy, conical beaks that let them crack hard seed coats.
- Represent majority of feeder birds
- Specialists, such as crossbills, can get to preferred foods because of unique beaks.
- The hull-less seeds found in "no mess" mixes are accessible even to birds whose beaks are not uniquely designed for cracking shells, and so are attractive to even more species.

grain eaters

Quail

Blackbirds, pigeons, doves, grouse, quail, wild turkeys, starlings, grackles, house sparrows

- A subset of seed eaters that includes more ground-feeding birds and those not equipped with beaks meant for cracking harder seed shells
- Many of the seed eaters will also eat grains, but sunflower and other oily seeds are much preferred.

nut eaters

Woodpecker

Woodpeckers, nuthatches, Clark's nutcracker, jays, chickadees, titmice

- A subset of seed eaters, including birds with sturdy bills that enable them to crack nutshells; shelled nuts are accessible to a much broader group of birds.
- See Chapter 2 for more information about birds that eat seeds and nuts.

suet eaters

Nuthatch

Chickadees, jays, woodpeckers, nuthatches, titmice, many others

- Suet blocks in traditional cage-style feeders limit access to birds that can cling.
- Crumbles of suet in a tray or on a platform feeder will attract bluebirds, catbirds, kinglets, mockingbirds, and yellow-rumped warblers; cardinals, juncos, and sparrows will eat suet served at ground level.
- Accessible suet also attracts starlings and crows, as well as cats, dogs, raccoons, and other mammals.
- High-fat food is particularly needed in cold weather and during migration.
- See Chapter 3 for more information about birds that eat suet.

like berries. The foods that our best-known feeder birds favor at backyard feeding stations provide a small and not entirely accurate picture of each bird's overall diet.

In the chapters ahead, we'll focus on specific types of feeder foods that birds seek out, plus the best methods for offering those foods at your feeding station. You'll also find plenty of plants with great bird appeal, to help you expand your bird-feeding efforts beyond basic seed and suet. To get you started, here's a quick look at some birds and their food specialties.

Waxwing

bug eaters

Woodpeckers, flycatchers, swallows, nuthatches, creepers, wrens, thrushes, robins, kinglets, waxwings, vireos, warblers, tanagers, many more

- Nearly all terrestrial (nonshore) birds eat insects during some part of the year.
- "Bugs" include spiders and other arachnids, arthropods, and invertebrates.

bark bug eaters

Woodpeckers, nuthatches, creepers

- Have strong, sharply pointed beaks that can withstand hammering; also have powerful rasping tongues
- Will visit suet and peanut feeders

flying bug eaters

Flycatchers, swifts, swallows, warblers, vireos, hummingbirds

- Have long pointed beaks and wide mouths
- Not often seen at feeders, but may be attracted to suet

ant eaters

Jays, robins, woodpeckers, flickers

- See Chapter 6 for more information about birds that eat bugs.

Hummingbird

nectar drinkers

Hummingbirds, orioles, woodpeckers (sapsuckers), house finches

- Have long curved beaks and long thin tongues that fit inside tubular flowers
- See Chapter 4 for more information about birds that drink nectar.

Tanager

fruit eaters

Northern mockingbirds, bluebirds, catbirds, thrashers, thrushes, robins, waxwings, orioles, blackbirds, vireos, tanagers

- Often also feed on insects
- See Chapter 5 for more information about birds that eat fruit.

Raven

omnivores

Large birds, mostly corvids (crows, jays, ravens), but many others

- Enjoy suet, many "people" foods
- See Chapter 7 for ideas on ways to serve "people" foods to birds.

Seasonal versus Year-Round Feeding

If you take your cues from the general retail market, you might easily conclude that bird feeding is strictly a wintertime activity. When fall rolls around, blocks of suet and bags of seed appear next to the seasonal decorations on the shelves of hardware stores and home centers, in pet supply and discount department stores, even at the supermarket. Suddenly you can buy a bag of sunflower seed or prettily packaged "wild bird mix" and a feeder to serve it in from the most unlikely places. It's winter! Time to feed the birds!

By spring (late January on the retail calendar), anything that remains is in the discount bin and those shelves are filled with Easter baskets and gardening gadgets. But the birds are still hungry and possibly still contending with freezing temperatures and snow-covered ground that limits their access to natural foods. Unfamiliar with the schedule that drives retail sales, they will thank you with their continued presence in your yard if you continue to fill your feeders into the warm weather of actual springtime.

By the time spring truly does arrive, the increasing abundance of natural foods and the limits of your bird-feeding budget may prompt you to take a break from bird feeding for a few months or to trade seed and suet dispensers for nectar feeders. This is a time when having plants in your yard to supply birds with insects, seeds, fruits, and nectar becomes especially useful. You can take down your feeders and take a guilt-free break from serving seeds while still enjoying the company of birds.

There are advantages and disadvantages

A simple wire cage and a preformed suet cake are all you need to invite downy woodpeckers and others to your yard. Birds that feed mainly on insects during warmer weather are especially drawn to suet in the winter months.

to feeding birds at any time of the year and reasons why many people choose to offer food only during winter months. Year-round feeding practically guarantees that you'll see more birds and different species of birds, but you'll spend more money on your hobby and more time cleaning feeders, too. Wintertime feeding brings a steady stream of customers to your feeders, so seeds are less likely to sit and spoil, and the cold weather keeps suet from becoming rancid if it lasts for any length of time.

Whether you feed birds all year long or only at certain times is entirely your decision. The birds will not fault you for taking down your feeders in spring, nor are they likely to starve if you go on vacation in December and the sunflower seed runs out. Almost all the time, birds get most of their nourishment from natural sources. Only in periods of extreme cold with snow cover that keeps birds away from their usual winter foods do feeders contribute to wild birds' survival. The rest of the time they serve to attract the birds to places where we can watch and enjoy them, which benefits us more than it does the birds.

Winter Feeding Tips

❄ Site feeders in locations that offer birds shelter from wind and snow.

❄ Use baffles or put up temporary covers to keep the feeders from becoming clogged with ice and snow.

"In winter, try a feeder with nothing but black-oil sunflower seeds. It will hold the attention of several species and will always keep chickadee and titmouse activity going, which attracts other species to the yard and to other feeders. My mom used to say when I was watching birds for the first time as a little kid that all we had to do after putting up a new feeder was wait for the chickadees to find it, and they'd eventually bring everyone else with them."

GEOFF MALOSH, Moon Township, Pennsylvania

❄ Make sure you can get to feeders to refill them in snowy or icy conditions.

❄ Keep a supply of seeds and suet on hand in case harsh weather keeps you from going out to shop for them.

❄ Supplement feeder foods with peanut butter treats, bacon grease, crumbled baked goods, and other tidbits from your kitchen. These can fill the gap if you run out of seed and can't get to the store. See Chapter 7: Kitchen Castoffs and Home Cooking for ideas on making bird-worthy treats from people (or pet) foods.

❄ Don't forget the water. If you don't have a heated bath, set out a shallow pan of fresh water once or twice a day.

❄ Take time to watch the birds at your feeders. Without the pressures of finding mates and defending breeding territory, the interactions among mixed flocks of birds are remarkably civil.

❄ Keep track of which seeds get eaten and which—if any—are tossed aside and adjust your seed purchases accordingly.

What to Serve and When

One of the biggest factors that determines what and how much birds eat is the time of the year. In the temperate regions of the world, birds reproduce in spring and early summer. For roughly 80 percent of the wild bird population in North America, that means a long migration north during which the birds expend a lot of energy. They need to stop and refuel frequently along the way. During these migration times, it's not uncommon to find an unexpected visitor—perhaps an indigo bunting or scarlet tanager in the East or a painted bunting or black-headed grosbeak in the West—helping itself to the sunflower seeds or other foods in your backyard feeders. These birds may have no intention of nesting anywhere nearby and may in fact leave your area completely after filling up on your bird feed. But they chose your feeders over the nearest fields or woodlands because the food was easy to get.

Birds that are preparing to migrate or that are passing through your neighborhood during migration will be especially drawn to high-fat foods, such as suet and black-oil sunflower seed. As a fuel for long migratory flights, fat supplies twice the energy of either proteins (from insects and seeds) or carbohydrates (from fruits or grains), making it the best option for birds on the move.

Spring Feeding Tips

❁ Shield feeders from rain and late snow-falls to keep the contents from becoming wet and moldy.

❁ Clean feeders thoroughly to remove caked food that's built up during winter months.

❁ Continue offering seed and suet as migrating birds pass through on their way northward or return to your area from their winter ranges.

❁ Watch for "rare" birds that may be pausing on their migration route or have been blown off course by spring storms.

❁ Tidy up fallen shells and spoiled seed beneath feeders and refresh mulch.

A Note from Arlene

SPRING SUET SEEKERS

In my yard in eastern Pennsylvania, from April through early July, so many woodpeckers come down from their nesting sites in the nearby woods to my suet that sometimes I have to refill it three times daily. I get a lot of activity at the suet year-round, but at this time of the year, I restock it more than I do even in the dead of winter.

❀ Offer crushed eggshells or crushed oyster shells to supply calcium as the breeding season approaches.

❀ Keep track of which birds are at the feeder as the seasons change. See who stays, who leaves, and when these comings and goings take place.

❀ Put out mealworms, suet crumbles, or peanut butter crumbles to tempt traveling insect eaters that may find natural insect populations still a bit skimpy.

❀ Plant red flowers to tempt hummingbirds in summer. Good choices include cardinal creeper (*Ipomoea quamoclit*), cardinal flower (*Lobelia cardinalis*), bee balm (*Monarda didyma*), and scarlet sage (*Salvia coccinea*).

❀ Put out hummingbird feeders.

Nutrition for Nesting Birds

When birds are getting ready to nest in spring, their hormones increase due to secretions from their endocrine glands. The levels of estrogen in females and testosterone in males rise, and both genders are in a heightened state of activity. While you might then assume that the more active a bird is, the more easily available food it will consume, that's not always the case. Sometimes individual birds are so focused on everything involved with the reproduction process that they might ignore your feeder offerings. That doesn't mean the birds aren't eating anything, because they have to eat to stay alive. It just means that they're taking advantage of whatever natural food is available near their nest site. In fact, nest sites are often chosen because of nearby food availability. Birds will only use your feeders during the breeding season if their nests are close enough that they're able to quickly fly to your feeders and just as quickly return to their nest areas. Birds such as woodpeckers, chickadees, titmice, and nuthatches nesting near a good supply of suet may actually come to it a lot during this time, and it may begin to disappear more rapidly than it did earlier.

Once nesting occurs, and a female (or the male, depending on the species) is incubating eggs, she is in constant need of food. It can be very hard for birds to eat enough while they're sitting on eggs. If it's a species in which only one of the adult birds takes care of the nest, as is the case with hummingbirds, the adult has to leave the nest for short periods of time to fly away and quickly grab something to eat. Even if one adult is feeding the other during this time, the need for a close food source remains. When species share incubation duties and the subsequent feeding of their young, as happens with rose-breasted and black-headed grosbeaks, survival is much easier for both of the adults.

Bringing Up Babies

As soon as the eggs in a bird's nest hatch, there are weeks of constant and strenuous activity ahead for the parent or parents. How long these young birds, known as nestlings, stay in the nest depends on their species. A normal span from hatching to fledging (leaving the nest) may be from 10 days to more than 2 weeks. Taking care of the young birds is a full-time activity and a steady drain on the adult bird or birds. Nestlings grow rapidly and have to be fed all day, although most feeding takes place in the morning.

Blind and Naked

Almost all of the birds that you'd expect to attract to your backyard have young that are helpless when they come out of the egg. The term for this is *altricial*, meaning their eyes are closed and they're naked except for a scant hair covering on their heads. The young grow rapidly—most species are ready to leave the safety of the nest sometime in the next 3 weeks, although they continue to receive food from their parents after they fledge. However, the young of birds (like woodpeckers, nuthatches, and some swallows) that make their nests in tree cavities or other such sheltered places can stay in the nest longer, because they're better protected than nestlings in open nests. As a result, the fledglings (what young birds are called when they leave the nest) of cavity-nesting species mature and manage on their own more quickly overall. Their parents don't have to

A Note from **Arlene**

FEEDING NEEDY NESTLINGS

One summer, an American robin built its nest on a thick grapevine that wound up through a black chokeberry bush outside my office window. The nest was well camouflaged from most angles, but clearly visible from where I sat at my computer desk. I was amazed watching how fast the nestlings grew on a daily basis and even more amazed at how many times the adult female fed them.

Most songbirds feed each young bird 4 to 12 times per hour and not in any particular pecking order. The nestling that gets to the food first is the one that gets it. The American robin is obviously not a bird that would normally use seed or suet feeders, but it's a common species and a good example of just how busy and strained all adult birds are when they're raising young. An easy and good source of seeds or suet for birds during this time, or a yard full of worms or grubs in the case of robins, will help them raise healthier young, and they'll brood earlier and more often if they're a species that raises more than one brood a year.

take care of them for as long once they're out of the nest. The North American species whose young stay in the nest the longest is the purple martin: It can be more than 4 weeks before the young leave the nest.

Regardless of what they eat as adults, nestlings are all fed the same thing: a protein-rich diet of insects and small invertebrates. It's not unusual during nesting season to see species like sparrows, buntings, blackbirds, bobolinks, and others—birds that normally eat seeds and nuts—carrying insects in their mouths as they perch atop weeds, on the branches of trees, or in flight. This is a sure sign that the bird is nesting somewhere in the surrounding area, because the insects it's carrying are for its babies. It doesn't automatically mean, though, that the nest is close to where the insect-carrying adult is perched. It may be relatively far away. When adult birds are confronted with the presence of something they perceive to be a threat to their young, they do a lot of things to divert the threat away from their nest location. If you encounter a situation like this, get as far away from the bird as you can, so it can feed its young.

While adult birds feed and take care of their fledglings for a while, gradually parents will wean young of their dependence and start to ignore their begging calls. Sometimes a parent bird will even withhold food from a nestling that should leave the nest but is hesitating to do so. Nothing spurs a young bird to "get with the program" more than hunger does. Parent birds instinctively know when it's time to let the youngsters fend for themselves, although sometimes a nestling will fall out of a nest. If that happens, and you find a young bird not yet capable of taking care of itself, leave it alone. Most of the time, the parent bird is around waiting to nudge the youngster back into the safety of a bush. The parent will continue to feed its young until they are able to fly on their own.

The High Cost of Badgering Birds

If you've ever spent time on coastal beaches during summer, you've probably seen shorebirds like plovers and sandpipers feeding in the surf, skittering back and forth in time with the waves. Perhaps you've also encountered sections of beach that were closed off to humans, because those same shorebirds were nesting there. Don't let pet dogs (or children) chase the feeding birds, even for the pleasure of seeing them run and fly in unison. Although enforcement of local, state, and federal laws protecting these birds tends to be limited, you can be assessed a stiff fine if you are found in violation.

Meanwhile, the cost of the birds' extra expenditure of energy while fleeing can be devastating to them. With their feeding time limited by the tides and further constrained by crowds of beachgoers, the birds need to "fill their tanks" when food is available to ensure that they have enough energy to seek a mate, to nest and lay eggs, to feed nestlings, to find more food, to sleep, and to migrate when the time is right. The extra energy it takes to flee from perceived threats, as well as the lost opportunity to gather food, can take a substantial toll and may even threaten the lives of individual birds.

Summer Feeding Tips

☀ Keep birdbaths clean and filled with fresh water. Add a mister or dripper to attract water-loving birds such as goldfinches and catbirds.

☀ Clean nectar feeders at least weekly, more often if the nectar becomes cloudy or mold becomes obvious.

☀ Plant sunflowers, zinnias, amaranths, millet, and other "seedy" bird favorites for home-grown treats at the end of the season.

☀ Clean seed feeders and let them dry thoroughly. Refill lightly for the fewer birds that will be visiting them and check regularly for damp or spoiled seed.

☀ Put a teaspoonful of uncooked rice or a bird-safe desiccant product into a tube feeder filled with nyjer or finch mix to keep moisture from spoiling your summer goldfinch party.

☀ Use processed "no melt" suet blocks that are meant for use in warm weather; keep even these in shady spots.

☀ Switch to shelled seeds (aka "no mess" mixes) in feeders near decks, patios, and walkways to avoid dropped shells in places where you and your family spend time outdoors.

☀ Check stored seed supplies for signs of insect infestations (webbing, larvae, or moths). Freeze, then compost or discard infested seed.

Fall Feeding Tips

🌿 Replenish supplies of seed and suet that have dwindled over summer. Watch for fall stock-up sales at your favorite bird-supply store or feed dealer.

🌿 Clean out storage containers and make sure no insect pests are lurking in the crevices before you refill them.

🌿 Secure supplies of seed in metal containers to protect them from rodents moving indoors for winter months.

🌿 Shop nursery sales for native plants with bird-friendly features and add a few new shrubs or trees to your yard.

🌿 Clear fallen leaves out of birdbaths and keep them filled with fresh water for feeder regulars and migrants stopping in to refuel.

🌿 Make sure all your feeders are in good repair and ready for the coming winter.

🌿 Watch for migrating flocks. Hundreds of birds traveling together make an impressive sight—and sound—as they pass overhead or pause to rest.

American goldfinches welcome summer with their bright yellow breeding plumage, which they wear well into the fall.

Enjoying the Empty Nest

During summer after breeding is over, there's an abundance of natural food, so backyard feeders may not get much use. Except for birds that double or even triple brood each season—or mourning doves that have been known to raise as many as five broods a season—the stress of breeding is over. It's a quiet time. But as fall migration approaches, all the birds that migrate, whether just a short distance or as far as Central or South America, have to bulk up to sustain themselves on their journey. Visits to feeders will then suddenly pick up, as the birds' hormones start making their metabolism increase, and they begin to accumulate a lot of fat. Depending on where you live, this starts happening as early as mid-July and can continue through November, because not all species migrate at the same time. Orchard orioles are almost all gone from the northeastern part of the country by the end of August, and by the end of September, the same is true for ruby-throated hummingbirds. Some sparrow species, however, can still be moving through as Christmas approaches.

The View from Deb's Window

There's Gold at Them Thar Feeders!

Although I tend to take a more relaxed approach to bird feeding during summer months, my lust for gold—gold*finches*, that is—keeps me from stopping completely. If I cease serving seeds when warm weather arrives, I'll miss the sight of male goldfinches, dressed in their bright breeding-season finest. These handsome yellow-and-black birds tend to hang about the feeders in small groups with their olive green–clad female counterparts, along with house and purple finches, too. All the finches sing sweetly and enjoy splashing in a birdbath, both of which make good entertainment for me on a summer afternoon. Male goldfinches wear their breeding plumage well into fall, keeping things colorful at the feeder when other birds are donning more somber hues.

To keep my golden companions close at hand while giving my bird-feeding budget a break, I usually cut back on black-oil sunflower seed through summer months, but keep a tube feeder filled with finch mix. The sunflower seed draws less action overall during the warmer weather and tends to get damp and then moldy in its hopper feeder. Many of the birds that gobble it down during the cooler months are off busy dining on natural foods, and the finches—both gold and rosy—are quite happy to have their own tube filled with nyjer seed, sunflower chips, and peanut hearts and outfitted with perches too small for their larger competitors. A modest amount of dropped seed from the finch tube makes a pleasant spot on the ground below it for mourning doves to find a meal, and I enjoy their soothing cooing sounds as well.

two

Seeds and Seed Mixes

From tiny grass and weed seeds to hefty acorns, seeds form the cornerstone of most backyard bird-feeding projects and are the staples of the feeder. The reason is clear: Seeds are easily gathered, stored, and served, and are a primary food source for a long list of songbirds. When we talk about "feeder" birds, we refer mainly to those that eat seeds.

Black-oil sunflower seeds attract a broad range of seed-eating birds.

Nutritionally, seeds make perfect sense for birds. A bird's speedy metabolism and accordingly high energy needs require it to eat a lot of calories each day. Nutrient-dense seeds, packed with fats and proteins, are just what birds need to fuel their activities.

This chapter focuses mainly on the seeds traditionally sold for bird feeding—the ones you'll find at the wild-bird supply store or on the shelf at the home center. But birds naturally eat a much broader range of seeds than the few kinds sold in 25-pound bags. To learn about some of the many plants—annuals, perennials, shrubs, and trees—that you can grow for their bird-attracting seeds, turn to Chapter 9.

Seeds and the Birds That Eat Them

To some extent, most wild birds are opportunistic feeders that will eat nearly any food that is readily available. Still, not every type of seed is equally attractive to every bird. A bird species may "specialize" in a particular kind of seed, because its bill is suited to cracking open the shell of that seed or because the seed plant and the bird are native to the same region. The presence of a preferred natural food may invite birds to nest in an area where it is abundant and may prompt them to claim territories, seek mates, and begin breeding. Even the type of feeder you use to offer birdseed and where you place it in your landscape can play a role in determining which birds will be attracted to it.

SEED TYPE	BIRDS ATTRACTED	TYPE(S) OF FEEDER TO USE
Canary seed	Buntings, house finch, purple finch, goldfinch, quail, common redpoll, native sparrows	Hopper, tube, low platform
Corn, cracked	Red-winged blackbird, grackles, thrasher, jays, woodpeckers, house finch, song sparrow, tree sparrow, fox sparrow, field sparrow, white-crowned sparrow, white-throated sparrow, juncos, buntings, towhees, mourning dove, American crow	Hopper, tube, tray, platform
Corn, whole kernel	Cardinal, jays, crows, woodpeckers	Hopper, tray, platform, on the cob
Millet	Red-winged blackbird, buntings, doves, finches, goldfinch, juncos, pheasants, quail, pine siskin, field sparrow, fox sparrow, song sparrow, towhees, varied thrush, Carolina wren	Tube, hopper, on the stem
Milo	Doves, game birds	Low tray, on the stem
Mixed seeds	Buntings, towhees, starlings, kinglets, California thrasher, chickadees, woodpeckers; vary according to contents of seed mix	Tube, hopper, tray, platform

Smart Seed-Shopping Strategies

Like almost any hobby, bird feeding is more enjoyable if you're not stressed out about how much you're spending. To keep your feeders filled, begin with an idea of how much you can afford to spend and a plan to help you stick to your budget. You can feed the birds without draining your bank account, but it's easy to go overboard when you start dreaming of all the birds that would flock to your feeders if only you were serving something special and tempting and different from whatever your neighbor's feeder holds.

SEED TYPE	BIRDS ATTRACTED	TYPE(S) OF FEEDER TO USE
Nyjer/niger ("thistle")	Finches, goldfinch, sparrows, chickadees, titmice, towhees, juncos, mourning dove	Tube, mesh "sock"
Peanuts, in shells	Jays	Tray, platform
Peanuts, shelled, pieces	Finches, juncos, sparrows, buntings, mourning dove	Tube, tray
Peanuts, shelled, whole	Jays, white-throated sparrow, juncos, buntings, towhees, red-winged blackbird, grackles, chickadees, titmice, nuthatches, starlings, yellow-bellied sapsucker, woodpeckers	Wire mesh tube
Poultry (or chicken) scratch	Purple finch, cardinal, game birds	Platform, low tray
Pumpkin and squash	Cardinal, chickadees, jays, nuthatches, titmice, woodpeckers	Platform, tray
Rapeseed (canola)	Buntings, doves, finches, sparrows, towhees	Tube, low tray, platform
Safflower	Cardinal, grosbeaks	Hopper, tube, platform, tray
Sunflower, black-oil	Cardinal, finches, white-crowned sparrow, juncos, crossbills, towhees, blackbirds, grackles, chickadees, titmice, yellow-rumped warbler, nuthatches, grosbeaks	Hopper, tube, platform, tray, on the seedhead
Sunflower, striped	Cardinal, jays, grosbeaks, woodpeckers, nuthatches, titmice	Hopper, tube, platform, tray, on the seedhead
Wheat	Blackbirds, doves, grouse, pheasants, quail, house sparrows, some native sparrows, starlings	On the stem, low tray, ground

Truly, the birds don't care how much you spend. Their "tastes" are guided by what's available, by what they are genetically programmed to eat, and by what they are physically capable of eating. And the foods you put in your feeders will only attract those birds that are already in your area—offering exotic foods won't make exotic birds appear unless they naturally live nearby, which probably renders them, by definition, less than exotic. The odd "rare" bird that turns up hundreds or thousands of miles from its usual range may partake of the same seeds, suet, or nectar that your feeder regulars enjoy, or it might make a meal of insects or berries in your landscape. There's little to be gained by serving specialty items in hopes of spotting a rarity, but much to be lost in spoiled, uneaten food or in feeding premium products to birds that would just as readily eat plain old sunflower seed.

To keep financial worries from spoiling your bird-feeding pleasure, start small and simply, offering one or two foods that you know are attractive to birds commonly found in the area where you live. If year-round feeding is beyond the scope of your budget, put out feeders when natural foods are scarce and take them down when insects and berries begin to capture birds' attention. As we've already mentioned, wild birds only occasionally rely upon feeder foods for their survival. Apart from times when harsh weather conditions prevent birds from finding natural food sources, a bird feeder full of seeds is a way to bring the birds to us so we can enjoy them, more than it is a way for us to help the birds. Filling your feeders from fall through winter and into spring offers the greatest benefit for birds—migrants and winter residents—and gives you the greatest number and variety of birds at your feeders in exchange for your investment.

In addition to seasonal feeding methods, a few other strategies can help you keep a lid on the expenses associated with feeder filling.

Location, location, location. Where you buy your birdseed can make a big difference in how much you pay. If possible, choose a local business with a good reputation. Even if its prices are a bit higher than those at chain stores, the difference in quality and service often is worth it. Ask other birders (members of a local Audubon chapter, perhaps) for recommendations on where to shop. If there's one within reasonable driving distance, a "feed and grain" store that

Birds That Eat Seeds

Some bird species feed almost entirely on seeds. When you offer seed, your feeders may be visited by sparrows, buntings, finches, woodpeckers, titmice, chickadees, jays, nuthatches, grosbeaks, cardinals, doves, juncos, and towhees, among others. If wild turkeys, grouse, quail, or other game birds live in your area, you may see them dining on fallen seed on the ground below your feeders.

sells livestock feed may be your best source of bagged seed at a reasonable price.

Wild-bird specialty stores (and their Internet iterations) tend to have the greatest variety of seeds and other foods and offer superior quality, as well as expertise on birds and bird feeding. Premium quality may come at a premium price, however, and stores and Web sites are filled with tempting gadgets and bird treats that can quickly put you over your spending limit. Online seed sellers may be an option if you don't have a nearby source of birdseed; watch for promotions offering free or reduced-price shipping, because birdseed is heavy.

If your area has an active chapter of the Audubon Society or another bird-watching group, see if it offers a cooperative seed-buying arrangement that's convenient for you. Even going together with several neighbors to make an annual or semiannual trek to a distant seed supplier can help keep a lid on seed costs.

Shop the sales. Watch for "preseason" sales in fall and stock up on seed and suet. Plan ahead, but only buy as much as you can reasonably store in suitable conditions. Be wary of spring sales on bags of seeds that have been sitting on shelves all winter. Such products may be spoiled or infested with insects, and as a result, will no longer be appealing to birds. Clearance items are only bargains if they're still fit for birds to eat.

Go solo. Although seed mixes are widely available, they often fail to deliver on their promise of attracting a wider variety of birds to your feeder. More often, part of the mix winds up on the ground below the feeder, as birds push aside less desirable seeds in their quest to get to their favorites. A bag of a single type of seed, such as black-oil sunflower, may cost more than the same size bag of a mix, but you'll be paying for seed the birds will eat, instead of filler seeds they won't.

Read the label—and the signs. If you do opt for mixed seeds, know what you're buying. Choose a mix of seeds that is suited to the birds that are likely to come to your feeders. While seeds such as milo, cracked corn, and wheat have their avian fans, these grains often get kicked off the feeder by songbirds that prefer sunflower and millet. Examine the bag of seeds, too, and look for signs of insect infestations. Check bag seams for webbing and/or larvae and watch for small brown moths fluttering about.

Do the Math Before You Shop

From the virtual aisles of online wild-bird supply stores to the shelves of your local garden center and everywhere in between, bags of seed mixes abound. Some are tailored for cardinals, others for finches; some specify *songbirds*, while others simply say *wild birds* on the label. If you've found a mix that seems to satisfy the birds at your feeders without a lot of waste, but that also seems a little pricey, you may begin to wonder if you can save some money by buying the ingredients of that mix separately and mixing them yourself.

A quick cost comparison often will support

your theory that you can make the mix for less if you buy its components separately. You might even save $2 to $3 per 5 pounds of seed mix, depending on how refined your local birds' palates are. Except . . . this savings is only real if you can find those ingredients readily and from no more than a couple of sources. If you have to order from multiple catalog outlets (and pay multiple shipping

> **"We feed black-oil sunflower seed, because so many of these birds down this way have small beaks and are able to crack black-oil seeds open, while the gray-striped ones are too big. We also feed white proso millet and suet, and that's about it. We never use mixes, because of all the crap in them."**
>
> **BOB SARGENT,** Clay, Alabama

fees) and/or have to drive to more than one store to get the seeds you need for your favorite blend, then—poof!—there go your savings.

Of course, this equation varies with the types of seeds you need and their availability, as well as your willingness to spend time to save money. If your local birds go for black-oil sunflower and cracked corn, and you are within reasonable driving distance of a feed store that stocks such items, skip the bagged mix and

make your own. But elaborate acquisition can make the price on a bag of premium seed mix seem rather reasonable. That's when you lay down the cash, pick up the bag, and get back home to watch the birds.

Sunflower Seed

Sunflower seed is the first and best choice for feeding wild birds. Bird-seed suppliers typically offer small black-oil seeds and large gray-striped seeds, as well as sunflower hearts or chips (broken kernels) whose hulls, or shells, already have been removed. Sunflower seeds are high in protein and fat. Nearly all of the seed-eating birds that come to bird feeders eat sunflower seeds, and many birds that are not primarily seed eaters will also nab this tasty treat when they have a chance. If you're just getting started feeding the birds, or you only want to offer one kind of seed at your feeders, sunflower seed is the way to go.

Black-oil sunflower seeds fill the feeders of experienced birders throughout North America, simply because it offers the greatest

Striped sunflower seed

Black-oil sunflower seed

return on investment—the greatest number of the most species of birds will turn up where black-oil sunflower is being served. Black-oil sunflower seeds are smaller than the heftier striped varieties, and their shells are softer, so even small birds and those with beaks that are not specialized for seed cracking can get to the tasty heart, or kernel, inside. Almost any form of bird feeder will work for offering black-oil sunflower: If you serve it, birds will come. To bring birds to a new feeder or feeding station, you may want to sprinkle some black-oil sunflower on the ground or serve it in an open tray or platform feeder. But these methods also make the prized seed available to diners that may be less welcome, including squirrels, raccoons, opossums, and skunks. Once birds discover your feeder or feeding area, limit the speed with which black-oil sunflower seed disappears by serving it in tube or hopper feeders that reduce its accessibility to four-footed wildlife and larger birds.

Gray-striped sunflower seeds contain just as much bird-worthy nutrition as black-oil sunflower and are nearly as popular at the feeder. Their larger size and harder shells limit their appeal among smaller feeder birds, such as chickadees, goldfinches, redpolls, pine siskins, and sparrows, which may be able to pick up the larger seeds, but then have difficulty cracking open their striped shells to reach the treat within. These smaller birds will take advantage of pieces of gray-striped sunflower kernels that fall into feeders or on the ground, although that doesn't happen as much with gray-striped sunflower seeds as it does with

Saving Some for Later

Some of the birds that favor sunflower seeds—and especially the ones who favor black-oil sunflower seeds—will cache, or store, food for later use. Some do this to get through the cold winter months, but others stockpile seeds year-round. A bird will fly away with as many seeds as it can fit in its mouth, and then hide them for later retrieval in bark crevices, under leaves, in the soft ground, under flower petals, or wherever it can find a suitable spot. Titmice, nuthatches, woodpeckers, chickadees, and crows all are known to practice this seed-hoarding habit. Not surprisingly, however, there is no honor among seed hogs—often one bird will find another's seed stash and steal it. Chickadees, in particular, are skilled at finding hidden food, and so are brown creepers, and it's relatively common for one white-breasted nuthatch to steal the seed that another white-breasted nuthatch has hidden away. It can be comical to watch a jay picking up sunflower seeds until its mouth is stuffed full. Birds that have a crop (or throat pouch), like evening grosbeaks and most of the northern finches, will take lots of sunflower seeds, pieces of them, or other seeds or nuts and store them in their crop for overnight digestion while they roost. This is nature's way of providing them with a means to survive in below-freezing temperatures.

"We do a whole raised bed of 'Mammoth' and a few other varieties of sunflowers. The goldfinches love them and pick the petals off one at a time, then start in on eating the seeds in the head. When everything is in full bloom, it's like they have a smorgasbord."

DONNA CHIARELLI, Kutztown, Pennsylvania

black-oil sunflower seeds. The bigger birds—jays, woodpeckers, nuthatches, and titmice—that can manage the sturdier gray-striped shells are unwilling to let many scraps of their prized food fall to the ground.

Grow Your Own Sunflowers are easy to grow and are superior in many ways to just about all other seeds you can provide for birds in your own garden. The small-seeded sunflower varieties are best, because almost all small birds can extract and eat their seeds. But the bigger types that produce striped seeds will get a lot of use, too, especially from bigger birds. Both kinds also attract insects, which birds of all sizes will gladly feed upon.

Growing a bed of sunflowers can be as easy as pressing some of the seeds from your bag of birdseed into the soil in a sunny location. But you can also browse your favorite garden catalogs to find an amazing selection of sunflowers. With petals ranging from near-white to shades of gold and bronze, and varieties that produce multiple small flower heads or single massive ones, there are sunflowers to suit almost any garden style and color scheme.

Choose a single variety to create a more formal effect or mix up different colors and

Allelopathy: When Sunflowers Attack

The covering of sunflower seed shells, or hulls, that builds up on the ground beneath a bird feeder is more than just an unsightly mess: It's also a threat to other landscape plants you have growing in that area. Sunflowers—and a number of other plants—contain compounds that are toxic to neighboring plants. Known as allelopathy, this property helps plants compete effectively for space in the wild, but it can have unintended consequences in landscape and garden settings. Not all plants are susceptible to the damaging effects of allelopathic compounds; many plants coexist quite happily next to sunflowers in a garden. But the problem can be compounded when seed hulls pile up and rainwater washes the toxins onto plants and into the soil below. Turf grass often succumbs, leaving a bare patch below the feeder, and any seeds you sow there will have a hard time germinating; seedlings will likely be weak and distorted, if they come up at all.

Serving hulled sunflower seeds in feeders where shells might otherwise put plants below at risk is one way to avoid this problem. Keeping the area below feeders clean and siting both feeders and landscape plantings appropriately are other ways to prevent casualties in the allelopathic battle between plants.

heights. The birds will appreciate any and all types and will be quick to start harvesting the seeds as soon as they begin to ripen. If you want to save some flower heads for homegrown seed dispensers later in fall and winter, you'll want to put a paper bag or netting over individual flowers to keep the birds from beating you to the finish.

When you feed black-oil sunflower seed, regardless of how well made or well placed your feeder or feeders may be, some of the hulls with small pieces of seed attached will inevitably fall or be dropped on the ground. Although it's messy, it's not all bad. The hulls themselves should get cleaned up every so often during the normal part of keeping your feeding area clean and healthy, which is covered in Chapter 8. But most of the small pieces of sunflower meat will be eaten by birds that like to feed on the ground, as well as by squirrels, chipmunks, and other critters. Not all of the birds that eat sunflower seeds do it in or near feeders. While finches, northern cardinals, grosbeaks, and sparrows eat their food right where they get it, jays, chickadees, titmice, woodpeckers, nuthatches, and others prefer to grab it and fly away.

Hulled sunflower seeds. If you don't mind paying premium prices for sunflower seed, then the way to go is to feed hulled sunflower seeds. While goldfinches, redpolls, pine siskins, chickadees, and other small-billed birds find gray-striped sunflower seeds extremely difficult to handle, they and just about any other species that eats seeds will freely flock to sunflower seeds that they don't have to crack open. Sunflower hearts, as the whole kernels are

called, and sunflower chips, as the broken-up pieces are called, are ideal from a seed-eating bird's perspective—they provide lots of nutrition for a relatively small expenditure of energy. Even birds that won't normally eat sunflower seeds—insect eaters and berry eaters like thrushes, mockingbirds, catbirds, bluebirds, thrashers, sparrows, and occasionally even flycatchers—will eat sunflower kernels when they're available. If you want to feed birds while keeping a meticulously clean backyard at the same time, there's no denying that feeding hulled sunflower seeds is the way to go.

Nyjer/Niger (aka "Thistle") Seed

Another seed valued for both its high oil and high caloric content is nyjer, or niger, seed. Although these tiny black seeds may still be found for sale labeled as thistle seed, they are actually unrelated to North America's thistles, those spiny, purple-topped, invasive weeds of the genus *Cirsium* that germinate freely anywhere their seeds are carried by the wind. Nyjer seed is imported from Africa and Asia and comes from a plant with yellow flowers whose botanical name is *Guizotia abyssinica*. But as long as birdseed companies continue to market it as thistle seed, it will probably keep that name. Also, it fits the profile of what

Nyjer seed

people think thistle seed looks like, and the birds that eat nyjer seed also make use of the seeds of native thistles, especially goldfinches and other small finches.

> *"Although some people who feed nyjer claim, as do the bird-feeding companies, that it is the top seed of choice among the small finches, I find that goldfinches often ignore it while preferring black-oil sunflower instead."*
>
> **TERRY MASTER,** East Stroudsburg, Pennsylvania

The big drawback to feeding nyjer seed is that it's expensive, which is why some birders call it "black gold." It's expensive because it has to be sterilized to prevent germination before being shipped across the oceans. Birdseed companies have to pay a lot of shipping fees before the seed is bagged, labeled, and transported to retail outlets. Most birders who offer it consider it worth the price, but there are just as many longtime birders who say it doesn't always live up to its billing.

Whether the birds in your backyard will devour or ignore nyjer isn't something that can be accurately predicted. What can be reliably predicted, however, is that almost always when there's a winter with a big irruption of northern finches due to a lack of natural food in the North, nyjer seed feeders see

A Note from Arlene

NYJER IS NOT ALWAYS FINCHES' FIRST CHOICE

Although some people feed nyjer seed year-round and regard it as the best seed they have for attracting the smaller feeder birds, many others who only feed it during winter to attract wandering northern finches often complain about it. Many times I've heard people say that their "thistle" seed is being ignored, and they assume it's because the seed is bad or spoiled. But that is rarely the case. I, too, have seen birds demonstrating a lack of interest in nyjer seed during even the coldest of Pennsylvania's winters, but I've never thought it had anything to do with bad seed. I think the birds just like the other food I put out more. When spring rolls around, I dump out the old nyjer seed from the feeder, clean it out, and refill it with fresh nyjer seed from the same bag that's been stored properly in the house. And when small flocks of American goldfinches begin showing up in spring, they gobble it all up.

I've also heard people complain that their "thistle" seed germinates under the feeders. But every time I hear those words, I wonder what the plant growing in the ground near or under their feeders really is. Nyjer is treated to prevent it from reseeding, and our North American climate doesn't suit its growth requirements. It's certainly possible that once in a while a few untreated nyjer seeds may fall to the ground and sprout. But even if that happens, they would never mature and spread.

lots of action. Such a winter occurred in the Northeast and other northern parts of the United States in the winter of 2008 to 2009. Flocks of birds like white-winged crossbills, redpolls, and pine siskins were everywhere. Backyard nyjer feeders, from the middle of cities to rural backyards to wooded northern mountainous areas, were hosting crowds of northern finches. Some siskin flocks numbered in the hundreds and stayed around so long that people were saying that they could no longer afford to feed them nyjer seed.

Safflower Seed

Like sunflower and nyjer, safflower (*Carthamus tinctorius*) is an agricultural oil crop that also produces seeds that birds like to eat. Depending on where you buy your birdseed, you may find safflower seed for sale on its own or as a part of seed mixes. Safflower seeds are plump, medium size, and usually white, although safflower seed with red-striped hulls is available from some birdseed suppliers. Safflower is widely billed as being a favorite food of northern cardinals, but whether cardinals actually prefer safflower over other seeds is a topic of disagreement among backyard birders.

Most birders find that the visitors at their feeders prefer sunflower seeds—black-oil or striped—over safflower seeds, but that the slightly smaller white seeds do get eaten

"We have three tube feeders with nyjer seed for the goldfinches and house finches, along with a tube feeder of black-oil sunflower seeds. I used to do a big wide feeder of the latter, but we have a lot of starlings, and they can take over a feeder quickly. I did switch the big feeder to safflower seed, which the starlings don't like; sadly, it seemed neither did the cardinals, or not as much, anyway. I throw some sunflower seed on the ground for them, and they pick up the leftovers from the one tube feeder. We seem to have at least a pair of cardinals hanging around every year."

DONNA CHIARELLI, Kutztown, Pennsylvania

eventually. It's possible that the harder shells of safflower make it less accessible to some birds, but the dedicated seed eaters seem to manage when it's the only food on the menu. Squirrels typically ignore safflower, so this alone may motivate you to try it in your feeders.

If you're offering safflower seed for the first time, start with modest amounts, served on a low platform or tray—the preferred dining format for cardinals—and mixed with black-oil sunflower. As you see the safflower being eaten, gradually increase the amount of safflower relative to

Safflower seed

other seeds. Jays reportedly don't care for safflower, either, so serving it can be a way of sending them and squirrels to raid feeders elsewhere.

Grow Your Own The plants that produce safflower seeds are not unattractive, so you may find a place to plant them in a flowerbed intended for producing bird foods. Safflowers are annuals that grow 10 to 30 inches tall and produce shaggy-looking yellow-orange flowers on rather prickly thistlelike plants. Sow the seeds after danger of frost has passed, in a well-prepared, sunny location. Safflower produces a taproot that makes it fairly tolerant of dry conditions, but it does not do well in humid weather or in competition with other plants. Harvest the seeds about a month after the flowers bloom, when the plants are mostly dry and brown.

Wear gloves to protect your hands while you rub the seeds free of the spiny plants. Or leave the dried stems and flower heads standing and see which enterprising birds fly in to dine on safflower on the stalk.

White Millet

White millet seed is small and round and comes from the seedheads of annual grasses grown for cereal or grain production. It's a favorite of small-billed birds like sparrows, juncos, buntings, and finches, but lots of birds with bigger bills will

White millet seed

A Note from
Arlene

TOPS WITH CARDINALS OR NOT?

Some people swear that the only birds they've ever seen eating safflower seeds are northern cardinals, while other bird-watchers—myself included—disagree. In addition to cardinals, I've seen purple finches, blue jays, house finches, and white-breasted nuthatches eat safflower. Some of the same birds that show up at feeders for sunflower seed will also eat safflower, but safflower has far fewer fans than sunflower. That's one of the reasons for serving it in your feeders, in fact.

In places where big flocks of blackbirds or grackles sometimes descend into feeding areas, safflower seed seems to help keep them away. Birds such as Brewer's blackbirds and great-tailed grackles apparently don't like it much. On my property in eastern Pennsylvania, I seldom feed safflower. I have a lot of acreage, and winter flocks of northern cardinals at my feeding stations sometimes number more than 30. But they seem perfectly content with eating black-oil sunflower seed and millet. When I do offer safflower seed in feeders or on the ground, it always gets eaten, but at a much slower rate than other seeds being served.

eat it, too. This is one seed that, like pieces of black-oil sunflower seed, will get eaten even by birds that don't normally eat seeds much at all. All of the ground-feeding species will readily help themselves to white millet, especially when it's put in a free-standing tray feeder on the ground. But no matter where you put it, it's always visited by lots of different species. Even during summer when natural seeds are abundant, many birds will come in to eat white millet seed in mixes or by itself.

Grow Your Own Millets are easy to grow, and different types combine readily with many garden styles. Any type of millet is perfect for feeding birds from summer through winter, because the birds pick every seed clean. Some millets shed their seeds and provide a banquet for sparrows and other ground-feeding birds. Others hold their seedheads intact on the plants, making sturdy landing pads for the finches that feed on the seeds.

You can buy millet seeds from companies that sell seeds for attracting wildlife, or you can sow a handful or two from a bag of birdseed onto a prepared seedbed in late spring. Proso millet (*Panicum miliaceum*) has an arching, branching seedhead that ripens in only 65 to 70 days. Siberian millet (*Setaria italica*), also called German millet, foxtail millet, or Italian millet, has long-lasting seedheads that droop like long fingers. Pearl millet (*Pennisetum glaucum*) bears cattail-like seedheads, and Japanese millet (*Echinochloa crusgalli*) produces a seedhead shaped like a turkey's foot.

Peanuts

Peanuts have a high oil content and are a great source of protein. They appeal more to larger birds than to smaller ones, but chickadees, titmice, and nuthatches will eat them, too. Peanuts are especially favored by woodpeckers, such as the Lewis's, acorn, and Gila in the West and the red-bellied, hairy, and downy in the East. If you're considering feeding peanuts, it's best to feed the shelled kind. You can put them in a conventional feeder, put them in with other seed mixes, or offer them separately in specially designed peanut feeders. You can also buy and feed peanuts in the shell, but only certain birds will pick them up and carry them away. Woodpeckers and titmice certainly do this, but the No. 1 species that will take as many peanuts as it can carry in its mouth is the blue jay.

It's fine to offer salt separately at your feeding station but better to stick with unsalted peanuts in your feeders. Although many birds—especially finches of all types—will visit a tray of rock salt or a salt block near your feeders, it's best to let them decide when, if, and how much salt they need in their diet. Occasional servings of salted nuts probably won't do any harm to the birds at your feeder, but it's generally preferable to provide plain, unsalted peanuts—with salt on the side, if you wish.

Peanuts

Grow Your Own Across much of the southeastern United States, peanuts are grown commercially. It's easy enough to grow your own crop of these legumes to eat yourself and to share with the birds at your feeders. While most peanuts need a long growing season, there are varieties that have been developed to produce a crop within the span of a short northeastern summer. Since peanuts can be among the pricier foods to purchase for feeder filling, growing your own is both a fun experiment and a way to stay within your bird-feeding budget, while offering a highly favored food at your feeders.

Choose a peanut cultivar that's suited to your local growing conditions. Plant peanut seeds (remove the shells but not the skins) 2 weeks after your area's last frost date, in well-drained, deeply tilled soil in full sun. Sow seeds 6 inches apart in rows 2 feet apart; after a month, thin plants in the row to 1 foot apart. Cultivate frequently to control weeds and to keep the soil loose, so the plants' "pegs" can stretch down into the soil to form the peanuts. Harvest when the plants start to turn yellow and the nuts have hard shells and pink or reddish skins. Dry whole plants with the peanuts attached in the sun for several days before hanging them to dry for several more weeks. Store dried peanuts in paper or cloth bags until you're ready to serve them in your feeders.

Seed Mixes

Seed mixes seem so promising—multiple kinds of food *in* the feeder should equal multiple kinds of birds *at* the feeder, right? In winter, when mixed flocks of birds often feed together wherever food is available, a seed mix may attract lots of activity and generate little waste. At other times of the year, you may find that birds are less inclined to share perch space at your feeders and, as a result, some of the less-favored foods in a seed mix are ignored or pushed out of the feeder. If the birds that stake out your feeder prefer sunflower seed, for example, they may pick it out of the mix and leave other seeds uneaten. They may even intentionally kick other seeds to the ground, along with the hulls of the sunflower seeds they love.

In a perfect world, ground-feeding birds would come along and happily clean up the cast-aside seeds from the feeder above, along with any bits of sunflower kernels that remain attached to the dropped shells. Reality is not always so tidy, however. Unwanted seeds tend to linger in a feeder, becoming damp and moldy. This happens on the ground under the feeder, too, where they mix with hulls and bird droppings to create unhealthy conditions for birds that might feed there and also become an attraction for rodents and other mammals.

If you're serving a seed mix in your feeder, pay close attention to which birds frequent the feeder and which seeds, if any, seem less popular with your visitors.

Birdseed mix

Use your observations to fine-tune your seed mix or to guide your decision to switch to a single type of seed in one or more of your feeders. Plenty of birds eat white millet, for example, but it may be a distant second choice in a mix with black-oil sunflower seed. Offering millet by itself in one feeder and black-oil sunflower in another can cut down on competition at the feeder between birds that prefer the sunflower and those that are attracted to the millet, and result in less wasted seed for you to clean up.

Choose—or Make—a Good Mix

A good seed mix is a combination of black-oil sunflower seed, gray-striped sunflower seed, sunflower kernels, cracked corn, and white millet, with shelled peanuts, safflower seed, and some nyjer occasionally mixed in. Avoid mixes that have a lot of buckwheat, flax, canary seed, milo, rape seed (aka canola), or red millet, because most feeder birds tend to ignore these ingredients.

If you can't find a mix that suits the birds that regularly show up at your feeders, buy seeds separately and make your own. Often this is a less expensive way to create a premium mix, and it lets you customize the combination of seeds to the birds in your area, so there's much less waste.

Like pieces of sunflower seeds or white millet that fall from feeders, seeds from a good mix that you purposely throw on the ground in winter will sometimes bring in birds that don't normally come to feeders. Rufous-sided towhees in the East and both spotted and green-tailed towhees in the West will come to birdseed on the ground under feeders in times of rough weather. Occasionally a vagrant spotted towhee or a

A Note from **Arlene**

CHECK THE LABEL: DON'T FALL FOR FILLER SEEDS

At times as an experiment, I've put cheap seed mix containing a lot of milo in one of my feeders, and it almost always has been ignored. Check the contents of your birdseed before you buy it. Its ingredients have to be listed on its bag or container. A seed mix with a lot of filler material will not only have milo but also wheatberries (the term for whole kernels of wheat) and other grain products listed on the label. These should generally be avoided. Many of these grains are attractive to birds when the grains are in their natural form in agricultural fields, but once they are harvested and put into birdseed, they seem to lose their appeal. When birdseed with a lot of filler material is put in feeders, the birds will just pick out the seeds they like, and either drop the others to the ground or drop them back into the feeder, where the uneaten seed often molds and clogs the feeder or messes up the other good seeds in that feeder.

green-tailed towhee turns up in the East far out of its normal range; when this happens, the bird almost always is feeding on seeds on the ground beneath a bird feeder.

Grow Your Own Sow a seed-mix garden with leftover birdseed in spring, and get to know the plants that produce your birds' favorite foods. In late spring, right around the time for planting gardens, activity at the bird feeder tends to drop off anyway, as natural foods become more available. And during summer months, that last bit of seed in the bottom of the bag will be more attractive to stored-grain pests than it will be to birds returning to your feeders in fall. So instead of tossing the remains of the bag or keeping it in hopes it will stay fresh, prepare a garden bed as you would for planting annuals, scatter the birdseed over the bed, and cover it lightly with soil.

Tend your birdseed garden just as you would an annual flowerbed. Watch to see what comes up and which birds show an interest in the plants as they begin to produce seeds. You can let the plants mature in place and leave the seeds for birds to eat directly from stem, stalk, or seedhead, or you can harvest your birdseed crop and serve the seeds in your feeders as fall arrives. You may see different birds enjoying the seeds in the garden from those that eat them at the feeder.

Milo

Milo is a small round grain that may be red, yellow, or white, depending on which kind of sorghum plant it comes from. In North America, milo is used primarily as animal feed, but in other parts of the world, it is ground up and used as a grain product. Milo is a common ingredient in inexpensive bird-seed mixes, but—except in parts of the Southwest and West where there are a lot of gallinaceous, or game, birds and different kinds of doves—it tends to be ignored by most birds at the feeder. That is not to say that milo is universally unloved by birds; rather, that its popularity depends on the region you live in and sometimes by the manner in which it is served.

Grow Your Own Despite its relative lack of popularity as a component of seed mixes, milo "on the stem" appeals to red-winged blackbirds, as well as to doves, grouse, pheasants, quail, and turkeys. Sorghum is easy to grow, too, and can provide an attractive vertical element to a birdseed garden. Prepare the soil as you would for any annual and sow sorghum in late spring after the ground is warm.

Until it raises its upright stalks of flowers in late summer, sorghum looks a lot like short corn, and so makes a nice backdrop for an annual flower garden. Once the seeds are set, you can leave them in your garden where birds will fly—or stroll—in to dine amid the drying stalks. Or you can harvest

Milo

some and stockpile them for fall and winter feeding. Combine stems of milo with those of millet and other dried seedheads from your garden to create your own edible dried arrangements for the birds.

Canary Seed

So named because of its use as food for pet canaries, small tan canary seed is the seed of canary grass (*Phalaris canariensis*). You may find canary seed as a component of seed mixes aimed specifically at attracting finches—these "wild canaries" appreciate canary seed nearly as much as their domesticated relatives do. Buntings, goldfinches, redpolls, and native sparrows also will eat canary seed, and so will quail and other game birds. But canary seed is not reliably popular with all birds or in all parts of the country. If you're experimenting with seeds and seed mixes to see which finds favor with your feeder guests, put out a small dish of plain canary seed and monitor how quickly it gets eaten, if at all. Or watch your mixed-seed feeder to see if canary seed gets eaten, left in the feeder, or kicked out with other unwanted seeds.

Corn

Ask any farmer or gardener and you'll hear that many birds will eat dried shelled corn, either as whole kernels or crushed up into the small pieces sold as cracked corn. Because it's easy for a wide range of bird species to eat, cracked corn attracts many of the same kinds of birds as does millet or mixed seed spread on the ground. When cracked corn is on the menu at your feeding

Myth or Truth: Rice and Birds

Throwing rice at a newly married couple as they walk out of a church has long been discouraged, sometimes on the basis of a widely held belief that if birds eat the rice, it will puff up in their stomachs and harm them. This has been shown to be untrue many times by bird experts, but myths and old wives' tales die hard. For dried rice to blow up in a bird's body, the rice would have to absorb a lot of moisture while being in extremely hot conditions for a long time—just as it is when it's boiled on a stove so that we can eat it. Those conditions don't exist in a bird's body, and in addition, birds digest their food rapidly. In the wild, birds such as bobolinks eat so much rice in commercial rice paddies that they're considered to be nuisances and are locally called "the rice birds."

The biggest danger from throwing rice at weddings or other functions is that rice underfoot is slippery for us to step on. So it's probably better not to throw rice at a wedding party, even though it has nothing at all to do with endangering birds. Better that you blow bubbles at the happy couple instead. As for rice, it's not popular with most birds, which is why it remains on church steps and walks to create a slipping hazard in the wake of weddings. But you can put a small amount of uncooked rice into the bottom of a tube feeder to draw moisture away from other seeds, thus helping to prevent clumping and spoilage. That's a use for rice that a bird lover can appreciate!

Like many birds, Northern cardinals will eat cracked corn served alone or as part of a seed mix. But cardinals' sturdy bills also enable them to dine on whole kernels of dried corn, a feat that birds with smaller, lighter bills cannot readily manage.

area, your guests may include sparrows, juncos, cardinals, doves, buntings, red-winged blackbirds, wild turkeys, and grouse or bobwhite. If you want to keep larger birds from eating all the cracked corn, spear a whole ear of dry corn on a large nail or screw driven through a board and mount the board on a branch or deck railing. Or you can hang an ear of corn with string or wire from a branch, shepherd's crook, or other pole. Jays, woodpeckers, and crows, and sometimes even nuthatches, will land onto the cobs and peck out the individual kernels. And just like they do with other nuts and large seeds, jays will take as many corn kernels as they can dislodge and then fly away with them. Squirrels will also perform whatever acrobatics are necessary to get to ears of corn and will take away whole kernels or even the entire cob, if they can free it from its holder.

Serve shelled corn in wire-mesh tube feeders like those used for peanuts. Kernels

Corn Forms a Quick, Bird-Worthy Hedge

If you're in need of a quick, single-season privacy screen, a few rows of corn can fill the bill while you shop for woody plants and perennials to create a longer-lasting hedge. When the ears mature, you can enjoy watching birds flit among the stalks as they feast on the harvest, or you can gather the ears and serve them more gradually through fall and winter.

To use corn as a screen, plant it a little more closely than you would in a garden. Sow the seeds 2 inches apart in three or more staggered rows spaced just 6 inches apart.

served on the ground or in tray or platform feeders will find favor with crows and squirrels and will quickly disappear. If deer are in your area, they may also show up for easily accessible dried corn, particularly if other food is scarce.

Grow Your Own You can buy ears of dried corn or bags of shelled kernels, but it's easy to grow your own corn for bird feeding. Interplant corn with tall sunflowers and create a vertical backdrop for a garden of birdseed plants, or use a stand of corn as a single-season hedge. Birds will dine on the corn on the stalk, or you can harvest the stalks and use them for fall decorations before stockpiling the dried ears for fall and winter bird feeding.

Birds aren't picky about which kind of corn you choose to grow. "Field" corn, also called "dent" corn, is preferred by most birds—and squirrels—but any dry type will do. The colorful kernels of Indian corn are attractive to the same birds that eat field corn, and you can use the ears as autumn décor and food for the birds. Likewise, popcorn appeals to many bird species, although its very hard kernels make it too tough for some smaller birds to eat. Grow the types you want for your own uses, and the birds will enjoy any corn you care to share with them.

Plant corn for harvesting in a prepared seedbed in full sun after the danger of frost is past. Sow seeds 1 to 2 inches deep, spaced 7 to 15 inches apart (thin seedlings to 15 inches apart when they are 2 to 4 inches tall). Use a covering of lightweight plastic netting over the area to keep squirrels and birds from making a meal of the newly sown seeds; leave the netting in place until seedlings are ready to thin, to prevent crows from eating the young plants. Nylon fishing line stretched between stakes at various heights and a few inches above your newly planted rows will also deter birds from feasting on corn seeds and seedlings.

Nuts

Nuts are just big seeds, and as such, they are popular with birds that are able get their beaks around them. While few backyard birds can manage the shells of walnuts and hickory nuts, many will gladly visit your feeders if you do the hard shelling work for them. Chickadees, jays, nuthatches, titmice, and woodpeckers will be among the first customers to frequent any feeders that you stock with nuts, although other birds will soon follow their lead. At wild-bird specialty stores, you can find fancy seed mixes and fruit-and-nut blends that contain shelled nutmeats for your birds' enjoyment, but the price of such treats may send you quickly back to the sunflower seed aisle.

If you do opt for the occasional treat of shelled nuts for the birds, save the nuts to serve in winter, so their fat and calories will be most beneficial in helping birds make it through cold weather when natural foods are scarce. You can serve birds nuts meant for human consumption, but unsalted, raw nuts are better for birds than the roasted, salted tidbits we prefer. And those rancid nuts that you found in the back of the cupboard are unlikely to appeal to birds any more than to your family, although the nuts

Going Nuts for Birds

Shelled nuts of almost any type will find favor at your feeders. You don't even have to pick the nutmeats free from the shells—just break the shells with a nutcracker or hammer and serve the cracked pieces in your feeders. The birds will do the delicate work of separating the good parts from the shells. While most nuts are generally popular with birds, some bird species do have their favorites. Here are the birds most likely to show up first when you put certain nuts in the feeder.

NUTS	ATTRACTS
Acorns	Chickadees, jays, nuthatches, quail, titmice, wild turkeys, woodpeckers, Clark's nutcrackers
Almonds	Cardinals, titmice, chickadees, crossbills, wrens, warblers
Hazelnuts/ filberts	Jays, woodpeckers, game birds
Hickory nuts	Chickadees, finches, sparrows, nuthatches, wrens, woodpeckers, titmice
Pecans	Chickadees, finches, sparrows, nuthatches, wrens, woodpeckers, titmice
Walnuts	Chickadees, jays, nuthatches, titmice, woodpeckers

might find favor with squirrels if you put them out in a feeder. When buying bird foods containing nuts, give them a sniff to check for freshness, just as you would if you were planning to eat them yourself. If they smell rancid or "off," skip the nuts and spend the money on more sunflower seed instead.

Grow Your Own Growing your own nuts—for your enjoyment and for the birds'—is a project that requires patience. While you can sow a bed of annual flowers and have bird-ready seeds within a couple of months, most nut trees take 5 to 7 years to begin producing a crop. Still, nut-producing trees and shrubs can be worthy additions to the landscape since they provide habitat as well as food for birds and other wildlife. In cold-winter areas, walnuts (*Juglans* spp.), hickories (*Carya* spp.), and hazelnuts (aka filberts, *Corylus* spp.) are popular landscape choices, while pecans (*Carya illinoinensis* and cvs.) and almonds (*Prunus amygdalus*) grow well in warmer climates. There are acorn-yielding oaks (*Quercus* spp.) suited to almost every region of North America. See Chapter 9 for more about choosing and growing nut trees in your yard.

Premium Seed Mixes: Are They Worth the Price?

You can get quite a "sticker shock" when you look at the price of the most premium of the premium mixes, the blends packed with shelled sunflower kernels, nuts, dried fruits, and peanuts. Sure, the birds will beat a path to your feeders for these favorites, but will your family have to survive on mac-n-cheese while the birds gobble the avian equivalent of filet mignon?

Commercial seed mixes are popular choices for filling feeders. And with just about every store—even those not remotely associated with nature—stocking some kind of birdseed, the choices can be overwhelming. If you're serious about bird feeding, don't waste your money buying the small bags of cheap seed found on many stores' shelves. Instead of the pretty songbirds pictured on the label, you're more likely to play host to unwanted species such as starlings, house sparrows, grackles, brown-headed cowbirds, and crows.

Read the label on any seed mix you're considering and be on the lookout for unpopular filler foods such as milo and wheatberries. Cheap birdseed is cheap because it has a lot of filler products in it, which contribute to the weight of the bag without adding an ounce of "bird appeal" to the mix. You don't have to pay premium prices for birdseed, but you should seek out well-known brands. Reputable seed companies sell different grades of birdseed mixes with prices that range from relatively inexpensive to very expensive. Even their least expensive mixes, however, are better than what you're likely to find on the shelves of your local pharmacy.

At the opposite end of the price spectrum from bargain mixes are the comparatively costly blends sold as "low mess" or "mess free."

"Cheap" birdseed mix

"Use logs for feeders. Place them on the ground and scatter seed on them. Some of the seed will fall off, but that's all the better. Ground birds will feed on and around the log. You can cut the log [lengthwise] to create a smooth surface, or just let the seed get caught in the bark. The birds will find it. Logs make great natural-looking feeders. I use a stepping stone in the same way. It's easy to sweep snow off it to clear it for seeds. White millet is a great seed for ground-feeding birds, such as sparrows and juncos, but other birds will eat it, including mourning doves and northern cardinals."

MIKE FIALKOVITCH, Pittsburgh, Pennsylvania

"Don't buy fancy feeders; the birds don't care."
ELAINE MEASE, Springtown, Pennsylvania

Made of shelled sunflower seeds, shelled peanuts, and other ready-to-eat bird treats, a mess-free mix is a great choice for a feeder over a deck or patio or any other place where the mess of sunflower shells is particularly unwelcome. Spending the extra money on a low-mess mix may be worthwhile if you have little time for cleaning up beneath your feeders. A mix that minimizes the mess is also a good choice if dropped seeds or shells are likely to wind up on a downstairs neighbor's balcony. You're unlikely to get birdseed sprouts popping up below a feeder filled with a mess-free mix, and using this kind of mix helps you avoid the allelopathic effects of sunflower shells on any garden plants you have growing around your feeder. Such mixes may seem pricey, but you're paying for almost 100 percent edible food without any of the waste of seed hulls. You may not be able to afford to fill all your feeders with mess-free seeds, but these mixes are worth considering when the tidiness of the feeder area is an issue.

Successful Seed-Serving Strategies

Knowing where birds prefer to dine will help you decide which kinds of feeders to use, as well as where to place them in your landscape. The smaller seed eaters, such as chickadees, finches, nuthatches, and titmice, are fairly agile and can take seeds easily from tube feeders and other hanging feeders that may swing in the wind. Larger and less adept birds, like jays and starlings, typically can't manage the small perches and tight-access ports of tube feeders, and thus can't gobble up seed from them as they tend to do from stationary tray feeders and accessible hopper feeders. Birds such as cardinals, doves, jays, juncos, sparrows, starlings, and thrashers that prefer to feed at ground level will usually find a low tray feeder to their liking, and they may also visit stable—not hanging/swinging—platforms or trays, at least for long enough to grab a seed to eat elsewhere.

Feeder Types and Features

There are so many different kinds of feeders to choose from that it can be overwhelming choosing the right one. There are hopper feeders, platform feeders, hanging tube feeders, "sock" feeders, rotating round feeders, feeders with battery-powered weight controls in them, plastic feeders, wooden feeders, metal feeders, brightly colored feeders, feeders shaped like barns or lighthouses, small feeders, large feeders, really cheap feeders, really expensive feeders, and homemade feeders. But what matters most is not the shape, design, makeup, or even the cost of the feeder: What matters most is what you put in it. So choose your birdseed the most wisely.

Perfect for Peanuts

Woodpeckers, blue jays, chickadees, titmice, and nuthatches all will make a beeline for a feeder filled with peanuts. It's no trouble to attract birds to these favorite treats, but keeping the feeder filled is another story. Peanuts in an open feeder will vanish almost before you get back inside the house after putting them out. In addition to the birds that love them, squirrels also are quick to find—and empty—a feeder that contains peanuts.

Slow the rate of peanut consumption and frustrate peanut-gobbling squirrels with a tube feeder made of sturdy wire mesh. You can buy a wire-mesh tube specifically designed for serving peanuts, or you can make your own by replacing the plastic tube from a commercial tube feeder with ¼-inch wire mesh. Quarter-inch mesh lets woodpeckers and other peanut lovers peck at the nuts, but keeps them from removing whole peanuts.

Converting an old plastic tube feeder to a wire-mesh tube is a fairly simple project, and it's a way to resurrect a plastic tube that has deteriorated from use or been damaged by squirrels. You'll need a piece of stainless steel ¼-inch wire mesh and a pair of needle-nose pliers with a wire cutter. Sturdy canvas or leather gloves are helpful for protecting your hands when you shape the wire into a tube. You can use a thin wooden dowel (or two) to create some perches, or you can leave this feeder perch free. Nuthatches, woodpeckers, and others will be able to cling to the wire mesh to extract the peanuts.

Step 1. Measure the circumference and height of the plastic tube feeder. (For example, some tubes measure 11 inches around and 12 inches tall.) Buy a piece of stainless steel ¼-inch wire mesh to correspond to those measurements. (Add about 1 inch to the circumference measurement to have enough wire to overlap and securely fasten your tube.) If you can't find stainless steel mesh, use ¼-inch hardware cloth.

Step 2. Roll the wire mesh into a shape and size to replace the plastic tube, overlapping the edges, then use pliers to bend the mesh over itself to create a secure "seam" along the length of the tube.

Step 3. Fasten the feeder bottom and top to the mesh tube. Usually, the bottom of the feeder will hold tight when the mesh is inserted into it, and the top will be held in place by the wire hooks at the base of the feeder's handle.

Step 4. Insert a perch or two, if desired, by sliding the dowel through the holes in the mesh.

Step 5. Fill with shelled whole peanuts, and hang the feeder in a spot where you can watch the visiting birds.

Conserve Seed with Feeder Selections

Not only will the types of feeders you use determine which kinds of birds will come to your yard, the feeders will also affect the rate at which seed is eaten from them. An open platform feeder may make its contents available to the greatest number and variety of birds, but it also allows "feeder hogs" to settle in and feast until there's nothing left for less-dominant species.

Tube Feeders

A tube-shaped feeder lends itself to serving almost any type of seed. Only the size of the

Small birds like chickadees and finches can eat from these tube feeders with ease, while the metal cage keeps feeder-raiding squirrels and larger birds from gobbling up the goodies.

feeding ports needs to change to make a tube suitable for chunky whole peanuts and striped sunflower seeds or for the tiny slivers of nyjer. Tube feeders are a practical way to control your birdseed expenses, because only one bird at a time can occupy a perch, and small feeding ports keep birds from taking more than a few seeds at a time.

Tube feeders are easy to maintain, too. Most have a lid that slides up on a wire loop that also forms the hanger, allowing you to easily lift the lid, pour in seed, and quickly replace the top. Depending on the size of the tube, you may only have to fill it once or twice a week. Features like metal-reinforced ports slow squirrels' efforts to chew through a tube feeder to get to its contents. While filling a tube feeder typically is quite simple, cleaning can be more difficult. Tubes are prone to developing a hard-to-clean layer of spoiled seed in the very bottom of the tube; this can be a lingering source of moisture and mold if you don't take the time to clean it out regularly. A tube feeder with an easily removable bottom is a worthwhile investment, because it lets you quickly scrape out any lingering residue every time you refill the feeder. See Chapter 8 for other tips on keeping feeders clean.

Some manufacturers offer "upside-down tubes," with the seed ports placed below the perches rather than above them. This arrangement is meant to limit house finches' access to pricey nyjer seed, while allowing more acrobatic goldfinches to hang upside down from the perches to reach it. If hoards of hungry house finches threaten to bust your nyjer seed budget, this type of feeder may at least slow them down, although some birders report that sufficiently motivated house finches eventually solve the puzzle of upside-down dining, even if it's not their preferred style.

Most tube feeders also limit access to birds that are cardinal-size and larger, because bigger birds are unable to fit easily on their perches. And birds that commonly feed on the ground will only occasionally attempt to dine from a tube feeder.

Seed "Socks"

A fine nylon mesh "sock" is an inexpensive way to deliver nyjer, one of the pricier foods you can offer your backyard birds. The small birds that prefer nyjer are able to cling to the seed sock to pluck the small black seeds through the mesh, while larger birds are unable to manage the necessary acrobatics to get to the costly contents. In terms of durability, a seed sock tends to be short-lived. Under the best of circumstances, you may refill it a few times before clinging and pecking birds take their toll, and the sock develops holes that let the contents leak out too freely. In the worst case, some creature other than birds takes an interest in the seed sock and makes off with it or chews it apart. Although nyjer is not generally attractive to squirrels and other mammalian feeder raiders, that doesn't guarantee that one of them won't give it a try at the expense of the sock and its contents. If you're crafty, you can buy mesh fabric and sew a small sack for a hand-made seed sock, adding a drawstring closure to the top. Or if you want a fun and frugal 5-second seed sock, cut a 12-inch length of clean, used pantyhose (from the toe up), fill with seed, and knot the top end. Hang from nylon cord or twine.

Hopper Feeders

The vast majority of commercially available bird feeders are based on the hopper model: a large central storage area that's filled from the top and lets seeds out into a tray at the bottom. Even tube feeders really are just tall, narrow hoppers with multiple access ports.

Variations abound, of course, and range from cosmetic features—feeders that look like

A hopper feeder accommodates birds of various sizes—from tufted titmice to cardinals to jays. Birds that can't easily land on narrow perches will be more at ease on the broader shelves of a hopper feeder.

barns or churches, for example—to practical baffles and barriers meant to keep squirrels and larger birds from cleaning out the contents. The key attraction of a hopper feeder is its ability to hold a lot of seed, reducing the duties of the feeder-filler even during the busiest times of the year.

The downside of a hopper feeder's large capacity is that it can allow a large quantity of seed to spoil, if the birds that frequent it suddenly move on.

Hoppers can be hard to clean, as well, particularly if they have features designed to hinder access by mammals. Because their large size makes them heavy, hopper feeders usually need to be mounted on fixed posts or other sturdy supports, which can also make it hard for you to get them thoroughly clean.

Tray and Platform Feeders

In contrast to tube and hopper feeders, trays and platforms mimic nature's delivery system and thus are welcoming to the greatest variety of birds. Species that normally feed on the ground will appreciate a low, stable platform, as will birds that don't fit on the perches of tubes or the narrow trays of smaller hoppers.

While the terms are largely interchangeable, *tray* typically describes a hanging feeder, while *platform* is used to refer to one

Containers made for both storing and pouring birdseed help to keep your seed supplies fresh and make it easier to refill feeders without wasteful spillage. If your storage container doubles as a feeder-filler, make sure it's light enough for you to lift and carry, even when full of seed.

that is fixed. Tray feeders more often have sides; platforms tend to be flat surfaces without any enclosure. Both tray and platform feeders are good for serving foods that don't lend themselves to closed feeders—dried fruits, large pieces of nuts, "kitchen" foods, crumbled suet, etc.—and they are a good way to offer your feeder birds new foods before adding them to other types of feeders. Because they are so simple, tray or platform feeders can be made out of things you have around the house, and they are easily cleaned and adjusted to allow for serving at different heights to attract different birds.

Unless you build or buy a cover, however, a tray or platform feeder's contents are fully exposed to the elements and always in danger of getting wet and becoming spoiled. Lightweight seed served in a tray may blow away in strong winds. Trays and platforms offer nothing to impede squirrels and other mammals from feasting on the foods you put out for the birds, nor do they restrict access to "feeder hogs" and bullies such as starlings, crows, and jays. You can use this knowledge to your advantage, however, by serving inexpensive foods to potential feeder pests in a tray or platform feeder placed away from other, more restricted feeders filled with pricier foods.

three

Suet, Peanut Butter, and More

On the face of it, suet may seem like an odd food choice for birds. Suet is animal fat, after all, and we don't tend to think of most songbirds as carnivorous creatures that would normally have a chance to eat animal fat in the wild. But suet, whether raw or "rendered" (melted and cooled) to make it more stable, approximates the nutritional return that birds naturally get from eating insects, and birds that mainly feed on insects will be the first ones to seek out any suet you choose to offer at your feeders.

A black-capped chickadee and a white-breasted nuthatch cling to a mesh bag of suet.

Birds That Eat Suet

Many types of birds—woodpeckers, nuthatches, chickadees, titmice, mockingbirds, wrens, starlings, catbirds, jays, brown creepers, and others—will regularly eat suet in whatever form you offer it. At times, you might be surprised by other species that will also eat suet—orioles, warblers, robins, kinglets, cardinals, towhees, sparrows, and members of the thrush family, including bluebirds and thrashers.

While *suet* specifically refers to the fat from around the kidneys of beef and mutton, the term is used more generally to describe a broad range of fat-based products that have been processed for feeding birds. For the birds, it's not about the source anyway, it's about the density of calories—the high-energy payoff that suet gives on a per-beakful basis. That's why peanut butter (and other nut butters) is often used as an ingredient in suet-style recipes and may be mixed with fats or used in place of them. Like animal fat, peanut butter is calorie-dense and packs the energy punch that birds need to sustain their speedy metabolisms.

Just as there are all kinds of seed mixes and different kinds of feeders specifically for certain kinds of seeds, there are many kinds of suet and suetlike products to choose from and feeders made to hold them. Deciding which suet product is best for your feeding area can be daunting, because almost every single one claims to attract more bird species than any other suet product does. Ultimately, though, they're all pretty similar—made of rendered fat, some with peanut butter or other fat added; "enhanced" with seeds, fruits, or flavorings; and presented in different consistencies or shapes.

As we've already mentioned, nearly all species of wild birds eat insects at least some of the time. Depending on how you serve it, suet may attract a remarkable number of different birds, including many you wouldn't expect. A block of suet in a wire-mesh suet cage may be accessible only to the most avid suet devotees—woodpeckers and nuthatches, for example—that are able to cling to a vertical surface to feed. But crumbles of suet served on a tray may attract the attention of bluebirds, while a low platform with bits of suet will welcome robins and cardinals.

Forms of Fat

Commercially available suet for birds is animal fat that has been rendered to form hard cakes or balls. The widely offered suet cakes are perhaps the easiest but not the only way to provide suet to the birds in your yard. Experiment with different forms and recipes for suet and see which ones your local birds find most appealing.

Suet and fat trimmings. Butchers often will sell (or occasionally give away) beef fat trimmings and suet, either of which typically costs less than processed suet cakes. The

Preformed cakes feature various flavorings and combinations of seeds and suet and other bird-tempting treats and are shaped to fit easily into standard-size feeders.

purest suet that you can get is a slab of raw fat from a butcher or the grocery store meat counter. In years past, butchers were glad to get rid of these slabs of fat and often gave them away, but that's rarely the case today. If you find a butcher willing to part with suet, it will almost certainly be as part of a normal retail transaction, albeit modest in com-

parison to those made for prime steaks and boneless chicken breasts.

In warm weather, you'll have to render this material yourself to keep it from spoiling quickly, or you can stash it in the freezer and offer prepared suet cakes at your feeders until cold weather returns. In winter, when the temperature stays at or below freezing most of the time, it's a different story. A slab of pure, unrendered fat can be an incredible draw to all kinds of birds and will last just as long, if not longer, than most commercially available suet products.

Rendered suet cakes. Cakes of plain, rendered suet may be found at wild-bird supply stores or other places where bird-feeding products are sold. Finding plain, unadulterated cakes can be difficult but worth the effort. Even though they're probably the least expensive commercial cakes, birds like them just fine, and you can soften them and add other ingredients to customize them for your feeder guests.

Serve Suet Responsibly

Birds are not the only wild creatures that find raw, unprocessed suet irresistible. If you notice one morning that the chunks of fat you've put out in an open feeder or a mesh bag have mysteriously disappeared— sometimes along with the feeder or bag that held them—your yard may be receiving nocturnal visits from mammals. Raccoons, skunks, feral cats, free-ranging dogs, rats, and even bears are among the unwelcome guests that may sniff out your suet supply and decide to claim it as their own. If you suspect that's the case, do yourself and your neighbors a favor and take raw fat off the menu at your feeders. Processed suet products that can be served in more secure wire cages tend to be less attractive to mammals. Even then, if you know that something bigger than a bird has been visiting your suet feeders, you may want to stop serving any form of animal fat for a week or two—or, at the very least, bring in suet feeders after dark until you're sure the nocturnal nibblers have moved on.

Besides the familiar rectangular cakes, rendered suet comes in other forms meant for fitting into different feeder configurations. It's also available in bigger blocks; in rounded "plugs" meant to be put into holes in logs; as small flavored suet nuggets or pellets that resemble rabbit food; as suet balls, bells, or logs with or without seed coverings; and in other shapes too numerous to list.

Bacon grease and meat drippings. Stockpile bacon fat and grease poured off cooked ground beef and mix it with cornmeal or bread crumbs to make a soft but serviceable suet stand-in. Bluebirds, jays, woodpeckers, and Carolina wrens will be tempted by bacon grease and tidbits at the feeder, as will starlings, crows, and ravens.

Lard. Lard, sold in the grocery store usually near the butter in the dairy case, is another soft but functional form of fat you can use in recipes for your birds. Vegetable shortening works, too, if you'd rather not buy meat products for your wild bird friends. They'll appreciate the high-energy fat in any form in which you choose to offer it.

Vegetable shortening. If you're not a meat eater and don't wish to serve animal products to the birds, substitute vegetable shortening in combinations with cornmeal, crushed crackers or cereal, or bread crumbs. You can also use vegetable oil to moisten bits of dried bread for the birds.

Shopping for Suet

The easiest way for most people to serve suet is by using the commercial suet prod-

A Note from *Arlene*

BEFRIEND A BUTCHER

While regular interactions with a butcher are not as common today as they were a couple of decades ago, it can be worth your time to seek out a butcher shop or meat counter that sells suet for feeding the birds. Anytime I make the trip to a local farmers' market, I make sure to go to the stand of a butcher who sells his products there. He grinds up fat and forms it into 4- to 5-inch compressed balls that are almost 100 percent suet and wraps them in mesh. I buy as many as I can carry or as he is willing to sell me. They're about equal in size to the suet cakes you'd buy in a store, but they last a whole lot longer because they're so dense. They're also much cheaper. I store them in the freezer, just like I do all the suet cakes and products I buy at all times of the year. Commercial suet cakes, especially those marked for year-round feeding, obviously aren't going to spoil, but it's easier getting them out of their wrappers and putting them in suet cages when they're cold. If I want to put one of the suet balls in a conventional suet cage rather than hanging it, I let it thaw out and smash it down with a plate. Because of the longevity of these suet balls, I sometimes have some left as summer approaches, but I don't put them out then. In the warm months, I switch back to commercial suet cakes that can take the heat without becoming spoiled and smelly.

ucts. But this is one of those cases in which the price you pay for them can vary, often dramatically, from one place to another. Shop around ahead of time before you decide what kind of suet you're going to buy and where. Check out suet prices at home improvement stores, general merchandise stores, grocery stores, and other places you frequent while going about your normal routine. At certain times of the year, processed suet cakes may be cheaper at the grocery store than they are in specialized bird, farm, or garden stores. And, unlike seed mixes, most commercial suet cakes are made by the same few companies, regardless of where you find them for sale. On the other hand, the grocery store may charge more for them, but you won't know until you check. When you find a good deal, buy suet cakes in quantity and freeze them for future use. Feeding the birds is a growing business, and suet is one of its most successful products. But the birds don't care where you buy your suet, so long as they get it.

Read the Label—or Not

You can find the actual amount of fat in a processed suet block by looking at the label, which will list the percentages of crude protein, crude fat, crude fiber, and moisture, along with any other ingredients. By comparing the protein and fat contents of different suet products, you may find big discrepancies. While you can get caught up

"Everyone always wants to buy the newest, fanciest, flavored suet cake because it's something different, and they think that it will attract different kinds of birds. But almost all of the suets have fruit, seeds, or nuts in them, and they will eventually attract the bane of the bird-feeding world—the squirrel. The best thing to do is to forget the flavors and buy plain suet cakes."

AL GUARENTE, Media, Pennsylvania

in seeking out products with the highest fat and protein content, it's not usually worth fishing out your reading glasses to inspect the fine print. Just use your eyes to visually evaluate any suet blocks you're considering: Look for suet that obviously contains a lot more fat than fillers or additives, even if those additives are nuts, dried pieces of fruit, or seeds. The fat is what wild birds want and need—often the extra tidbits are more attractive to human suet buyers than they are to the birds that supposedly flock to them.

When you start looking at suet blocks, you'll find a variety of flavors and ingredients that promise to attract particular desired species of birds to your feeders. These may seem like a good idea, but birds almost never read labels. From their perspective, fat is where it's at, and flavorings and vitamin additives matter little, if at all. I have no recommendation as to which kind of suet cake you should buy. The choices are endless. But you should know that the different flavors that are heavily advertised as attractants really don't matter at all to the birds. In fact, nuts, berries, and seeds in the suet can actually be more of a problem than a benefit. Birds are most interested in the suet, but other wildlife may take an interest in your suet feeders because of the extra goodies embedded in the fat. If you buy suet with seeds or nuts in it, the squirrels will like it as much as the birds do. If you have squirrels in your neighborhood, rest assured that they will find it and be as pesky about raiding your suet feeders as they are at getting into seed feeders.

Render It Yourself

If you find a butcher who will supply you with raw fat, you may want to render some of it yourself to increase its stability when you put it into your feeder. Here's how.

1. Chop the fat into small pieces or run it through a meat grinder. A butcher may be willing to do this for you. Remove all traces of meat.

2. Heat the chopped fat on low until it is liquefied. Don't try to speed the process by turning up the heat, as this could lead to scorching or fire.

3. Carefully strain the liquid fat through cheesecloth or a fine mesh sieve placed over a heatproof bowl to remove any particles. Do this several times to purify the suet.

4. Pour the still-liquid suet into a shallow metal pan to cool. Once it has solidified, you can cut it into cakes to fit your suet feeders or chop it up to serve on a tray or platform.

Warning: Few people find the odor of melting suet appealing. If you have an electric skillet and access to an outdoor outlet, you may want to take suet outside to render it rather than have the smell in your kitchen. Take all the same precautions as you would indoors to minimize the risk of fire or of burning yourself while pouring the hot fat.

Serve a Suet-y Spread

Spreading suet or peanut butter on a tree trunk, branch, or feeder made specifically for that purpose is another way of serving fat to the birds. If you're concerned that plain peanut butter poses a risk to birds that might get their bills gummed up by it, mix in bread crumbs or cornmeal to reduce its stickiness and to put your mind at ease. (Evidence of birds being harmed by plain peanut butter is both scarce and anecdotal.)

Knowledgeable backyard birders have been spreading some form of suet or peanut butter mixture on hard surfaces for years for the birds to eat, but bird food manufacturers have only recently spotted this trend and now offer the convenience of commercial spreadable suet products. Whether you stir up your own suet spread or buy a tub at the wild-bird supply store makes little difference to the birds.

The same birds that feed on suet cakes and other forms of fat also will eat suet and peanut butter spreads. And as with any other foods you offer, the way in which you serve this softer version will play a role in which birds are attracted to it. Woodpeckers, creepers, and other birds that are adept at clinging to vertical surfaces will help themselves to fat spread on the trunk of a tree, on a wooden post, or on a wooden shingle hanging from a branch or feeder pole. You can also spread this treat in the corner of a tray feeder or on a flat surface at ground level for less acrobatic birds. Be aware that these high-fat spreads will leave a greasy stain on feeders and any other surfaces

A Note from
Arlene

THE BENEFITS OF YEAR-ROUND SUET

Whether you should or should not feed suet in summer months is a matter of preference. Some people do; others say they never have and never will. I don't think there's a right or wrong answer here. Personally, I'm in the camp that feeds suet year-round, because the variety and number of birds that come to the suet in my yard during the breeding season and through summer months far surpass the variety I see during winter. But I've spent years developing a good wildlife habitat that's visited by lots of birds on a daily basis. I'm also in a good geographical location in a big valley, surrounded by farm fields with a northeast-to-southwest wooded ridge across from the house. That ridge is a great migration route and the valley has a "sink" effect, meaning birds drop down into it to feed. However, I still wouldn't see as many different birds as I do if I didn't offer a variety of foods, including suet, year-round.

The woodpecker parade at the suet I put out is nonstop. During the breeding season, both adult male and female hairy, downy, and red-bellied woodpeckers are at it constantly. They fly down from the woods, eat some of the suet, and then fly back off, often with suet in their beaks that they're almost certainly taking back to feed to their young. When the young leave the nest, become fledglings, and are able to travel around with the adults away from the nest area, it's not uncommon for me to see a whole family at the suet at the same time. At first, the young will perch on the dead tree trunk on which I've got the suet mounted and wait for the adults to break off a piece and bring it to them. Eventually the young begin to come to the suet on their own, sometimes even attempting to chase off the adults.

At times, unexpected visitors like warblers or kinglets may come to suet, especially in winter. In the Pacific Northwest, the Townsend's warbler is one that has been known to frequent suet feeders. Once a ruby-crowned kinglet spent the winter eating the suet in my yard in eastern Pennsylvania, and during another winter a pine warbler did the same thing, although the pine warbler also occasionally ate the remnants of black-oil sunflower seeds. Another time I was asked to confirm the identity of a northern parula warbler coming to a suet feeder north of Trenton, New Jersey, in what was a brutally cold and snowy season. All these warblers were eating suet as a replacement for the protein they'd normally be getting from insects.

"I hang a suet feeder on the garage at the end of the yard for the downy woodpeckers. I am amazed to get those in town. I can't serve suet on a regular basis, though, because the starlings move in. They seem to be worse in spring when they are nesting."

DONNA CHIARELLI, Kutztown, Pennsylvania

where you spread them—the railing of your deck or porch is probably not a good serving site. Keep in mind that other wildlife may also seek out suet or peanut butter spreads, so factor that into your selection of places to offer these treats.

Should You Serve Suet in Summer?

Because unrendered fat quickly becomes rancid and smelly when the weather turns warm, many birders stop offering suet at their feeders during summer months. Certainly it's true that raw suet and fat create an unpleasant, insect-attracting mess when the thermometer starts to climb. Fortunately, rendering and other processing results in commercial suet products that are much more stable at high temperatures and can be served to birds year-round.

Just as it happens at seed feeders, activity at your suet feeders may decline in late spring and through summer, when natural foods are abundant. Keep watch to see which birds, if any, continue to visit the suet you're serving. If you've been filling multiple suet feeders during winter, late spring may be the time to take down all but one or two. Make sure any suet feeders you plan to leave up during summer are placed in shady spots—even "year-round" suet products can melt and turn rancid when exposed for hours in the hot summer sun.

Beyond rendered suet blocks processed to help them hold up in hot weather, peanut butter–based products and recipes can help you keep suet-loving birds happy when the temperature turns your usual suet servings

With or without added ingredients like seeds and fruit, processed cakes of rendered suet let you keep offering this fatty food to chickadees and other summer residents during the warm months of the year.

sticky (or stinky). If you (or someone you know) like peanut-butter-and-bacon sandwiches, you'll see the logic of some of these recipes. They're basically PB-and-bacon treats for the birds!

Suet's Biggest Fans

Suet attracts all kinds of birds. Woodpeckers, most of which are nonmigratory species, are its primary visitors, but there's also a constant parade of others. Nuthatches, titmice, chickadees, creepers, northern mockingbirds, Clark's nutcrackers, wrens, and kinglets are some that visit it often. The Carolina wren in the East and its western counterpart, the Bewick's wren, are frequent suet visitors. Reports of hummingbirds and Baltimore orioles at suet feeders are heard occasionally, but it's likely those birds were going after the bugs around the suet, not the suet itself. Suet can also attract unwanted species at certain times of the year. In early spring, when big mixed flocks of grackles, cowbirds, European starlings, and blackbirds are still traveling together, they may arrive at your feeding area in huge numbers and fight over every little bit of suet. There's really no solution to this problem, except to wait it out or to take down the suet feeder for a while. All of the various crows will eat suet, too, although they don't usually visit yards in big numbers. Feeders designed to exclude birds that are unable to cling to vertical surfaces can also deter starlings and other potential suet hogs.

One of the few species that can go down a tree trunk head-first, a nimble red-breasted nuthatch has no trouble getting a meal from a wire suet cage.

Make Your Own Suet Foods

Homemade "suet" recipes vary, but they all follow a basic template: a fat, usually peanut butter or lard, mixed with cornmeal, flour, cracker crumbs, bread crumbs, peanut bits, and raisins or other dried fruits. If you want to make suet that's soft rather than firm, use more fat than the solid ingredients. Spread it wherever you want—on tops of posts, on boards attached to trees, or on tree trunks or branches themselves. Just be aware that wherever you spread it, it will leave a stain.

Some people's suet recipes have become famous, including the three that follow.

SOUTHERN SUMMER "SUET" TREAT

Birds that eat suet will go for these suet-style treats wherever you serve them. In the Southeast and Texas, potential takers may include downy and red-bellied woodpeckers, white-breasted and brown-headed nuthatches, Carolina chickadees, blue jays, and summer tanagers.

INGREDIENTS AND SUPPLIES

1½ cups water

1 cup uncooked oatmeal

¾ cup lard or bacon grease, melted

1 cup uncooked hot wheat cereal (such as Cream of Wheat)

1 cup corn meal

½ cup raisins or similar dried fruit

1½ cups creamy peanut butter (chunky is acceptable, if that's all you have)

Waxed paper

Baking sheet

Resealable plastic bag

DIRECTIONS

1. Bring the water to a boil and add the oatmeal. Turn down the heat and let simmer for 1 minute.

2. Remove the oatmeal from the heat and stir in the remaining ingredients in the order listed above.

3. When the mixture is cool enough to handle—without sticking to your hands like glue—mold it into rough patties about an inch thick and 2½ to 3 inches in diameter.

4. Set aside any patties that you plan to use immediately. Place the rest on a waxed paper-lined baking sheet and put them in the freezer.

5. When the patties are frozen, store them in the resealable plastic bag in the freezer.

6. When you're ready to serve a patty to the birds, let it thaw until it's soft. Then you can set it in a bird feeder, hang it in a mesh bag, or press it onto the surface of a pinecone.

YIELD: 6 TO 8 PATTIES

MARTHA SARGENT'S SUET RECIPE

Martha Sargent and her husband, Bob, run the nationwide Hummer/Bird Study Group in Clay, Alabama. They catch and band all kinds of birds at Fort Morgan on the Gulf Coast and are internationally known hummingbird banders who train other qualified people to band hummingbirds. Here is Martha's suet recipe.

INGREDIENTS AND SUPPLIES

2 cups crunchy peanut butter

2 cups lard (do not substitute for this)

4 cups quick-cooking oats

4 cups yellow cornmeal

2 cups flour (any kind)

$\frac{2}{3}$ cup white sugar

1 cup (or more) hulled sunflower seed chips

12" x 8" baking pan

Waxed paper

Plastic food storage box

DIRECTIONS

1. Melt the peanut butter and lard in a large bowl in the microwave. Start with 1 minute on high power, then stir and continue microwaving in 30-second increments until completely melted. Stir in the remaining ingredients.

2. Spread in a 12" x 8" inch baking pan and let cool.

3. Cut into eight 4" x 3" inch squares (to fit a standard suet cage).

4. Wrap the squares in waxed paper and store in a box in the freezer. You can put frozen cakes right into your suet cage, or soften a square and press it into whatever kind of feeding container you'd like to use.

YIELD: 8 SUET CAKES

EASY SPREADABLE SUET-AND-CEREAL

Frank and Barbara Haas live in Narvon, Pennsylvania, not far from Philadelphia. Twenty-two years ago, they started **Pennsylvania Birds**, *the state's official and highly acclaimed quarterly birding magazine. That led to the formation of the Pennsylvania Society for Ornithology and the state* **PABIRDS LISTSERV,** *which is handled by the National Audubon Society. Frank and Barb have two of the longest bird lists in Pennsylvania, and they've taught many birders through the years. Their suet recipe may be adjusted to make as much or as little as you (and the birds) want, and can be soft and spreadable or crumbly.*

INGREDIENTS AND SUPPLIES

Lard

Peanut butter

Rolled oats

Crisped rice cereal

Wheat germ

Cornmeal

Flour

Electric mixer

DIRECTIONS

1. Melt equal parts of lard and peanut butter in a large bowl in the microwave. Start with 1 minute on high power, then stir and continue microwaving in 30-second increments until completely melted. Thoroughly stir until smooth.

2. Using a mixer, mix in the remaining ingredients in desired amounts to get the consistency you like, making sure the mixture is thick but not dry.

3. Store in the refrigerator and use as needed. This mixture works great in suet logs.

RUDY'S BASIC BUDGET SUET

Rudy Keller is past president of the Baird Ornithological Club in Reading, Pennsylvania, and of the Pennsylvania Society for Ornithology, and is a counter of migrating birds at Hawk Mountain Sanctuary in Kempton, Pennsylvania. He combines three inexpensive ingredients to make his suet.

INGREDIENTS

12 ounces peanut butter

14 ounces lard

1 large loaf white bread

DIRECTIONS

1. Melt the peanut butter and lard in a large bowl in the microwave. Start with 1 minute on high power, then stir and continue microwaving in 30-second increments until completely melted.

2. While the fats melt, tear the bread into small pieces.

3. Stir the bread into the melted peanut butter-lard.

4. Store the mixture in the refrigerator to make it firmer or in the freezer to harden it. Serve crumbled in a tray or cut into cakes to fit your feeders.

Seeds with Suet on the Side?

You've likely seen some version of a combination feeder that has a central hopper for serving seeds plus a cage for serving suet on one or both ends. While this seems like a nice arrangement—maybe the equivalent of offering meat and potatoes to the birds?—it's probably more of a convenience for the person who refills the feeder than it is a desirable setup for birds.

The suet will be more attractive to its usual fans when served on its own, away from the activity of the seed feeder. The seed feeder will be more welcoming to smaller seed-eating birds, without the suet there to attract jays, starlings, and other potential feeder bullies. And, while the combined feeder lets you make one-stop refills of both seed and suet, it makes cleaning the feeder a more complicated process. The need to clean out spoiled seed may not coincide with the timing for cleaning the suet holder and vice versa. The perceived convenience of the combo feeder exceeds the reality for both you and the birds. Serve suet in a separate area away from your seed feeder, and you'll find that both feeders are visited more frequently.

FRUITY SUET SMORGASBORD

Many of the birds that eat suet also are attracted to fruit. But few of us have the budget to treat birds to fruit out of season. Fortunately, birds are not as particular about spotted, bruised, or insect-nibbled fruits as our families may be. If you have a cherry tree—or know someone who does—collect imperfect fruit that falls on the ground during the harvest, cut it into halves and quarters, and dry it in a dehydrator for serving to the birds. This recipe uses cherries, but also works with raisins or other dried fruit. You can also replace the cherries in this recipe with shelled sunflower kernels and pieces.

INGREDIENTS AND SUPPLIES

1–1½ pounds beef fat

⅓ cup cracked corn

¾ cup chopped dried cherries

Heatproof bowl

Small containers, such as plastic margarine tubs

Waxed paper

DIRECTIONS

1. Melt the fat in a saucepan over low heat. As the fat melts, pour off the resulting liquid into a heatproof bowl to prevent it from burning.

2. Let the liquid fat cool slightly, then stir in the other ingredients.

3. Line containers with waxed paper and pour in the mix.

4. Cool in the refrigerator, then store in the freezer until ready for use. To serve, just pop a cake out of the container and put it in a mesh bag or wire suet cage.

YIELD: ABOUT 4 CUPS OF SUET

SIMPLE SUET-PEANUT BUTTER BIRD SNACK

Combinations of suet and peanut butter are easy to make and find favor with many wild birds.

INGREDIENTS AND SUPPLIES

1 cup rendered suet

1 cup peanut butter

3 cups cornmeal

½ cup flour

Small containers, such as plastic margarine tubs

(Optional: Pinecones, string, waxed paper, cookie sheet)

DIRECTIONS

1. Melt together rendered suet and peanut butter.

2. Stir cornmeal and flour into the liquid fats and mix well.

3. Pour into containers and refrigerate or freeze until ready to use.

A Western scrub-jay clings precariously to a pinecone to get at the peanut butter mixture packed between its scales.

You can substitute lard or shortening for the suet in this recipe and add any tidbits your birds respond to. Or tie pieces of string to pinecones, and when the fat mixture is still liquid, coat pinecones with it, chill them on a cookie sheet until the coating solidifies, and hang them outside.

Suet Stir-Ins

Birds like suet just fine without any additions, so there's no need to put extra ingredients in your suet creations. But if you have treats to include, or you want to use other ingredients to stretch your supply of rendered suet, choose tidbits that birds that eat suet would normally eat. Chopped nuts, bits of dried fruit, cracked corn, and shelled sunflower kernels or pieces are all good choices. Avoid small seeds that suet-eating birds don't normally eat, and avoid sunflower seeds with shells—birds may have a hard time cracking open seeds that are slippery with suet.

FUN AND FESTIVE SUET SHAPES

Nearly any suet or suetlike mixture can be made into decorative shapes using cookie cutters or molds meant for gelatin or candy. Use this recipe to make Christmas "cookies" to hang on trees in your yard, and soon your trees will also be adorned with hungry songbirds.

INGREDIENTS AND SUPPLIES

1 cup lard

1 cup crunchy peanut butter

2 cups rolled oats

2 cups cornmeal

1 cup flour

Baking sheet

Waxed paper

Cookie cutters

A chopstick or skewer for making holes

Ribbon or yarn

DIRECTIONS

1. Cover a baking sheet with waxed paper and place the cookie cutters on it.

2. Melt the lard and peanut butter in the microwave, heating in 30-second intervals on high power until they are completely liquefied. Add the remaining ingredients and stir well to form a thick mixture.

3. Pour or spoon the mix into the cookie cutters to a depth of about 1 inch.

4. With the chopstick or skewer, poke a hole through the suet near the top of each "cookie." Make the hole large enough to thread ribbon or yarn through.

5. Put the tray of filled cookie cutters into the freezer for several days.

6. Lift the "cookies" off the tray and push them out of the cookie cutters; peel off any adhering waxed paper. Thread ribbon or yarn through each and hang them outside.

YIELD: APPROXIMATELY 8 COOKIES

Suet Serving Suggestions

The way you serve suet to your birds will depend both on the type of suet you're offering—"original" style (raw, unrendered fat), preformed cakes or logs, or a soft and spreadable form—and on your aesthetic preferences. Not everyone appreciates the sight of a mesh bag full of chunks of fat hanging from a tree, but the birds will enjoy it.

Mesh bags—the sort that onions and oranges and other produce are sold in—make a fine delivery system for chunks of suet from the butcher shop. Suet-eating birds such as woodpeckers and nuthatches have no problem clinging to the mesh to peck away at the treats within. The disposable nature of these bags also lends them to this task: When there's nothing left of the suet but old, nasty bits and a greasy mesh bag, the entire thing can be tossed into the trash.

The main downside of mesh bags is that they offer no resistance to other wildlife that also finds suet mighty attractive. From roaming cats and dogs to raccoons and other critters, a bag of suet is a tempting treat. If you wake one morning and find the bag missing, suspect a raccoon at work and suspend your suet serving for a few days.

Suet cages are made of sturdy, sometimes vinyl coated wire that provides the same sort of cling-holds for birds as mesh bags do, but cages are a little more vexing to undesirable animals interested in their contents. Most suet cages are made to hold the square suet cakes that are ubiquitous in stores from fall into late winter. You may also find larger cylindrical cages meant to hold seed or suet "logs" but also serviceable for holding chunks of raw suet.

These basic cages are relatively inexpensive and serve quite well to give birds access to suet, while giving some degree of resistance to foraging animals. Raccoons are clever enough to figure out how to open a wire cage, though, so it's important to clip the cage's "door" shut and to secure the cage on its hanger so a hungry 'coon doesn't simply carry

Most feeders made for serving preformed suet cakes are based on a rectangular wire cage. Additional features may include a covering to protect the contents from the elements, clips or latches to keep mammals from swiping the whole block of suet, and double cages for added serving capacity.

away the whole thing. A twist tie or short piece of flexible wire works well both to hold the cage shut and to fasten it to its hanger.

Based on the same premise as the simple wire mesh cages, fancier vertical suet feeders hold the suet upright in a mesh cage and also feature an extension below the cage to help woodpeckers and other clinging birds balance as they hang on and peck away at the contents. This arrangement limits the ability of starlings and other pesky birds to get to the suet, because they are generally less adept at clinging and balancing. Even more confounding to starlings are suet feeders that require birds to cling to the underside of the feeder to get to the contents. You can find these in wild-bird supply stores.

Such stores sell all kinds of other suet delivery systems and the proper shapes of suet to fit them—boards with shallow holes to spread with suet "butters," wooden feeders with larger, deeper holes to hold small cups or cylinders of suet, and an array of other configurations. Any of these will do the job of delivering suet to your birds, or you can create similar feeders using a few basic tools. A short log, 10 to 12 inches long and about 3 to 4 inches in diameter, needs only a few holes—roughly 1 inch deep and 1½ to 2 inches wide—drilled into it to become a rustic-looking suet server. Add a long eye-screw in one end, pack the holes with suet or a suet-peanut butter mixture, and hang it where you can enjoy the view.

A rough cedar shake, or shingle, makes a fine way to serve soft, spreadable suet or peanut butter mixes. Fasten it to a tree or feeder post and spread it with suet—that's all. You can even spread suet on the bark of

A suet feeder with a tail support below the wire cage lets woodpeckers cling to the feeder just as they would naturally hold on to a tree trunk or vertical branch.

a tree, where plenty of birds (and other wildlife) will be able to take advantage of it. Oily suet and peanut butter spreads will leave greasy stains on surfaces, however, so you may prefer to use a feeder rather than permanently mark your tree.

Tray and platform feeders make suet in crumbly (or whole chunk) form available to many bird species that can't manage the clinging act favored by woodpeckers and their kin. Thrushes, robins, bluebirds, and cardinals are just a few of the birds that will enjoy wormy-looking suet crumbles served on a low tray or platform. Starlings and crows will like these, too, and may show up in large numbers for unsecured suet. You may have to take suet "off the table" in this form for a few days if pest birds or other creatures become a problem. Or you can offer them their own suet serving area (give them a few large chunks of raw suet rather than fancy crumbles) away from the area where the songbirds dine.

Convert a Coconut for Small Birds' Convenience

One way to keep crows, jays, starlings, and other feeder hogs from gobbling up special treats is to serve the goodies in a feeder that makes it difficult for potential pests to get to them. This coconut feeder lets small birds, like chickadees, alight on it, but larger birds set it rocking. You can use it to serve suet- and peanut butter–based foods like "Southern Summer 'Suet' Treat" or "Simple Suet-Peanut Butter Bird Snack." A small hollow gourd can be used instead of a coconut for this project.

TOOLS AND SUPPLIES

One small coconut, about 5 inches in diameter

Hacksaw or keyhole saw

Spoon for scraping

Pencil

Drill with small drill bit ($^3/_{32}$ or similar size)

One small eye-screw

One small piece of scrap wood, about $^3/_4$ inches
    square and thick

One $^1/_4$-inch-diameter dowel, about 8 inches long
    (the length depends on the size of the coconut)

Glue

String or wire to hang

Try a feeder made from a coconut or a gourd for offering soft suet to small birds such as chickadees and wrens. Jays, crows, and other suet hogs are too large to feed from this delicately balanced diner.

DIRECTIONS

1. Saw a hole about 2½ inches to 3 inches in diameter in the top of a coconut—the end that has indentations. (Coconuts crack easily, so handle it gently.) Scrape out the contents of the coconut.

2. Balance the coconut on the tip of a pencil inserted in the hole. When you find the spot where the pencil tip will balance the coconut, mark that location on the outside of the shell. Carefully drill a hole there using a small drill bit. Move the bit around so that the hole is slightly bigger than the threaded end of the eye-screw.

3. Drill a hole only $^1/_{16}$ inch deep in the center of the small piece of scrap wood. Place the scrap wood inside the top of the coconut, aligning the drilled holes. Poke the eye-screw through the coconut and thread it into the wood.

4. Saw a notch at the base of the large opening, then slide the dowel into the notch, touching the back of the coconut. Glue the dowel into place inside the coconut and in the notch. Pack softened suet or peanut butter mixture into the back of the feeder and hang it with string from a tree.

four

Nectar for Hummingbirds and Others

Hummingbirds are certainly among the most popular of the birds for which people fill and maintain feeders. Hummingbirds' small size, their jewel-like colors, and the way they zip and zoom around appeal to people who otherwise might not feed any backyard birds at all. Following close behind in popularity are the orioles, because they're big, loud, colorful, and interesting to watch. Both hummingbirds and orioles will visit sugar-water feeders, even though providing a man-made equivalent of the natural nectar from flowers is a relatively new thing in the world of bird feeding. Only in the past couple of decades has interest in tending nectar feeders skyrocketed to the point that there are now almost as many nectar feeders available as there are seed and suet feeders.

A male ruby-throated hummingbird visits a nectar feeder.

Like the other birds we enjoy at our feeders, hummingbirds do not rely upon the food we provide for their survival. Nectar feeders attract hummingbirds to our yards so that we can see the tiny birds up close and admire their dazzling colors and their physics-defying flight, but the feeders are for our benefit—not the hummingbirds'. They have gotten along without man-made nectar for countless centuries and would be fine even if no feeders were ever put out for them again. Hummingbirds use nectar feeders because they're available and full of free food. If you truly want to make a difference for the hummingbirds that live in your area, create an inviting backyard habitat for them that includes trees and shrubs to offer shelter and nesting sites, as well as flowering plants to provide nectar and attract the tiny arthropods—insects and spiders—that make up most of a hummingbird's diet.

"My one goal since I moved here was to try to get hummingbirds. Being in town is tough. I tried bee balm and most any red flower with a tubular shape, but what worked in the end was cardinal climber [Ipomoea x multifida]. The first year we planted it, we got ruby-throated hummingbirds. Now the little hummers visit all the other plants we put out for them, too. And we see hummers visiting our sunflowers and hyssop that aren't red. I have a hummingbird feeder out, too, but they visit the flowers far more than the feeder."

DONNA CHIARELLI, Kutztown, Pennsylvania

On the Hummingbird Menu

Hummingbirds instinctively know where and how to get the nutrition they need, and it comes from far more than just nectar. They also eat tiny arthropods, such as spiders, fruit flies, midges, and countless others so small they're referred to as "no-see-ums." Some biologists and others who have studied hummingbirds extensively think of them as little flycatchers, because they consume so much protein from the insects they eat along with the carbohydrates they get from nectar. Hummers will explore every flower they find, but they quickly learn and remember which ones produce the most nectar or have the largest supply of insects. People unfamiliar with what and how hummingbirds eat often mistakenly think the tiny birds are getting nectar from some flowers just because they're red, when in fact they're poking their bills into the blossoms because there are lots of insects in them. If you observe hummingbirds a lot, you'll see that they fly out from perches, grab insects with their open bills, and fly back to the perches just like flycatchers do.

Hummingbirds' bodies, like human bodies, are designed to process and digest the

"People think they feed hummingbirds to make or keep them healthy, but that's just not true. People do it for the enjoyment. They also think that if a 1:4 mixture [of sugar to water] is good, then 1:3 is better— but that's wrong."

BOB SARGENT, Clay, Alabama

You can make your own sugar-water solution (1 part sugar to 4 parts water), stir up nectar from a powdered mix, or buy ready-to-serve nectar to fill your hummingbird feeders. It's all the same to the birds.

foods they eat in a certain way. In the wild, the birds naturally choose flowers that produce nectar that is 20 to 30 percent sugar. To mimic that, the sugar-water solution you serve in your feeders should be 1 part sugar to 4 parts water: for example, ¼ cup of sugar in 1 cup of water.

Use only white sugar, and don't make the mistake of thinking that if 1:4 is good, then 1:3 is better—because it's not. Don't make your sugar-water solution any stronger than 1:4, and don't use sweeteners other than white sugar. Never use honey, brown sugar,

molasses, powdered sugar, or any sugar substitute. You may meet people who tell you they've substituted another sweetener for sugar in their nectar solutions without any ill effects on the hummingbirds at their feeders. But the truth is that there's little way of knowing what happens to birds once they leave our feeders. In exchange for the pleasure we get from watching birds, the least we can do is offer foods that are appropriate and unlikely to cause any harm.

When you make up a batch of sugar-water solution to put in a nectar feeder, you can

Birds That Drink Nectar

Hummingbirds and orioles are the two main groups of birds that feed on nectar, but other species may surprise you by showing up at your nectar feeder to have a drink. Most of them don't have the right kind of bill to get to the liquid, but that doesn't stop them from trying. Small-billed birds like warblers, chickadees, sparrows, wrens, and finches all may be occasional nectar-feeder visitors. Woodpeckers, catbirds, mockingbirds, tanagers, cardinals, titmice, jays, and even grosbeaks are among the other birds that sometimes will have a go at drinking from a nectar feeder.

make it with boiling water or hot tap water, or just use running water as long as you make sure the sugar is completely dissolved before you pour the nectar into the feeder. Some people feel that boiling the water keeps the nectar solution from spoiling as quickly, while others disagree and say that it really doesn't matter. During migration, there are people who feed hundreds of hummingbirds on a daily basis; they don't boil the water for their nectar solution, because they don't have time given the volume of nectar they're serving each day. Others who feed hummingbirds are rigorous about the nectar-making process: boiling the water, stirring in the sugar, then cooling the solution in the refrigerator for hours before putting it in a feeder. As with most types of bird feeding, the key is to develop a system that suits your level of interest and ability to maintain it, while offering the birds appropriate foods in adequately clean conditions.

If making homemade hummingbird nectar is not your cup of tea, there are numerous commercial nectar products sold either as ready-to-serve liquids or in powder forms that you mix with water and put in a hummingbird feeder. Many of these products contain red dye, because it's well known that hummingbirds are attracted to the color red. But the use of red coloring in nectar solutions is an ongoing source of controversy—some hummingbird experts feel it may be harmful to the birds, and many believe it is at least unnecessary. While it's true that hummingbirds are attracted to the color red, they're also attracted to all the colors in the high end of the color spectrum.

Many of these prepared nectar products also advertise that they contain vitamins and minerals for the hummingbirds' benefit, but that's a subject on which experts actually agree: Such additives are unnecessary and a waste of money. Hummingbirds get all the nutrition they need from the natural foods they eat. Plus, by the time a ruby-throated, Anna's, rufous, black-chinned, or other species of hummingbird is lapping up the artificial nectar solution in your feeder, most added vitamins and minerals are long gone.

A Speedy Nectar-Making Solution

One way to ensure that the sugar in your solution dissolves fully and quickly, even without boiling water, is to use superfine sugar in place of regular granulated sugar. Also called bar sugar and caster/castor sugar, superfine sugar is used by bartenders and in uncooked desserts, such as meringues, because of its rapidly dissolving property. If you don't find superfine sugar on the grocery store shelves, you may be able to buy it from a restaurant supply store. You can also make your own superfine sugar by putting granulated sugar in a food processor or blender and processing it until it's powdery. (Don't use confectioner's, or powdered, sugar in place of superfine—it often contains a small amount of starch to prevent clumping and is not suitable for making hummingbird nectar.)

Choosing and Using Nectar Feeders

Hummingbird feeders come in all shapes and sizes. It really doesn't matter to the birds what a nectar feeder looks like, as long as it is clean and contains a suitably sugary solution. That leaves matters of aesthetics and practicality up to the person who will look at, fill, and clean the feeder on a regular basis.

Because you may find yourself cleaning and refilling a hummingbird feeder every 2 to 3 days during summer months, finding a feeder that's easy to take apart, clean thoroughly, reassemble, and refill is essential. A feeder that looks like a miniature hot air balloon may be adorable, for example, but it will quickly lose its appeal if you find it hard to open the nectar reservoir to refill it, or if its elaborate decorations require a lot of extra cleaning.

Feeders for serving nectar are every bit as simple in concept as hopper feeders are for serving seeds: a reservoir that holds nectar and openings where birds can feed from that reservoir. Hummingbirds don't sip liquid; they lap it up with their barbed tongues. When you're shopping for nectar feeders, consider the following features:

Simple construction. The fewer parts there are, the easier a feeder is to take apart, clean, and reassemble. Highly decorative feeders may be attractive or quaint, but cracks and crevices in extra adornments tend to gather grime and result in nectar solution that spoils more rapidly.

Reservoir size. Ideally, you want a feeder or feeders that hold as much nectar as your local hummingbirds will lap up within a

Choose a hummingbird feeder based on ease of use rather than aesthetics. In general, the more adornments, the harder a nectar feeder is to keep clean.

couple of days and not too much more. A feeder with a super-size reservoir may result in a lot of nectar down the drain, while one that's too small may keep you busier than you'd like while cleaning and refilling it. If you live along a hummingbird migration route, you may want to put out bigger feeders at times when many more birds are present, and use smaller ones during the rest of the feeding season.

Materials. Most nectar feeders are glass, ceramic, or plastic, and each of these has some advantages, as well as disadvantages. Glass and ceramic feeders may be dishwasher safe and, therefore, be easier to keep clean, while plastic feeders typically are more durable and less at risk of shattering if they fall from their hanger. Whatever a feeder is made of, one with a transparent reservoir will make it easier for you to see when its contents are running low, and/or when it's cloudy and in need of refilling with fresh solution.

Accessibility. Hummingbirds can hover as they lap nectar, and so perches aren't absolutely necessary on the feeder. Other nectar lovers will make use of perches, if present; while hummingbird feeders may be perch free, oriole feeders will have perches. On hummer feeders, look at the orientation of the feeding ports. Feeders with a vertical bottle-type reservoir usually have ports that are mostly horizontal and angled slightly upward, much like real flowers. Flat or saucer-style feeders often have ports that face almost directly upward. While flat feeders have simple construction that makes

them easy to clean, it's important that the feeding ports on top of the feeder are angled rather than straight up. Hummingbirds have been known to get their bills caught in openings that weren't at least slightly angled.

Hang hummingbird feeders near flowers, shrubs, or trees. The flowers will attract and feed the hummingbirds, and the trees and shrubs will protect them from predators. If you can, put a tomato cage or shepherd's crook near a feeder so hummingbirds can perch on it if they wish to rest.

Beware Sticky Drips

When choosing a place to hang a nectar feeder, your main goal, of course, is to put it where it will catch the attention of hungry hummingbirds. You'll also want to pick a site that makes it easy for you to get to the

SUPPORT YOUR LOCAL HUMMINGBIRDS

A Note from **Arlene**

When they're available, I'll pick up political posters left along roadsides long after they should've been removed and use their metal frames as both flower supports and bird perches. I learned this years ago, and it's one of the most useful things I do in my yard to make hummingbirds more visible—and it doesn't cost any money. When there's a perch close to a feeder and flowers, the hummingbirds will sit on it both before and after eating. They'll often also use it as a guard lookout, near what they perceive to be their own personal property there: the feeder.

feeder for regular cleaning and refilling, as well as one that affords you a clear view of the birds that fly in to drink the sweet contents. In the midst of all that, it's easy to forget that sweet equals sticky, and even the sturdiest nectar feeder is prone to occasional spills and drips.

Factor the risk of sugar-water spills into your plans for a nectar feeder's location, and save yourself the time and trouble of scrubbing nectar from surfaces you never intended to get sticky. Avoid hanging a nectar feeder over patio furniture, for example, or where its contents may dribble onto a frequently traveled walkway. If you're thinking to yourself that you don't mind a little stickiness, bear in mind that puddles of sugary stuff are also nectar for ants, wasps, and other insects that may be equally unwelcome in the area below your feeder.

The Case for Multiple Feeders

Because of their diminutive size, we humans often think of hummingbirds as "cute." As you get to know these tiny birds, you may be surprised to discover that "aggressive" and "territorial" are perhaps more accurate descriptions to apply to hummingbirds, particularly when there are nectar feeders involved. Sharing does not come naturally to hummingbirds, no matter how cute we may find them, and a single nectar feeder likely will be claimed by a single bird that will dedicate itself to keeping any other hummers from drinking its contents.

Putting up more than one feeder is the way to deal with hummingbirds' unwillingness to share and, by extension, the way to see more hummingbirds. Maintaining several hummingbird feeders means more time spent cleaning and refilling, but you should always have more than one feeder, regardless of how small your yard is. Several one-port feeders will give the birds in your area choices, and you'll probably be surprised to

"Try putting up several hummingbird feeders. Cram as many into a small space as you can. Eventually there's a threshold beyond which even the most aggressive birds give up trying to defend the area. This is the trick to making your yard a hummingbird free-for-all. If you have only one or two feeders, one or two birds will defend them and drive all the other hummingbirds out."

GEOFF MALOSH, Moon Township, Pennsylvania

see that there are more hummers around than you thought. Banding operations—in which licensed banders catch birds, band them, weigh and measure them, blow on their breasts with a straw to see how much fat is under their skin, and then release them—have shown time and time again that there are always more hummingbirds around at any given time than you'd think.

Other Fans of Nectar and Sweets

Just as hummingbird feeders often are red or have red accents, nectar feeders for orioles are almost always orange, presumably because a lot of orioles are orange and/or because orioles seem to especially like cut orange halves.

A Bullock's oriole and a Gila woodpecker represent some of the non-hummingbird species that will drink from a nectar feeder that has ports and perches to accommodate them.

In form and function, oriole feeders resemble hummingbird feeders, only they're larger to accommodate the much bigger birds. You can fill them with commercially available oriole nectar if you like, or you can make your own. Because orioles like their nectar a little sweeter, make their mixture with 1 part sugar to just 3 parts water (¼ cup sugar in ¾ cup water, for example). At least as popular as a nectar feeder for orioles is one that offers the big orange-and-black birds pieces of oranges and other fruits. Orioles also like jelly, probably for its sweetness, and grape jelly is the kind most often offered by bird lovers, with orange marmalade coming in second. Feeders with cups attached, or even feeders designed to hold a whole jelly jar, are available.

Orioles eat a lot of caterpillars and other insects and don't depend on nectar nearly as much as hummingbirds do, but they certainly drink their share. In the process, they also pollinate flowers, more so in the tropics but also in North America. A favorite way orioles get to nectar is by piercing blossoms. The orange or yellow tubular flowers of trumpet creeper vines (*Campsis radicans*) are especially favored.

A Note from Arlene

HIDDEN HUMMINGBIRDS REVEALED

During migration, the rule of thumb is that you can multiply by 3 or 4 the number of birds in view at the same time. I didn't think this was true until Scott Weidensaul, an internationally known author of nature and conservation books, came to my place to band [birds] and caught 28 in a few hours—even though I had only been seeing four or five at the same time.

Limiting Insects at Your Nectar Feeder

Even though hummingbirds and orioles eat insects as well as nectar, the birds don't favor the two foods together, and few of us feeder-keepers are putting out nectar in hopes of attracting insect pests to our yards. One of the biggest problems associated with nectar feeders is the flying insects, especially wasps, they attract. Nectar and sugar-water solutions often will drip from a feeder or spill out while it's being filled or hung, and this often is enough to catch the attention of sweet-seeking pests.

If your nectar feeders feature yellow guards over the ports, sometimes removing them takes away a visual attractant for wasps and bees, but this may not work if the insects have already found your feeders. Serving a stronger sugar solution (1 part sugar to 2 parts water) in a shallow pan on the ground near but not too close to your feeders can help to draw wasps away from the feeders, but may also bring more of them to the general area. Wasp traps that feature a reservoir for juice or sugar water also can help, but watch carefully to ensure no birds accidentally get caught in them. Perhaps the best thing to do is to hang more hummingbird feeders in a different place and wait until the wasps eventually go away.

Another insect problem is that of ants in or on nectar feeders. Fortunately, they are much easier to deal with than wasps. When a worker ant discovers a good source of food, it goes back to the colony and communicates this to the other ants; then they follow the scent trail that the "finder" ant left and make their way down into the feeder

> *"The inside of the bottle part of a hummingbird feeder can and often does mold easily during extremely hot weather, especially if the feeder's put in the sun. But it's often extremely difficult to reach all the mold. Use a small handful of [uncooked] rice in soapy water and shake the mixture in the bottle. Then rinse it out well."*
>
> **AL GUARENTE,** Media, Pennsylvania

through the ports. A few ants aren't a problem: The birds will ignore them. But when the ants get so numerous that they clog the ports, they are a problem. The best solution is to move the feeder to a different place. But if you can't or don't want to, you can buy an ant moat to fasten to the hook or chain from which the feeder hangs. You fill the moat with water, and when the ants march down the hanger, they end up in the moat. You may see recommendations for deterring ants by putting oily or greasy substances on feeder hangers and around their ports, but this is ineffective in stopping the ants and dangerous to birds that come to the feeder. Some of the ants are sure to make it through the slippery substance, dragging it with them and polluting the nectar with it. If a bird, especially a hummingbird, gets oily goo on its bill, it may have difficulty feeding and die as a result.

Take It Easy, but Keep It Clean

Keeping nectar feeders clean is important for the health of the birds that use them. Preemptively change the nectar on a regular schedule and monitor feeders closely for signs of mold. Change the sugar water in them when it begins to look cloudy, or at least every 3 days during warm weather. Avoid hanging nectar feeders where they're in the sun all day long, because this speeds the mold growth and spoilage that makes the nectar hazardous to birds' health. The only exception is if you hang a hummingbird feeder near really good nectar-rich flowers, in which case you'll have to pay closer attention to the condition of that particular feeder. Be sure to put other feeders nearby, either in fully or partly shaded spots, so the hummingbirds have a choice other than the feeder in full sun.

There are many ways to clean nectar feeders, so choose the one that works the best for you. It doesn't matter, as long as any and all of the sticky remnants of the sugar water are removed. Everyone, it seems, has the "best" approach. But the best thing to do is to buy feeders that don't have a lot of parts to them and that are easy to dismantle and clean. Put the disassembled parts into a pail of 10-percent bleach solution (1 part bleach to 9

A female broad-billed hummingbird visits a thistle flower. Blossoms don't have to be red or tubular to serve hummingbirds' needs. Even flowers that don't produce a lot of nectar will attract small insects that form a large part of hummingbirds' diets.

parts water) and soak them for a few hours. After you've checked to make sure there's nothing solid left inside that needs to be brushed out, rinse them with cold water and let them dry before refilling. Soapy water works just as well, but be sure to rinse all of the soap out.

Using baking soda and very hot water is another way to clean nectar feeders. The bubbles that form from the baking soda cleanse the inside of the feeder, but again, be sure to check it and follow up with a brush if necessary. Some feeders advertise that they can be put into a dishwasher, but follow instructions carefully if you go that route. Dishwater temperatures vary a lot, and plastic parts may melt or warp. But, above all, don't obsess too much about keeping your feeders clean: If you do, you won't enjoy the birds using them.

Nectar Plants for Hummingbirds and Others

The list of nectar-producing flowers, shrubs, and trees that hummingbirds use is long. But when you select plants, don't get hung up on choosing only red-flowering plants. Flower shape and nectar content are what really attract hummingbirds to their favorite plants. Red attracts hummingbirds, but it won't keep them coming back for more if there's not much nectar. Some of the best

"In western Oregon, . . . in summer's enduring sunshine, a hummingbird feeder sprouts mildew faster than I can clean and refill it. Fungus-infested feeders can pass on a fungal infection to the tiny birds, causing growths and thickening of their bills that interfere with feeding and lead to starvation. Feeders [would] need to be cleaned at least every 2 days in the heat, so summertime feeders are strictly off-limits for my family. . . .

"In colder weather, I can get away with washing the feeder once every 5 to 7 days, but once spring hits, a good cleaning is needed about every 3 days. I use plain hot water and let the feeder air-dry before filling it up again. A simple nectar solution—4 parts boiling water and 1 part white sugar—keeps those little guys visiting my garden and keeps me smiling during the darker months."

JEN H., Eugene, Oregon

nectar flowers for hummingbirds include coral bells, penstemons, salvias, monardas, milkweeds, columbines, zinnias, turtlehead, jewelweed, lilies, hostas, four o'clocks, phlox, fuchsias, bleeding hearts, foxgloves, lantanas, pentas, and crocosmias.

Everblooming trumpet honeysuckle (*Lonicera sempervirens*) bears long, tubular, red or yellow flowers that are full of nectar. If it's planted in the right place, it will produce flowers all summer long. Butterfly bushes (*Buddleia davidii*), so called because butterflies love their blossoms, are also great for hummingbirds. Many flowering shrubs are attractive to hummingbirds as much for the insects their blooms attract as for any nectar the blossoms provide. The big blossoms of buckeye trees, particularly the small south-ern red buckeye (*Aesculus pavia*), are full of nectar, as are the airy flowers of mimosa trees (*Albizia julibrissin*) and most flowering fruit trees. The flowers on scarlet runner beans (*Phaseolus coccineus*) and the tiny red blossoms of red morning glories (*Ipomoea coccinea*) are also highly favored by hummingbirds.

If red flowers don't fit your color scheme, but your garden is packed with plenty of nectar flowers, try this simple trick to bring hummingbirds in for a closer look: Stock up on red fake flowers at the next craft store sale and fasten a few of these false blossoms around your garden. Hummingbirds will for-give your subterfuge when they discover nonred nectar sources and the tiny insects that most flowers attract. Once they find food sources in abundance, they'll keep coming back, regardless of the color of the flowers.

A pot of bright red geraniums (*Pelargonium* hybrids) will attract hummingbirds even when there's no garden around—and without the mess and fuss of a nectar feeder. On a townhouse patio or apartment balcony, brighten the setting with a few containers of hummingbird-friendly flowers and watch as the hummers stop in for a nectar meal.

Flower shape is a big draw for hummingbirds, too, because the birds' long narrow bills and even longer tongues are meant for

A female ruby-throated hummingbird displays the long tongue that allows a hummer to lap nectar from the depths of tube-shaped flowers like the cardinal creeper (*Ipomoea x multifida*) shown here.

plumbing the depths of tubular blooms. Deep blue and purple flowers are just as attractive to them as reds, but any tube-shaped blossoms, from tiny mints to hefty hibiscus, will capture their attention and bring them to your garden.

Agastaches (anise hyssop and others) are good examples of nonred flowers that are surefire hummingbird attractors. Most have foliage with a delicious licorice scent, which has given more than one species the nickname licorice plant, or anise hyssop. But it's the whorled spikes of small tubular flowers that are the prime attraction for hummingbirds.

Native mostly to the American Southwest and Mexico, agastaches include many plants of surprising cold hardiness. Agastache species and hybrids offer a variety of flower colors, including blue-purple, salmon, rosy orange, pink, and pale blue. Hummingbirds love them all.

In western gardens, Anna's hummingbirds are among the species likely to seek nectar from the small tubular flowers of hyssops (*Agastache* spp.), which are hummingbird favorites.

Welcome Travelers Home

Hummingbirds returning north after spending winter in warmer climes are on the lookout for nectar to refuel after their long flights. Early-blooming plants make your garden extra enticing in spring, when hungry hummers are on the move and many flowers have yet to appear.

To provide reliable nectar in early spring, choose flowering trees, shrubs, and perennials suited to your local climate. For example, in the Pacific Northwest (and throughout Plant Hardiness Zones 6 to 8), red flowering currant (*Ribes sanguineum*) is a good choice. A graceful shrub or small tree, flowering currant bears dangling clusters of red-to-pink fragrant flowers in very early spring. In your perennial garden, include wild columbines (*Aquilegia canadensis* and *A. formosa*), eastern and western natives that open their elegant spurred flowers in early spring, just as the hummingbirds are on the move. Columbines are long-blooming, too, keeping hummingbirds supplied with nectar for weeks until other flowers come along.

Annuals for Nectar

While waiting for perennials and woody plants to reach blooming size, annuals can fill the gaps in your nectar-flower offerings and let you change them from year to year for different colors and textures in your garden. Potted annuals also fill the bill on patios and in small gardens. Here are some good annuals to bring hummingbirds in for a visit.

- Calibrachoa
- Cardinal creeper (*Ipomoea* x *multifida*)
- Cypress vine (*Ipomoea quamoclit*)
- Four o'clocks (*Mirabilis jalapa*)
- Fuchsias
- Geraniums, zonal (*Pelargonium* spp.)
- Impatiens
- Jewelweed (*Impatiens capensis*)
- Lantanas
- Morning glories (*Ipomoea* spp.)
- Pentas (*Pentas lanceolata*)
- Petunias
- Salvias, sages (*Salvia* spp.)
- Texas bluebonnet (*Lupinus texensis*)
- Zinnias

Native Nectar Plants for Hummingbirds

Filling your landscape with native nectar plants is a more reliable way to attract—and keep—hummingbirds, without going to the trouble of cleaning and filling nectar feeders. Trees, shrubs, perennials, and vines give hummingbirds places to perch, nest, and hide from predators; plants also attract the tiny bugs that make up as much, or more, of a hummingbird's diet than nectar does. Many of the plants listed below also produce fruits or seeds eaten by birds and other wildlife.

TREES AND SHRUBS FOR NECTAR

- California buckeye (*Aesculus californica*), Plant Hardiness Zones 7–8
- Red buckeye (*Aesculus pavia*), Zones 5–8
- Firecrackerbush (*Bouvardia ternifolia*), Tropical and subtropical
- Eastern redbud (*Cercis canadensis*), Zones 4–9
- Desert willow (*Chilopsis linearis*), Zones 8–9
- Ocotillo (*Fouquieria splendens*), Desert conditions
- Swamp rosemallow (*Hibiscus grandiflorus*), Zones 7–11
- Tulip tree (*Liriodendron tulipifera*), Zones 5–9
- Mock oranges (*Philadelphus* spp.), Zones 5–10
- Pink azalea (*Rhododendron periclymenoides*), Zones 4–9
- Red flowering currant (*Ribes sanguineum*), Zones 6–8
- New Mexico locust (*Robinia neomexicana*), Zones 5–9
- Fragrant sage (*Salvia clevelandii*), Zones 8–10
- Basswood (*Tilia americana*), Zones 3–8
- Weigela (*Weigela florida*), Zones 5–9
- Soaptree yucca (*Yucca elata*), Zones 4–9

Another Source of Sweetness

Flower nectar and sugar-water solution are not the only sweet liquids that birds seek in the landscape. Tree sap is the sweet treat of choice for sapsuckers, which are woodpeckers that drill holes in trees specifically to get to it. Other birds will also stop in for a drink when sap is available, and they will take advantage of holes made by sapsuckers as well as sap flows resulting from insect damage and branches broken by ice or wind.

Hummingbirds will come to flowing sap as readily as they do to nectar feeders. Orioles, house finches, and other woodpeckers also feed on sap when it's available. Many other birds find a sap flow attractive, too, because of the insects that are also drawn to the sticky fluid.

PERENNIALS FOR NECTAR

Anise hyssop (*Agastache foeniculum*), Zones 6–10

Sunset hyssop, (*A. rupestris*), Zones 5–8

Eastern and western columbines (*Aquilegia canadensis, A. formosa*), Zones 3–9

Milkweeds (*Asclepias* spp.), Zones vary by species

Butterfly weed (*Asclepias tuberosa*), Zones 3–9

Turtlehead (*Chelone glabra*), Zones 2–9

Bleeding hearts, Dutchman's breeches (*Dicentra* spp.), Zones 3–9

Foxgloves (*Digitalis* spp.), Zones 3–9

Coral bells (*Heuchera* spp.), Zones 4–9

Hostas, Zones 3–9

Lilies (*Lilium* spp.), Zones vary

Cardinal flower (*Lobelia cardinalis*), Zones 2–9

Great lobelia (*L. siphilitica*), Zones 3–8

Virginia bluebells (*Mertensia virginica*), Zones 3–9

Four o'clocks (*Mirabilis jalapa*), Zones 7–11

Bee balms (*Monarda* spp.), Zones 3–7

Sundrops (*Oenothera* spp.), Zones 3–9

Penstemons, Zones 3–9

Phlox, Zones 2–9

Obedient plant (*Physostegia virginiana*), Zones 3–9

Salvias (*Salvia elegans, S. splendens, S. coccinea*), Zones 8–10 and tropical

Mexican sunflower (*Tithonia rotundifolia*), Tropical or annual

VINES FOR NECTAR

Trumpet vine (*Campsis radicans*), Zones 3–9

Yellow jessamine (*Gelsemium sempervirens*), Zones 7–9

Trumpet honeysuckle (*Lonicera semper virens*), Zones 4–9

five

Berries and Fruit to Bring in the Birds

When and where there's an abundant and regular supply of fruit, whether from wild or cultivated plants or served at feeders, you will always find birds there, even the ones that normally eat seeds. Most birds are opportunists, and fruit is an opportunity that a majority of them will take advantage of when they can.

Gray catbird with grapes

Even if you don't have your own backyard orchard or berry patch, you can enjoy the company of the many species of birds that will show up when fruit is on the menu. By adding a feeder (or two) for serving fruit, you can invite birds that don't stop in for seeds to visit your yard. Fruit offerings are especially attractive at times of the year when natural sources of fruits and berries are scarce. In spring, birds migrating northward may be drawn to a tray feeder sprinkled with berries that you stockpiled over winter in your freezer. Winter feeder birds, while mostly seed and suet eaters, will gobble up bits of dried fruit or pieces of a freshly chopped apple. Woodpeckers will turn their powerful beaks to the task of pecking at a whole apple skewered on a large nail, and once they've exposed some of the juicy inner flesh, other birds will stop by to partake, too.

Birds digest fruits and berries quickly, so once a good source of these foods is found, the birds often will stay around or return to it repeatedly until all the food is gone. For example, berries pass through and out of the digestive systems of cedar and Bohemian waxwings in about half an hour, so they have to eat a lot of them—and often.

Serving Fruit for Birds

Even if it's dried, most fruit is less stable— that is, more prone to spoilage—than are the seeds we put out for birds. Rule No. 1 of fruit feeding, then, is to start with small quantities. This is especially important when you're offering a fruit for the first time at your feeders and are not sure when or if birds will discover it. Better to put out a small amount and have to replenish the feeder when it is quickly gobbled up, than to have to clean up a tray full of rotting or moldy fruit that has gone uneaten.

Timing also matters when you're experimenting with offering fruit at your feeders. In summer, when natural foods of all kinds are abundant, even established feeders filled with birds' favorite foods sometimes are ignored. A new feeder with food that's unfamiliar to

Birds That Eat Berries and Fruit

A lot of birds eat berries and fruit—some year-round and others when such foods are easily available. Members of the thrush family, which includes the American robin and bluebirds, are year-round berry eaters, as are northern mockingbirds, thrashers, orioles, cedar waxwings, and vireos. Jays, never ones to pass up any kind of food, also eat a lot of berries and fruit, as do grosbeaks. Blackbirds, cardinals, catbirds, chickadees, crows, house finches, purple finches, flickers, grackles, magpies, tanagers, titmice, woodpeckers, and wrens all will eat fruit when they have a chance at it, and in the case of the smaller birds, when the fruit is small enough to eat.

your local birds may attract little interest from them, but it may bring unwanted guests like starlings, raccoons, and insects. In fact, the insects attracted to decaying fruit may be of more interest to birds during summer than the fruit itself.

Plan Ahead

Just as you might for your own family, store up fruit during summer months when it's cheap and plentiful, and prepare it for easy serving at times when birds' natural foods are scarce. Birds are far less particular about things like bruises and worm holes than we are, so feel free to stock up on "seconds" at the farm stand or supermarket and windfalls at the orchard, and save the unblemished produce for your own use.

◯ If you have space in your freezer, fill up resealable bags with slightly shriveled berries and chopped-up cherries, apples, and plums—all bird favorites. It's helpful to chop fruits into beak-size bites before you freeze them, so they are ready to thaw and serve when business is brisk at your feeders and other food is in short supply.

◯ Drying is another option for securing fruits for future feeder fillings. Dry apple slices, berries, grapes, cherries, and other fruit just as you would for your own use, using a dehydrator, good old sun power, or a warm oven. Wild-bird supply stores sell dried fruit (separately or in mixes with seeds or nuts) for birds, or you can treat your feeder visitors to raisins and other dried fruit from your grocery store shelves, although the cost of these goodies may convince you to dry your own for bird-feeding purposes, or at least to limit such offerings to occasional treats.

◯ Shop the sales for deals on pricey treats. In the wake of holidays, supermarkets often give deep discounts on seasonal products such as dried fruits meant for baking. Look for bargains on raisins, currants, and other tidbits your birds will enjoy. Stock up and stash the goodies in your freezer until you're ready to put them in your feeder.

◯ You probably won't go to the trouble just for the sake of feeding birds, but if your talents include making homemade fruit preserves, consider putting up a few extra jars of grape jelly, strawberry preserves, or

"I put raisins on the rim of the living room picture window and American robins, gray catbirds, and northern mockingbirds all come in to get them. When we had a collie dog, she would lie inside looking out at them, and they got so comfortable with each other that when the dog went outside, she'd check the mockingbird nest that was in a bush close to the window and the birds just watched. There was no animosity whatsoever. But any other cat or dog that wandered into the yard and got near the nest got instantly attacked."

JOAN SILAGYI, Leesport, Pennsylvania

blackberry jam for serving at the feeder. Orioles will come to a feeder to feast on jelly, as will catbirds and woodpeckers. This may be good news if you're trying your hand at jelly making for the very first time—birds won't mind if the sweet treats filling the cups at their feeder are from a batch that failed to gel properly.

Skewers, Trays, Jelly Jars, Garlands, and Baked Goods

Serving fruit at your feeders requires a little more creativity than offering seeds or suet, particularly if you want to keep pest birds and mammals from dominating fruit feeders and gobbling up the treats before less aggressive birds get a chance. The sticky, juicy nature of most fruits means you can't just pour them into a secure hopper as you would premium seeds. An open tray or platform readily accommodates the variable shapes, sizes, and consistencies of different fruits, but grants access to any bird or critter that comes along. This may be fine if you only occasionally have fruit to serve to the birds. If fruit is a regular feature at your bird-feeding area, you may find it worthwhile to serve it in feeders customized for holding fruit and for limiting its availability to a particular clientele.

Commercially available fruit feeders, often sold for feeding orioles, typically consist of

"*Baltimore orioles will slurp up grape jelly from a hanging yogurt cup. There's absolutely no need to spend money on a fancy store-bought fruit or jelly feeder. Skewer orange slices on tree branches or plant hooks, or put them in a suet cage. Put grapes or jelly in recycled lids from peanut butter or mayonnaise jars placed on a picnic table, or poke a few holes in their sides and hang them with string or twisty ties from a hook, branch, or clothesline.*"

CINDY AHERN, Huntingdon Valley, Pennsylvania

Fruit is especially tempting to birds like this Bullock's oriole in winter, when natural sources of these favorite foods are hard to find.

The View from Deb's Window

While there are many sleek and attractive feeders available to buy, the birds they're meant for are very forgiving about aesthetics. This works to my advantage when I turn my limited carpentry skills to constructing feeders and other bird-oriented projects. The birds really don't mind what a feeder looks like. They'll visit with the enthusiasm of tourists at Buckingham Palace if the contents are to their liking.

Thus my very basic fruit feeder sees just as much bird action as the much nicer store-bought feeders elsewhere in my yard. Based on the cage feeders made for serving commercial suet cakes, my fruit feeder is a simple wood frame with suet-cake dimensions (roughly $4\frac{1}{2}$ inches square and $1\frac{1}{2}$ inches thick) nailed to an 8-inch-long piece of 2-inch by 6-inch lumber that serves as a back and as a part to mount the feeder. A long nail driven from the back into the center of the wood frame creates a skewer for holding an apple or orange half; a second long nail driven partway into the front of the board just below the frame serves as perch. A piece of $\frac{1}{2}$-inch wire mesh fits over the frame to keep feeder raiders from stealing fruit off the skewer. The mesh is "hinged" at the bottom of the frame by a

6-inch piece of coat-hanger wire that fits into holes drilled on the sides of the frame and is woven through the wire mesh. This lets me flip the mesh open, slide a piece of fruit onto the skewer, and then close the mesh over the fruit. A small piece of wood, loosely nailed at the top of the frame, makes a simple latch to hold the mesh closed.

It's far from beautiful, but it serves quite well for woodpeckers and nuthatches that can cling to the wire mesh and for any birds small enough to perch on the nail. Starlings and crows can't manage it, except on occasions when a squirrel opens the latch and the wire mesh opens out like a handy landing pad. When I don't have fruit to put on the skewer, my homemade feeder works just fine for serving suet, too.

A simple homemade cage for offering fruit or suet may not win any beauty contests, but hungry birds won't mind when the contents are to their liking.

some combination of skewer(s) to hold the fruit and places for diners to perch (sometimes also with a roof or other shield against the elements). Fruit feeders aimed at orioles may include cups for serving jelly. If you buy a combination feeder like this, make sure the jelly cups are removable for easy cleaning, because they'll require more frequent washing than other parts of the feeder.

A basic wire-mesh suet cage works well for

Fruits at the Feeder

Because they are easier to eat, fruits at the feeder attract a broader bird clientele than those same fruits growing in your garden or in the wild. That is not to say that birds don't eat many of the fruits listed below anywhere they find them—some, such as blueberries, are among the most popular foods sought by birds in the wild. By comparison, apples chopped into beak-size bites are quite popular at the feeder, but few birds eat cultivated apples while they're on the tree. (Crabapples are quite another matter.)

FRUIT	BIRDS ATTRACTED
Apples, crabapples	Blackbirds, bluebirds, chickadees, grackles, jays, magpies, mockingbirds, robins, starlings, thrashers, titmice, towhees, Carolina wren
Blackberries (and other bramble fruits)	Blackbirds, bluebirds, bobwhites, buntings, cardinals, catbirds, chickadees, crows, grackles, grosbeaks, grouse, jays, mockingbirds, orioles, pheasants, quail, robins, sparrows, tanagers, thrashers, thrushes, titmice, towhees, turkeys, waxwings, woodpeckers, wrens
Blueberries	Blackbirds, bluebirds, flickers, magpies, mockingbirds, robins, sparrows, brown thrasher, thrushes, towhees, woodpeckers, Carolina wren
Cherries	Grosbeaks, robins, sparrows, thrushes, titmice, woodpeckers
Figs	Grosbeaks, magpies, orioles, thrushes, yellow-rumped warblers, woodpeckers
Grapes	Bluebirds, cardinals, catbirds, grackles, grosbeaks, jays, magpies, mockingbirds, robins, sparrows, tanagers, thrashers, thrushes, woodpeckers, wrens
Oranges	Bluebirds, cardinals, house finches, mockingbirds, orioles, robins, starlings, woodpeckers
Peaches	Orioles
Pears	Orioles
Persimmons	Kinglets, yellow-rumped warblers
Strawberries	Catbirds, crows, grosbeaks, grouse, mockingbirds, pheasants, quail, robins, sparrows, thrashers, thrushes, towhees, turkeys
Watermelon	Catbirds, flickers, mockingbirds, thrashers; hummingbirds may drink juice

serving fruits like apples and oranges. Simply cut an apple in half and slip one or both halves into the cage. Woodpeckers and other birds with the ability to cling will enjoy this treat, while starlings will mostly be unable to get to it. A variation on the rectangular cage is a hanging spring-style feeder. To put a piece of fruit in it, you bend or stretch the feeder to open the coils, then allow them to spring back once the fruit is in place.

You can also make a very basic fruit feeder out of a board—call it a platform feeder if it makes you feel better—with a few nails driven through it. Place it on any flat surface with the nails pointing upward, skewer fruits on the nails, and voilà! Slightly "fancier" is the same board with a plastic margarine tub or a low-sided can (as from tuna or cat food) glued or nailed to it for offering jelly or berries or even mealworms along with the skewered fruits.

Serving Fruit Nature's Way

From a bird's-eye view, there are many more sources of fruit in the wild and in man-made landscapes than we poor humans recognize. This is good news for the birds, because it means they are able to find plenty of foods to eat beyond the handful of cultivated fruits that we consider edible, and it's good news for us for the same reason.

Although birds may find our carefully tended berry patches and orchards a convenient source for meals of fruit, "our" fruits are not the only ones available to them. This can ease the bird pressure on our home fruit crops and make the idea of sharing (or not sharing) more palatable to us. If you take steps to prevent birds from feasting on your strawberries, for example, you can do so with the knowledge that they won't go hungry because of your love of strawberry shortcake. Denied access to your strawberry patch, the birds will find foods elsewhere, although they'll quickly gobble any less-than-perfect berries you care to serve in a feeder.

Including fruit-producing plants in your landscape is a much easier way to feed the birds than serving fruit at your feeders. A greater variety of bird species will visit

A halved apple, orange, or other fruit served on a skewer or in a wire suet cage will quickly attract the attention of any fruit lovers in the vicinity. Catbirds, mockingbirds, and woodpeckers are among those likely to partake.

Berries and the Birds They Bring

Berries that birds love come from many more wild and cultivated plants than the ones we think of as producing palatable fruits. Here are some of the most common berry producers and the birds likely to visit them.

PLANT NAME	BIRDS THAT EAT THE BERRIES
Serviceberries, shadbush, Juneberries (*Amelanchier* spp.)	Bluebirds, catbirds, jays, mockingbirds, orioles, tanagers, thrashers, thrushes, waxwings
Hollies (*Ilex* spp.)	Bluebirds, bobwhites, catbirds, doves, flickers, grouse, jays, mockingbirds, quail, robins, sapsuckers, sparrows, thrashers, thrushes, towhees, wild turkeys, vireos, waxwings, woodpeckers
Cedars, junipers (*Juniperus* spp.)	Bluebirds, catbirds, crossbills, finches, flickers, grosbeaks, jays, mockingbirds, Clark's nutcracker, robins, sapsuckers, tree swallow, thrashers, hermit thrush, yellow-rumped warbler, waxwings
Spicebush (*Lindera benzoin*)	Bluebirds, bobwhites, catbirds, pheasant, robins, thrushes
Mulberries (*Morus* spp.)	Bluebirds, cardinals, catbirds, doves, flickers, grackles, grosbeaks, jays, mockingbirds, orioles, robins, tanagers, thrashers, thrushes, titmice, waxwings, woodpeckers
Virginia creeper (*Parthenocissus quinquefolia*)	Bluebirds, catbirds, chickadees, flickers, mockingbirds, nuthatches, robins, sapsuckers, tree swallow, thrashers, thrushes, titmice, woodpeckers
Buckthorns (*Rhamnus* spp.)	Catbirds, mockingbirds, robins, sapsuckers, thrashers, thrushes, pileated woodpecker
Sumacs (*Rhus* spp.)	Bluebirds, bobwhites, cardinals, catbirds, crows, finches, flickers, evening grosbeak, grouse, jays, juncos, magpies, mockingbirds, pheasant, quail, robins, tanagers, thrashers, thrushes, wild turkeys, woodpeckers, wrens
Blackberries, raspberries, thimbleberries, wineberries (*Rubus* spp.)	Blackbirds, bluebirds, bobwhites, buntings, cardinals, catbirds, chickadees, crows, grackles, grosbeaks, grouse, jays, mockingbirds, orioles, pheasant, quail, robins, sparrows, tanagers, thrashers, thrushes, titmice, towhees, wild turkeys, waxwings, woodpeckers, wrens
Elderberries (*Sambucus* spp.)	Blackbirds, bluebirds, buntings, cardinals, catbirds, flickers, grosbeaks, grouse, jays, kinglets, magpies, mockingbirds, nuthatches, orioles, pheasant, robins, sapsuckers, sparrows, tanagers, towhees, wild turkeys, waxwings, woodpeckers, wrens
Snowberries (*Symphoricarpos* spp.)	Bobwhites, purple finch, evening grosbeak, grouse, magpies, pheasant, robins, thrushes, towhees
Viburnums (*Viburnum* spp.)	Cardinals, grouse, pheasant, robins, thrashers, thrushes, wild turkeys, waxwings, woodpeckers

fruit-bearing plants, because they instinctively recognize them as food sources. Not all birds that feed on a kind of fruit in the wild will come to feeders for that fruit, perhaps because the feeder is not in the right situation for some birds, or because they don't naturally feed in proximity to other bird species. We don't always know what brings birds to a feeder or keeps them away; foods that are most like what birds normally seek in nature, in general, seem to be most attractive to the most birds.

By providing fruits "on the plant," you can enjoy birds in your backyard without buying, filling, and maintaining feeders. You won't have to worry about running out of food or about cleaning spoiled, uneaten fruit out of a feeder. And fruiting plants offer birds advantages beyond food—they also provide places

"An excellent native perennial for birds is spice-bush (Lindera benzoin). It has yellow flowers in spring, aromatic leaves that turn yellow in fall, and bright red, high-energy berries eaten by many species of migrant birds. It's also a host plant for the spicebush and eastern tiger swallowtail butterflies. It's a wonderful addition to any bird garden."

BETSY MESCAVAGE, Seemsville, Pennsylvania

to perch, roost, and nest, and give birds shelter from the elements and cover from predators. See Chapter 9 for more about the benefits of gardening for the birds.

Birds and Brambles

Bramble patches are great places to find birds. Raspberries, gooseberries, blackberries, and just about any other berries that grow on spreading, spiny branches are easy pickings and relished by birds. Not only do

(continued on page 93)

MULBERRIES BRING IN THE BIRDS

In my yard there's a large mulberry tree not far from our deck that starts producing berries in early June. When the berries start appearing, bird species I don't normally see in the yard during breeding season—birds like scarlet tanagers and great-crested flycatchers that nest in nearby woods, and brown thrashers that nest in the fencerows of our fields—suddenly show up, along with a lot of waxwings, to eat the mulberries long before they're ripe. The mulberries on this tree are white, but mulberries can range in color from white to deep purple. I planted this tree as a sapling from one with deep purple berries that grew in the yard of my parents' home. When I planted it, my husband, David, looked at me skeptically and asked if I knew what I was doing, because purple mulberries stain anything and everything they touch. But I was determined to have a mulberry tree near the house, because I knew it attracted birds, and I had the last laugh when the tree began producing its berries years later and they were white.

Select Native Fruiting Trees and Shrubs for Birds

PLANT NAME	HEIGHT X SPREAD	BEST REGION(S)*	PLANT TYPE/ HARDINESS ZONES
Catclaw acacia (*Acacia greggii*)	8 feet x 8 feet	Desert Southwest	Shrub; Zones 8–10
Red buckeye (*Aesculus pavia*)	20 feet x 15 feet	Humid South	Tree; Zones 5–8
Serviceberries (*Amelanchier* spp.)	12 feet x 12 feet	Most regions have at least one native species.	Shrubs and small trees; hardiness varies by species
American beautyberry (*Callicarpa americana*)	6 feet x 5 feet	Humid South; Texas	Shrub; Zones 5–9
Hackberries (*Celtis laevigata, C. occidentalis*)	70 feet x 50 feet	Mountain West; Midwest/Great Plains; Pacific Coast Northwest	Trees; Zones 5–9 (*C. laevigata*); Zones 2–9 (*C. occidentalis*)
Spiny hackberry (*Celtis ehrenbergiana*)	18 feet x 18 feet	Desert Southwest; Florida	Shrub; Zones 7–11
Blueblossom (*Ceanothus thyrsiflorus*)	20 feet x 20 feet	Coastal California and Oregon	Shrub; Zones 8–10
Flowering dogwood (*Cornus florida*)	20 feet x 25 feet	Continental East; Canadian North	Tree; Zones 5–8
Pacific dogwood (*Cornus nuttallii*)	40 feet x 25 feet	Pacific Coast Northwest	Tree; Zones 7–8
Red-osier dogwood (*Cornus sericea*)	7 feet x 7 feet	Continental East; Canadian North	Shrub; Zones 2–8
Hawthorns (*Crataegus* spp.)	30 feet x 25 feet	Most regions have at least one native species.	Trees; hardiness varies by species
Black hawthorn (*Crataegus douglasii*)	30 feet x 25 feet	Pacific Coast Northwest	Tree; Zones 5–9
Mayhaw (*Crataegus aestivalis*)	30 feet x 25 feet	Humid South	Tree; Zones 6–11

*Best Region(s) indicates the area where a plant is most likely to grow well, but many of the plants in this table can grow successfully in a broad range of conditions.

PLANT NAME	HEIGHT X SPREAD	BEST REGION(S)*	PLANT TYPE/ HARDINESS ZONES
Persimmons (*Diospyros virginiana, D. texana*)	15–50 feet x 20–35 feet	Midwest/Great Plains; Continental East	Trees; Zones 4–9
Salal (*Gaultheria shallon*)	4 feet x 5 feet	Pacific Coast Northwest	Shrub; Zones 6–8
American holly (*Ilex opaca*)	50 feet x 40 feet	Humid South	Tree; Zones 5–9
Yaupon holly (*Ilex vomitoria*)	25 feet x 15 feet	Humid South	Shrub; Zones 8–10
Rocky Mountain juniper (*Juniperus scopulorum*)	40 feet x 20 feet	Mountain West	Tree; Zones 4–7
Eastern red cedar (*Juniperus virginiana*)	50 feet x 25 feet	Continental East; Canadian North	Tree; Zones 3–9
Spicebush (*Lindera benzoin*)	10 feet x 10 feet	Continental East; Canadian North	Shrub; Zones 5–9
Southern magnolia (*Magnolia grandiflora*)	50 feet x 50 feet	Humid South	Tree; Zones 7–9
Oregon grape holly (*Mahonia aquifolium*)	3 feet x 5 feet	Pacific Coast Northwest	Shrub; Zones 6–9
Pacific crabapple (*Malus fusca*)	35 feet x 30 feet	Pacific Coast Northwest	Tree; Zones 5–8
Red mulberry (*Morus rubra*)	40 feet x 40 feet	Continental East; Canadian North	Tree; Zones 5–9
Northern bayberry (*Myrica pensylvanica*)	8 feet x 8 feet	Continental East; Canadian North	Shrub; Zones 3–6
Mountain ninebark (*Physocarpus mono- gynus*)	3 feet x 3 feet	Mountain West	Shrub; Zones 5–8
Western sandcherry (*Prunus besseyi*)	6 feet x 6 feet	Mountain West	Shrub; Zones 4–8
Carolina cherry laurel (*Prunus caroliniana*)	25 feet x 20 feet	Humid South	Shrub; Zones 7–10

(continued)

Select Native Fruiting Trees and Shrubs for Birds—cont.

PLANT NAME	HEIGHT X SPREAD	BEST REGION(S)*	PLANT TYPE/ HARDINESS ZONES
Chokecherry (*Prunus virginiana*)	30 feet x 25 feet	Continental East; Canadian North	Tree; Zones 3–8
Coffeeberry (*Rhamnus californica*)	15 feet x 10 feet	Pacific Coast California	Shrub; Zones 7–9
Carolina buckthorn (*Rhamnus caroliniana*)	30 feet x 20 feet	Humid South	Tree; Zones 5–9
Skunkbush sumac (*Rhus trilobata*)	6 feet x 8 feet	Mountain West	Shrub; Zones 4–6
Staghorn sumac (*Rhus typhina*)	15 feet x 15 feet	Continental East; Canadian North	Shrub; Zones 3–8
Flowering currant (*Ribes sanguineum*)	10 feet x 6 feet	Pacific Coast Northwest	Shrub; Zones 6–8
Nootka rose (*Rosa nutkana*)	8 feet x 6 feet	Pacific Coast California	Shrub; Zones 3–9
Brambles (*Rubus* spp.)	8 feet x 8 feet	Midwest/Great Plains	Shrubs; hardiness varies by species
Blue elderberry (*Sambucus mexicana*)	20 feet x 20 feet	Pacific Coast California	Shrub; Zones 7–10
Mountain ash (*Sorbus americana*)	40 feet x 25 feet	Continental East; Canadian North	Tree; Zones 3–8
Dwarf mountain ash (*Sorbus scopulina*)	12 feet x 5 feet	Mountain West	Tree; Zones 3–7
Blueberries (*Vaccinium* spp.)	6 feet x 6 feet	Continental East; Canadian North	Shrubs; hardiness varies by species
Viburnums (*Viburnum* spp.)	15 feet x 10 feet	Continental East; Canadian North	Shrubs; hardiness varies by species

*Best Region(s) indicates the area where a plant is most likely to grow well, but many of the plants in this table can grow successfully in a broad range of conditions.

they provide food for the birds, they also provide protection from predators while the birds are eating them. Beware: Just as is the case with berries and fruit produced on trees or shrubs, the birds will begin to eat bramble berries long before they're palatable to the human tongue. So if you have a fruit crop you want to harvest for yourself, don't wait until the berries are ripe to protect it.

Where there are berries and birds that are eating them, there will also be bramble seedlings, sown by those same birds. This is good for the birds, because most like nothing better than a thorny thicket to take shelter in while they feast on berries in season and hunt for insects and seeds at other times of year. People tend to prefer their berry patches a bit tidier. Fortunately, most berry canes are easily kept in check with proper pruning techniques and by mowing along the edges of your berry planting. If you have the space, consider planting a berry patch just for birds in an out-of-the-way corner, where it can grow a bit tangly without offending anyone's sense of landscape propriety. A bird berry patch will quickly become the most bird-intensive spot in your landscape, because it offers food and more. In a separate spot, tend *your* berry patch, keeping it carefully pruned and protected from foraging birds.

Berry-Sharing Techniques

If you love homegrown berries and have illusions of enjoying at least some of your crop yourself, you may be chagrined to learn that birds are not very good at sharing. In fact, if any sharing is to take place, it will be up to you to secure your portion before the birds come for theirs. This applies to any home fruit plantings that are likely to catch birds' attention—blueberries, bramble fruits, cherries, and strawberries, to name a few.

To ensure that you get to enjoy the fruits of your labors, you'll probably need to use a combination of methods to deter fruit-eating birds. Once birds discover desirable fruits in your landscape, they can be extremely persistent in their efforts to eat them.

○ Where it's possible, use some sort of barrier to physically keep birds away from your fruit. Lightweight black plastic mesh is preferred by most home gardeners because it is inexpensive and easy to use. Once in place, plastic netting is almost invisible in the landscape, it is flexible to fit over different plant sizes and shapes, and it lets sunlight and rain get to your plants while discouraging birds trying to get to the fruit beneath it. When putting plastic mesh over your plants, you'll want to support it above the fruit-bearing branches—not because it's too heavy, but because birds will otherwise learn to perch on the net-covered branches and pluck berries though the openings in the mesh. Bamboo poles at least 6 inches taller than your berry bushes work well for this task of holding the mesh aloft. It's equally important to anchor the netting at the base of your plants, to stop birds from slipping under the edges and feasting inside the enclosure. Robins and other ground-level feeders are especially adept at getting under netting that's draped over fruit bushes but not fastened down. Be sure to put netting in place well in advance of fruit ripening, or birds will harvest your crop before you enjoy so much as a single berry.

◯ In addition to preventing—or at least slowing—birds from reaching your berries, offer them an alternative that draws them away from your crop. One of the best distractions is a mulberry tree. Many birds eat mulberries and even seem to prefer them to other fruits that ripen around the same time. Given the choice between raspberries under netting and unrestricted mulberries, most birds will go for the fruit that's easier to get. If you don't have the space for a mulberry tree—or don't relish the potential

mess—a tray feeder stocked with fruit and placed away from your berry patch will provide at least a little bit of a diversion. Use it to serve berries that are bug-bitten or otherwise unpalatable to you, but still appealing to the birds.

◯ You can use basic bird-deterring techniques to further discourage them from visiting your berry patch. Hang pie tins, old compact discs, or other shiny things that will sparkle and wave in the breeze above your fruit planting. Move these around every couple of days; to avoid annoying the neighbors, keep them in place only during the time when you're harvesting berries.

A Note from **Arlene**

FERMENTED FRUITS AND TIPSY BIRDS

Birds can get intoxicated if they eat too many fermenting berries. In this condition, they have trouble walking, hopping, and flying, and may fly into branches, windows, or each other. This state also makes them vulnerable to predators. Weather conditions determine if berries ferment, so there's not much you can do about this. The ill effects the birds feel will wear off, just like alcohol does in humans, although I doubt they get the equivalent of a hangover. Cedar waxwings are the species most mentioned by people who've seen "drunk" birds.

Many years ago, I was called by an alarmed neighbor who wanted to know what he could do about the birds in his yard that were dropping to the ground and staggering around. He lived close by, so I went to see what they were, almost certain they were cedar waxwings. It was early spring, and the waxwings were gorging themselves on holly berries that had been on a large bush all winter. All I could tell him to do was to wait it out and hope for the best, because there really wasn't anything he could do about the situation—except for stripping the large bush of all the berries, and that wasn't a feasible option. I told him that these feeding flocks usually move around a lot, and that this one would probably soon leave, as it did the next day, with the birds none the worse for wear. The experience gave my neighbor a great story about his drunken birds that he still tells to this day.

In the Pacific Northwest, huckleberries are favorites of many western birds, and they often cause the same kind of intoxication in birds there. Blue grouse love huckleberries and will take as many of them as they can, but they put them in their crops, which seems to keep the birds from becoming intoxicated.

First-Rate Berry Bearers

There are many shrubs and trees, both wild and cultivated, that bear fruits that birds find palatable. Many are fine landscape plants and are worth considering to give birds both food and shelter. In Chapter 9 you'll find more about all kinds of garden and landscape plants that attract birds, but here are some good fruit-producing trees and shrubs that bear long-lasting fruits. Birds may seem to ignore the fruits on these plants but will eventually turn to them when other resources become scarce.

Red chokeberry (*Aronia arbutifolia*), Zones 4–9

American beautyberry (*Callicarpa americana*), Zones 7–9

Cotoneasters (*Cotoneaster* spp.), Zones 6–9

Cockspur hawthorn (*Crataegus crusgalli*), Zones 4–6

Glossy hawthorn (*C. nitida*), Zones 5–9

Washington hawthorn (*C. phaenopyrum*), Zones 5–9

English holly (*Ilex aquifolium*), Zones 7–9

American holly (*I. opaca*), Zones 6–9

Winterberry holly (*I. verticillata*), Zones 4–9

Crabapples (*Malus* spp.), Zones 3–7

Bayberry (*Myrica pensylvanica*), Zones 4–9

Firethorns (*Pyracantha* spp.), Zones 5–9

Sumacs (*Rhus* spp.), Zones 3–8

Mountain ash (*Sorbus* spp.), Zones 4–7

Snowberry (*Symphoricarpos albus*), Zones 4–7

Linden viburnum (*Viburnum dilatatum*), Zones 5–8

Tea viburnum (*V. setigerum*), Zones 6–8

American cranberrybush (*Viburnum trilobum*), Zones 3–8

Keeping Birds Safe

To safeguard birds that might overindulge in fermented fruit, avoid positioning near roads or driveways those plants that hold their fruit through winter. Birds "under the influence" of alcoholic fruits may be unable to take flight quickly enough to move out of the way of cars, putting them in danger of being killed by passing vehicles. Even unfermented fruits can put birds at risk, if favorite fruits are dropping onto roadways and luring birds into danger. The birds endangered by fruit and other foods placed too close to roadways include raptors that may be hunting smaller birds that are drawn to the food source. Keep birds safe by keeping fruiting plants (and feeders) away from roadsides.

Mark Your Calendar for Fruit and Berry Times

Know when the berries on the shrubs or trees you plant will ripen, so you can choose those plants that will give birds a steady supply of natural food in your yard. This scheduling will vary depending upon where you live. Look around local woods, other people's yards, and in public gardens to see what's blooming and fruiting and when. Get a calendar on which you can see all the months at once, then mark what berries or fruit are available each month. You'll be able to see where there are gaps to fill.

Fruiting Groundcovers and Vines

Berry-producing groundcovers and vines are important not only for their berries, but also because their tangles give protection to birds as they eat. Some of the best and most easily grown are Virginia creeper (*Parthenocissus quinquefolia*), wild grapes (*Vitis* spp.), and honeysuckle (*Lonicera sempervirens*). Poison ivy in the East and poison oak in the West (*Toxicodendron* spp.) are plants to be avoided by humans, but they're worth

Select Native Fruiting Groundcovers and Vines for Birds

PLANT NAME	HEIGHT	BEST REGION(S)	PLANT TYPE/HARDINESS ZONES
Hairy manzanita (*Arctostaphylos columbiana*)	8 inches	Pacific Coast Northwest	Groundcover; Zones 7–10
Bearberry (*Arctostaphylos uva-ursi*)	8 inches	Mountain West	Groundcover; Zones 2–6
American bittersweet (*Celastris scandens*)	30 feet	Continental East; Canadian North; Midwest; Great Plains	Vine; Zones 3–8
Wild strawberry (*Fragaria californica*)	6 inches	Pacific Coast California	Groundcover; Zones 7–10
Trumpet honeysuckle (*Lonicera sempervirens*)	20 feet	Humid South	Vine; Zones 4–9
Chollas (*Opuntia* spp.)	3 feet	Desert Southwest	Groundcovers; hardiness varies by species
Virginia creeper (*Parthenocissus quinquefolia*)	Indefinite	Continental East; Canadian North	Vine; Zones 3–9
Greenbriers (*Smilax* spp.)	20 feet	Humid South	Vines; hardiness varies by species
Grape (*Vitex* spp.)	Varies by species	Species suitable for every region are available	Vines; hardiness varies by species

mentioning because they produce white berries that birds seek out, especially in winter. When flocks of yellow-rumped warblers spend the cold months in northern areas, they will almost always be found eating poison ivy berries. Native bittersweet (*Celastrus scandens*) is another vine that gets full of ornamental berries that birds love.

Saving Some for Spring

When you see a holly bush or a mountain ash loaded with berries untouched by birds through winter months, you may think that the birds are ignoring what appears to be perfectly good food. Don't mistake their fly-over for dislike or disinterest—the birds instinctively know what they're doing. The berries and fruits that birds leave on bushes and trees in late summer and fall are ones that need to be weathered before they are palatable. By freezing and thawing, aging, and even fermenting over winter, some kinds of fruits are softened and sweetened and made ready for birds to eat them.

The plants that hold their fruits into winter—rather than dropping them after they ripen—are particularly useful to birds that feed primarily on fruit. It's not an uncommon thing to see a pyracantha shrub loaded with berries go through an entire winter without being touched. Then suddenly in spring, the birds will begin devouring the berries. They know when it's the right time. Migratory fruit eaters would be out of luck upon their return to northern breeding areas if there were not plants such as crabapples holding last season's fruits, now adequately prepared by winter's exposure to the elements for the birds to eat. Because almost no plants in the temperate regions produce fruit in early spring, last season's leftovers, finally, look mighty good to hungry birds.

Birds aren't the only beneficiaries of this natural form of food processing. When you're choosing bird-friendly plants for your landscape, you'll want to include a few of these winter-long "fruit keepers" for their aesthetic value, too. It's fun in fall to watch a flock of birds descend on a flowering dogwood and feast until there's not a single fruit left on its branches. But once the fruits are gone, that tree's visual interest—and its bird appeal—are pretty much over until it blooms or leafs out in spring. When winter reduces the landscape to white and gray and brown and dark evergreen, bright holly berries or deep red crabapples are a welcome sight for our eyes, as well as a necessary food source that birds will turn to when it—and they—are ready.

Here's a hint if you want to enjoy colorful berries in your yard throughout winter and to later offer natural foods for birds: Choose fruiting shrubs and trees with berries in colors other than red. Birds seem to go for red berries first and leave yellow fruits until late winter or early spring. This phenomenon has been observed with cherries, for example—trees with yellow fruits generally are less at risk of being stripped of their crop by birds than red-fruited ones.

six

Creepy-Crawly Treats

In addition to natural foods, such as berries and seeds, and any kind of birdseed or suet that you put out for the birds, nearly all of them also eat insects when they're available. It's not uncommon to see birds you might think of as "feeder" birds—sparrows, jays, and woodpeckers, for example—fly out from a perch and then right back to it, grabbing a free-flying insect along the way. In the northern parts of the country in warm months, and all year-round in areas that remain free of ice and snow, birds that eat seeds most of the year supplement their diets by taking advantage of nature's abundant supply of insects. When insects are in good supply, your usual backyard birds may largely ignore your feeders, and it's nothing to be concerned about. The birds will be back on the perches of your feeders when insects become less plentiful.

Eastern bluebird bringing food to nestling

Meanwhile, take the opportunity to clean your feeders while your regular customers are dining elsewhere, then refill them sparingly to avoid having seed that becomes damp and spoiled before it gets eaten. Take a break from the frantic feeder-filling days of late fall and winter, and enjoy watching bird activity that's not dependent on hefty bags of black-oil sunflower seed. You may even come to appreciate the insects for helping to keep your bird-feeding expenses in check—and the birds for helping to keep the insects in check.

Seeing Bugs: A Bird's-Eye View

Creepy-crawly creatures are found all over the place in the wild. They're under bark or logs, under or on leaves, in the grass, and on or around every garden or other plant there is. All plants, whether they're big or small, attract insects, caterpillars, and other crawly things that birds like to eat. But some plants attract more insect life than others, and the birds know which ones will provide them with the most food. That's why you see so many birds working their way through leaf canopies, in goldenrod fields, on compost piles, through piles of fallen leaves, and even on bare tree or shrub branches in the middle of winter. At that time of year, it may not look to us like there's anything to eat there, but the birds know better.

Even the plants that we think of as providing seeds, fruit, and nectar for birds often are visited by birds just for their insects. It makes sense, then, to note that the insects a bird eats are those that it encounters in its regular habitat. Birds that live high in the treetops eat insects that feed on tree leaves, such as the tent caterpillars that are favored by many bird species; birds that live near open fields eat flying insects that hover over, or grasshoppers and others that live in, grasslands. Robins, grackles, and wood thrushes hunt on the ground and feed on earthworms and grubs in the upper layer of the soil.

Bugs and insects are high in protein, and when they're available, birds will always take advantage of a free meal—even birds that usually eat seeds. Members of the

Birds That Eat Bugs

Although the birds that feed almost exclusively on insects are rarely seen at backyard feeders, most birds—nearly 90 percent of all species—will eat insects, spiders, and other small invertebrates when they're available, even bird species that are regulars at the seed feeder. Additionally, roughly 97 percent of all terrestrial (nonshore and water) birds feed insects to their nestlings, making insects more important to birds' survival than any other type of food.

thrush family are especially fond of soft, creepy-crawly treats, but so are mocking-birds, thrashers, flycatchers, and many others. If you sit and watch a tent caterpillar or fall webworm nest, you'll see just how many different birds come and pick out the caterpillars from it. Cuckoos, both yellow-billed and black-billed, will gorge themselves on these caterpillars. Analysis of the stomach contents of one yellow-bellied cuckoo showed it to contain 217 fall webworms, and another yellow-billed cuckoo's stomach had 250 tent caterpillars in it. So unless there are so many pest nests around that they're doing major damage to your trees, leave these nests alone, because they're a major source of food for many birds.

Northern mockingbirds most often visit feeders when fruit is on the menu, but, like nearly all species of songbirds, they raise their babies on a steady diet of insects.

"Serving" Insects in Your Yard

With a few exceptions, we don't generally go to the wild-bird supply store to buy insects by the bagful or in preformed cakes, as we do with seeds and suet. Apart from mealworms and a few other "buggy" treats found at bird-specialty stores and on Web sites, any insects we "serve" to the birds in our yards are those that occur there naturally. For the most part, that's just as well—even the most dedicated birders are unlikely to run out to the store for a 50-pound bag of ants.

But that's also the beauty of feeding insects—and other multilegged critters—to birds. You don't have to buy anything. In fact, most of us can provide wild birds with

more insects simply by doing *less*. For starters, adopt a more relaxed view of the insects you encounter in your yard and garden. Where are they? Are they causing you harm or doing significant damage to your plants? We've been sold on the idea that perfection in our gardens equals beauty, that any sign of caterpillars nibbling leaves means we must take action to stop them, because holey leaves somehow diminish our garden's visual appeal. In our pursuit of this unattainable and unsustainable perfect beauty, we've lost sight of true beauty—a landscape that's brimming with life, including colorful butterflies and birds.

With three simple actions—two of which

are actually inactions—you can increase the populations of insects in your yard, and by doing so, make your yard more inviting to a greater variety of birds. If increasing insects in your yard sounds like the last thing you'd want to do, rest assured that the vast majority of the bugs that make up birds' diets are not pests that are bothersome to humans. You can make your landscape more bug friendly—and thus more bird friendly—without spoiling your own enjoyment of the outdoors around your home. In most cases, you won't even be aware that more insects are present, except when you notice that there are more birds, or when you see adult birds taking insects to feed their nestlings. Such sights are certainly worth a few nibbled leaves here and there.

Choose Native Plants

When you're making a new garden, installing a new landscape, or renovating part of your yard, make every effort to choose plants that are native to your region. The food web—of which we and birds and insects all are a part—depends on green plants to convert solar energy into food for every other living thing. But it turns out that not just any green plants will do. In our quest to fill our yards with the biggest, brightest flowers, we've carried plants from around the world to our doorsteps and installed them in place of the adequately pretty plants that naturally grow there. Often, to our delight, we find that insects seem to bypass these showy aliens, so we buy more and fill our gardens with nonnative beauties, never realizing that

A Note from Arlene

BIRDS ARE WHERE THE BUGS ARE

It's not uncommon for me to see ruby-throated hummingbirds hovering and picking at the seedheads of the many sunflowers we plant on our property. When I first noticed it, I was stumped, wondering why I hadn't known that sunflowers produce a lot of nectar. But a close look revealed that the birds weren't after the seeds, but rather were eating insects from between the seeds and in the foliage around the seedheads.

Corn tassels are also a major source of insects for birds, because tassels have lots of tiny insects and spiders in them. On our property, we leave the stalks of field corn and occasionally even those of sweet corn standing in our fields for extended periods of time. The field corn is often left in place for 3 years, while the sweet corn will be left standing through winter and sometimes even through the next summer. The reason we do this is because not only do these stalks make great perches for the birds, but the stalks also are a constant source of insects as they gradually decay. Most homeowners can't do this because they don't have the space, but the same thing can be done on a smaller scale with just a bed of sunflowers or other tall, sturdy-stemmed plants. Mexican sunflowers [*Tithonia* spp.], which produce round orange blossoms that attract birds and butterflies, are a good choice for this. They grow 6 feet tall or more, and their stalks are sturdy enough to withstand the rigors of winter.

we're reducing our landscapes' bird appeal as we do so.

As often happens, well-intentioned actions can have outsize and unforeseen consequences. The natural environment is vast and complex and responds to our "adjustments" in unexpected ways. But this part of the equation is quite simple: Birds need bugs, and bugs need native plants. Some 90 percent of plant-eating insects are specialists that feed only on a particular species or closely related group of plants. If insects can't find plants to feed on because they've been replaced by alien species, the insects die out. If birds can't find the insect species they eat and/or feed to their young, they go elsewhere in search of their preferred food. To enjoy more birds in your landscape, include as many native plants in your yard as you can. These will support the insects naturally found in your part of the country—and the birds know this. Everything evolves to eat or be eaten by some other living thing.

Delay Garden Cleanup

In addition to overreacting to every creepy-crawly we encounter, we humans also tend to go a little overboard about keeping our landscapes tidy. We snip off every faded flower, saw off every dead limb, and vacuum up every fallen leaf, not realizing in our zeal that we're taking bird food out of our yards as we work. When fall arrives, many gardeners are too quick to clean up their flowerbeds, removing dry stems and seedheads along with dried leaves and twigs. Besides removing seeds that sparrows, chickadees, finches, and others would eat into winter months, fall cleanup also takes away all sorts of insects

You may hear an Eastern towhee rummaging in dried leaves before you see it. If you happen to follow the sound of rustling to one of these brown (female) or black (male), white, and orange-red birds, watch its characteristic backward hop as it hunts for insects.

that would otherwise serve as cold-weather food for bluebirds, woodpeckers, nuthatches, wrens, and many other birds.

Insects overwinter in and on dried flower stems as well as tucked into the crevices of tree bark and hidden beneath a layer of fall leaves. You may think the chickadee perched on a dried goldenrod or aster stem is eating lingering seeds, and it may be—but it may also be mining the stalk for insect pupae. Thrushes, thrashers, robins, and towhees hunt for their food in leaf litter, nabbing crickets and grubs, as well as earthworms in warmer weather. As much as you can bear to, put off your garden cleanup until spring, leaving a feast of hidden insects to help birds make it through winter. Keep a corner of your landscape leafy—or create a low compost pile of chopped leaves—where robins and others can scratch for grubs. In spring, it will become an ideal earthworm hunting ground for them. And while it's not possible in every landscape, try to allow a dead tree or limb to stand, providing food for woodpeckers, creepers, and nuthatches as well as potential shelter for cavity-nesting birds.

Cut Back on Chemicals

When we spray pesticides to get rid of aphids on the roses or codling moths on the apple trees, the cause-and-effect relationship is clear: Fewer insects equal less natural food for the birds that eat them. But we might not immediately make the connection between a lush green lawn and less bird food, although the result is much the same from a robin's point of view. Strong fertilizers applied to a lawn wash down into the soil and either drive earthworms deeper, where birds can't reach them, or simply drive worms away. Products that kill grubs take food out of the beaks of grackles and starlings that hunt for them, just as sprays that kill caterpillars eliminate food for a wide variety of birds and their nestlings.

In addition to taking away sources of their food, insecticides may sicken or kill birds directly. A bird may mistake pesticide granules on the ground for food and eat them. Or it may gobble up dying caterpillars that have been sprayed with poison and thus ingest a lethal dose of toxins along with its meal. Depending on the time of year, pesticide-coated insects may be fed to hungry nestlings. Birds that eat insecticides may not die as a direct result, but they may be affected in ways that are hard to measure. Pesticide exposure and ingestion may interfere with mating and reproduction, may cause young birds to fail to thrive and mature normally, and may reduce birds' ability to forage for food—and any of these effects can cause gradual decline and death.

When you think of chemical use in those terms, the better choice for the health of birds in your landscape is to forgo using pesticides and to at least limit use of other chemicals. Even biological pesticides, such as BTK (*Bacillus thuringiensis* var. *kurstaki*), a control for caterpillars, have downsides. Although birds won't be sickened if they eat caterpillars that have been sprayed with BTK, they will find fewer caterpillars to eat. And you may notice fewer butterflies in your yard, too, because BTK kills all sorts of caterpillars, even those that would grow into beautiful butterflies.

Mealworms and More

Although bluebirds will eat pieces of sunflower seed, other seeds, or suet when insects and caterpillars are in short supply, they're primarily insect eaters. In the parts of the country where it gets cold in winter, bluebirds have to change their diets a lot, because their favorite foods aren't easily available. Even in far northern areas, however, flocks of wintering bluebirds can be found surviving mainly on insects that live in honeysuckle, grapevine, or other thickets in the shelter of the woods. In warm months, bluebirds spend most of their time perched on top of fences, fence posts, or tree branches, looking down into grassy fields for movement from grasshoppers, cicadas, and other insects, or scanning the air around them for mosquitoes and other flying insects. But they especially relish mealworms, the epitome of creepy-crawly creatures. Even if nature provides enough food for bluebirds to eat, they'll pick mealworms first when they're available.

Mealworms

Mealworms, the larvae of the darkling beetle (*Tenebrio molitor*), are favored by bluebirds as well as other insect-eating birds. You can buy mealworms from different sources—wild-bird supply stores, pet stores (where they're sold for feeding snakes and lizards), or bait shops—or you can raise them yourself. But you have to have patience and a good work ethic to raise them, especially when you first start, because it takes at least 3 months for you to get your first good

Creepy-crawly mealworms are bluebird favorites. You can raise your own mealworms or buy them by the tubful. Serve them in a separate mealworm feeder to invite bluebirds to your yard.

mealworm "crop." For example, if you want mealworms to put out for bluebirds in April or May, you have to start them in January or February. Growing your own mealworms instead of buying them can save you a lot of money, but it may also help you understand why these insect larvae command a premium price at the bird-food store.

Raising Mealworms

To raise mealworms to serve in your feeders, start with a large plastic box—with at least a 5-gallon capacity—that has a snap-on lid. Shallow plastic boxes, such as those sold for storing sweaters, make good mealworm incubators. Use a hammer and nail or an awl to make about 20 holes in the lid for ventilation. Prepare bedding and install your "starter" mealworms in the box as follows:

1. Combine equal parts whole wheat flour, oatmeal, and cornmeal to make enough food and bedding to fill the container 2 to 3 inches deep. Gently stir in several dozen live mealworms or a few adult beetles. If the store where you buy your mealworms raises its own supply, ask if it will sell you adult beetles, as this will shorten the time it takes you to raise your own larvae.

2. Cut a small potato in half and place it cut side down on top of the bedding. Lightly mist the surface of the bedding and put the lid on the box. Keep the container in a warm, dry place.

3. Each week, remove the old potato and replace it with another one, or with a wedge of cabbage, the core from a head of lettuce, or another moist vegetable. Change the vegetable more often if it becomes moldy.

4. Every couple of weeks, use a colander or just your gloved hands to sift the $\frac{1}{2}$-inch-long, dark brown or black beetles out of the bedding that holds the eggs and small larvae. The beetles may be added to a new container of bedding or served at the bird feeder.

5. The larvae take about 10 weeks to reach maturity (about 1 inch long), but you may offer them to birds at any time. To collect a few mealworms, lay two sheets of damp paper (such as brown craft paper) over the top of the bedding material. Within a few hours, mealworms will gather between

A Note from Arlene

DO MEALWORMS MAKE BETTER BLUEBIRDS?

Mark Blauer, who lives in Nescopeck, Pennsylvania, near Hawk Mountain Sanctuary, has several bluebird boxes on his property. He puts out mealworms for the bluebirds, and in the summer of 2010, the birds successfully raised three broods. Mark saw the young from one of the first two broods helping to feed the young from the last brood. This is something that's always mentioned in literature about bluebirds, but I've never personally seen it happen or known anyone who did before I talked to Mark. I don't know if having a constant supply of tasty, protein-rich mealworms made the adults and young stronger or better off, but it may have.

the papers or beneath them. Put as many worms as you need into a separate container to take to the feeder, or store them in a container—labeled clearly!—in the refrigerator in an inch or so of uncooked oatmeal until you're ready to serve them to the birds.

6. To remove adult beetles from your original large box, press quarters of apple into the bedding and leave overnight. Scoop up the apple pieces with beetles clinging to them and drop them quickly into a newly prepared box, to expand your mealworm production.

7. About once a month, sift mealworms out of the soiled bedding and frass (mealworm poop) and use this waste material to fertilize your garden or add it to a compost pile. Clean out the box, replace the worms, and add fresh bedding.

Loved by Lots of Birds

If you're going to the trouble of raising mealworms, and even if you just buy them, you may or may not be pleased to learn that many birds other than bluebirds will eat them, too. The list is long and includes warblers, woodpeckers, sparrows, jays, blackbirds, robins, thrashers, catbirds, chickadees, cardinals, wrens, finches, grosbeaks, kinglets, orioles, tanagers, vireos, and more. If you want to keep the mealworms just for the bluebirds, you'll have to either buy or make a mealworm feeder that's only accessible to them. And even that won't solve the exclusivity problem completely, if you see it as a problem. Although feeders designed just for bluebirds often are enclosed in wire cages, they still don't keep out all unwanted birds.

Some "bluebirders," as they call themselves, don't like this reality. Other people are happy keeping out just the larger birds and sharing the mealworms with the smaller ones. Most enthusiastic bird lovers appreciate the need to share the wealth. Bluebirds don't live alone in fields and at woods' edges, so neither should they be the only ones to get good food.

Earthworms and Grubs

Earthworms and grubs are high in protein and a major food for American robins, but many other species of birds eat them, too. European starlings and house sparrows will actually steal this protein-rich food from other birds if they can, and robins are often easy targets. In spring, huge flocks of migrating robins drop down onto lawns as they wing their way north, separating into breeding pairs along the way. The reason

American robins are often seen hunting earthworms in lawns after a rain has softened the ground and prompted the worms to move closer to the surface.

they do this is because the ground has finally softened up, and earthworms and grubs are there in droves for the taking. Compost and leaf piles are also good sources of worms and grubs for robins, other thrushes, and towhees.

Ants

Nobody likes having an anthill near the kitchen door, around picnic areas, or near hummingbird feeders, but ants are a major source of food for some birds. Like every-thing else in nature, ants have a role, so if you have an anthill on your property in a place where it's not doing you any harm, let it be. Flickers in particular love ants. Scientists examining the stomach contents of two yellow-shafted flickers counted 3,000 ants in one and 5,000 in the other.

Apart from having a picnic, another way to attract ants is to put a piece of old wood or a rotting log at the edge of the yard away from your main bird-feeding area. Most birds that feed on ants don't usually come to

"Bugs" and (Some of) the Birds That Eat Them

Insects and other creepy-crawly things provide food at least part of the time for nearly all the birds we see around us. Even the birds we think of as being mainly seed eaters or fruit eaters will make a meal of insects when the opportunity arises. The following list represents just a few of the bugs that birds eat and only some of the familiar feeder birds that eat them. In nature, the numbers on both sides of the equation are far greater, reflecting the immense complexity of the natural world.

BUGS	BIRDS THAT EAT THEM
Ants	Flickers, common grackle, juncos, yellow-billed magpie, orchard oriole, chipping sparrow, song sparrow, white-throated sparrow, starling, downy woodpecker, pileated woodpecker
Aphids	Indigo bunting, cardinal, orchard oriole, titmice
Beetles	Red-winged blackbird, bluebirds, indigo bunting, cardinal, common grackle, grosbeaks, blue jay, juncos, yellow-billed magpie, orchard oriole, robin, song sparrow, white-crowned sparrow, white-throated sparrow, woodpeckers
Cankerworms	Red-winged blackbird, indigo bunting, painted bunting, grosbeaks, orchard oriole
Caterpillars	Blackbirds, painted bunting, cardinal, black-capped chickadee, grosbeaks, jays, juncos, orioles, chipping sparrow, song sparrow, white-crowned sparrow, tufted titmouse, downy woodpecker
Cicadas	Indigo bunting, cardinal, chickadees, common grackle, robin, warblers, downy woodpecker

feeders, although once in a while a flicker might. As the log decays, it will become filled with ants for flickers and other birds to dine on. If you're lucky enough to have pileated woodpeckers in your area, your "ant farm" may also attract them.

Spiders

Spiderwebs feed birds as well as the spiders that catch insects in them. Some birds will take advantage of insects caught in webbing and make a meal of them before the spider gets a chance. Some will also eat the spider that made the web. When you can, leave spiderwebs in place under the eaves of your house, on bushes, or atop plants in your gardens. The birds will find them and either eat insects caught in them or use the webbing in their nests. Hummingbirds, for example, eat tiny spiders as well as other small insects and arthropods. And the little birds regularly incorporate spiderwebs into the construction of their nests.

BUGS	BIRDS THAT EAT THEM
Crickets	Eastern bluebird, western bluebird, painted bunting, cardinal
Earthworms*	Common grackle, robin, thrushes
Flies	Painted bunting, common grackle, black-headed grosbeak, black-billed magpie, white-crowned sparrow, white-throated sparrow
Grasshoppers	Blackbirds, eastern bluebird, western bluebird, buntings, cardinal, common grackle, black-headed grosbeak, rose-breasted grosbeak, blue jay, magpies, orchard oriole, robin, chipping sparrow, song sparrow
Grubs (beetle larvae)	Red-winged blackbird, common grackle, starling
Mosquitoes	Indigo bunting, white-crowned sparrow
Moths	Red-winged blackbird, cardinal, black-capped chickadee, downy woodpecker
Spiders*	Red-winged blackbird, cardinal, black-capped chickadee, black-headed grosbeak, blue jay, juncos, chipping sparrow, white-crowned sparrow
Termites	Cardinal, robin
Wasps	Painted bunting, black-headed grosbeak, juncos, yellow-billed magpie, chipping sparrow, song sparrow
Weevils	Mountain bluebird, buntings, juncos, chipping sparrow, downy woodpecker
Wood borers	Woodpeckers

*Birds don't count legs when they're dining on arthropods and other invertebrates—earthworms are not insects, of course, nor are spiders.

seven

Kitchen Castoffs and Home Cooking

Because of their fast-paced metabolism and limited storage capacity, most wild birds need abundant energy-dense foods to enable them to go about their daily lives. At times of the year when birds are migrating, seeking mates, raising young, or just surviving in subfreezing temperatures, their energy needs are even higher, and finding food becomes an almost full-time activity.

Western scrub jay with cracker

When we say a person "eats like a bird," we mean almost exactly the opposite of how birds actually eat. A person who truly eats like a bird would spend almost every waking hour of every day gobbling as much high-calorie food as possible. Clearly this is not a recipe for human health, as we have neither the metabolism nor the activity level for genuine bird-style dining. The flip side is that birds, generally, do not and should not eat like people, either.

That is not to say that some of the same foods we feed our families can't also find a place at the bird feeder. It depends on what's in your pantry, what you're willing to share with your feathered friends, and which birds you're willing to share with. As a rule, "people foods" that are closest to their natural form—whole grains, fresh or dried fruits, eggs, and meat scraps, for example—are the things that are most appropriate for feeding wild birds. The more processed a food is, the less likely it is to find favor among the birds at your feeders and the more likely it is to be attractive to scavengers and nonnative species such as starlings and house sparrows.

Even birds that seem to spend all their time at feeders are actually getting much of their daily nutrition from natural sources. If you worry that serving food meant for humans will jeopardize birds' health, bear in mind that what you see birds eating at the feeder is only a part of their diet and probably not the biggest part.

A diet of nothing but scraps and discards from your kitchen would certainly be unsuitable and unhealthy for wild birds, but birds are unlikely to eat such a diet. Birds can incorporate occasional "treats" such as crumbled baked goods into their diets probably better than we can without any harm. And diversifying the foods you offer to birds might attract new species to visit your yard.

At times of the year when birds' natural diets are constricted by ice and snow, food scraps and other goodies from our kitchens can actually benefit birds by providing nutrients that aren't found in the seeds and suet in our feeders. Because birds' needs may coincide with the strain of winter's uptick in seed consumption on our bird-feeding budgets, it works well for both the birds and people who feed them to augment feeder foods with kitchen castoffs and goodies. This is the best time to experiment with baked goods customized for birds' tastes and to try unfamiliar foods at your feeders. Hungry birds are far more likely to consider new foods than those same birds would at times when natural foods are plentiful.

Just as the birds at your feeders will vary according to the seeds and suet you're offering, so will the cast of guests lining up for your kitchen castoffs. Crows, jays, magpies, pigeons, house sparrows, and starlings may be your first and best customers for things like food scraps. But other birds, such as blackbirds, chickadees, woodpeckers, titmice, orioles, thrashers, and Carolina wrens, will also turn up when the menu is to their liking—foods that are similar to what they normally eat in the wild or at feeders—and when the presentation meets their needs. Low platform and tray feeders make "people foods" available to the broadest number of bird species.

What to Serve

Whether you're cleaning out stale but still serviceable items from your cupboards or scrounging in the kitchen for something—anything!—to keep the feeders filled when your seed stocks are running low, the foods that are most like those that birds naturally eat in the wild should be your first choices for offering at the feeder. Whole grain products, seeds, and fruits—plus meat drippings and scraps, peanut butter, even bits of cheese—all can become satisfactory stand-ins and special "sides" for birds' usual feeder fare.

Breads and Baked Goods

Just about everyone at one time or another has tossed old, stale bread out onto the lawn "to feed the birds." For people living in the city, that used to be the primary method of providing food for city birds, and for some people it still is. Years ago, birdseed as we know it today wasn't available; even if it had been, few people would've been likely to buy it. Feeding wild birds didn't gain true popularity as a pastime until the last part of the 20th century.

Bread in small quantities won't really hurt the birds, but it doesn't fulfill many of their nutritional requirements. A lot of birds will eat it, but if you consistently throw out bread, the species that you'll attract will be ones you probably don't want around. All of the grackle species, especially common grackles in the East and great-tailed grackles of the West, are attracted to bread. Grackles are opportunistic feeders that will take anything that's offered. They often carry pieces of stale bread to water to wet it before they eat it. Jays, house sparrows, European starlings, and of course crows, will also quickly learn where a good supply of stale bread is available, and they'll continue to visit your feeding area as long as bread is being put there.

Fatty baked goods such as doughnuts make fine treats for birds during winter, and the chickadees—often the first to check out new foods at the feeder—won't care if the doughnuts are stale. Of course, for the birds, plain doughnuts are best—they don't care much for colorful sprinkles or chocolate icing. If you want to add bird appeal to a doughnut or bagel, spread it lightly with peanut butter or soft suet.

A Note from Arlene

HER BIRDS LIKE BAGELS

I don't make a habit of throwing out bread or other baked products, but every once in a while I will toss out a stale bagel, and it doesn't take long for it to disappear. I've read that if you provide any kind of baked products for the birds, bagels are the ones to pick, because they have more nutrients in them than bread does. I don't know that to be true, but a bagel—either whole or sliced—fits handily into a suet cage, which makes it easy to serve without attracting crowds of starlings.

Birds Aren't Bread Snobs If you're baking, and things don't turn out quite right, put the "failures" out for the birds. You may find that you end up baking just for the birds. A loaf that fails to rise in your electric bread maker, for example, may not get much interest from your family, but the birds won't mind making a meal of your flops. People who go from serving birds baking "mistakes" to baking especially for the birds report that birds are a resoundingly appreciative audience and not fussy at all. You may actually spend more on custom-baking goods for the birds than you would buying day-old bread from a bakery outlet, but your customized treats can include goodies the birds will welcome and that you wouldn't find on the supermarket clearance shelf.

Cupboard Clean-Outs

A rainy or wintry day spent cleaning out your pantry can yield plenty of odds and ends that you can transform from unwanted "people food" to tasty treats for the birds in your yard. Once you discover the possibilities of stale crackers and cereal crumbs, you'll start setting these things aside for the birds, instead of shoving them to the back of the cupboard. Bird-food ingredients you may encounter during your cupboard quest include:

Broken or stale crackers
"Bottom-of-the-bag" cereals, such as granola, shredded wheat, bran flakes, and other whole grain cereals
Cornmeal or grits
Oatmeal
Hot wheat cereals
Bread crumbs
Graham cracker crumbs
Stuffing mix
Croutons
Dried fruit remnants

If cupboard cleaning comes at a time when birds are well supplied with natural foods, stash your goodies in the freezer until they're needed for feeder filling. A heavy-duty resealable storage bag, clearly labeled as *bird food*, is handy for storing all the tidbits from the bottom of cereal and cracker boxes and lets you add to it or pour out what you need when the time comes. Mix crushed or crumbled crackers, grain meals, or cereals with bacon grease, meat drippings, shortening, or peanut butter and press into empty yogurt cups or shape into balls and freeze for easy serving. You can also moisten dry foods with vegetable oil to make them easier and more nutritious for birds to eat.

Cheese

Feeding cheese to birds is something of a questionable practice, because it's not clear how well birds are able to digest milk-based products. Bits of stale, hard cheese are the easiest to serve and are readily eaten by birds. Limit cheese options to mild-flavored cheeses like American or Cheddar and avoid soft cheeses that are likely to spoil rapidly. Crusts and scraps from grilled cheese sandwiches, torn into bill-size bits, are more stable than cheese alone and will attract birds' interest served on a low tray or scattered on the ground.

Cooked Pasta and Rice

Few birds, if any, will bother with uncooked pasta, but leftovers from your spaghetti dinner or other types of pasta may find favor with jays, starlings, magpies, and crows. If your left-over noodles are bare, toss them with some vegetable oil to moisten them for the birds. Cooked rice also will appeal to some birds, but be sure to break up any clumps before you put it in the feeder so the birds can manage it.

The View from Deb's Window

Cupboard cleaning used to fill my kitchen trash can, but now it provides ingredients for a variety of bird-feeder treats. Instead of feeling guilty about the open box of crackers that got pushed to the back of the shelf and grew stale, I feel good that the birds, at least, will be nourished by the food we didn't eat.

When the temperature dropped suddenly and unseasonably into a stretch of subfreezing days and nights late last fall, I turned to my stockpile of cupboard clean-out ingredients to whip up a couple of high-fat concoctions to augment the usual seeds and suet in my feeders.

The first was a cracker and bacon spread, made from stale crackers and whatever bacon fat I had stashed in the refrigerator. This was a breeze to make using my food processor: I put in the crackers and a few small pieces of stale bread and turned them into about a cupful of crumbs, then added the bacon grease—about ⅓ cup—and processed everything into a thick, almost crumbly paste. I spread a thick layer on a piece of dry bread and inserted it into a suet cage, then spread the rest over the surface of a hanging wooden feeder that has shallow holes drilled in it for such spreadable offerings. Downy woodpeckers and nuthatches didn't take long to start feeding at both spots, and a Northern mockingbird even made the effort to cling awkwardly to the hanging feeder to get to the cracker-and-bacon combo.

I made another batch of crumbs from a loaf of bread too dry and hard for human consumption and added it to a mix of old turkey broth from the back of the freezer, combined with about ⅓ cup of peanut butter and a similar amount of lard. I melted the broth, peanut butter, and lard together in the microwave, then stirred in the bread crumbs and enough cornmeal (roughly 2 cups) to make the mixture crumbly. This mix I scooped into a hanging tray feeder. By the time I was back in the house, a tufted titmouse had checked it out, taken a bite, then flown away. It quickly came back and grabbed a piece large enough to hinder its flight as it returned to a branch to eat its prize. Chickadees, nuthatches, titmice, downy woodpeckers, blue jays, a Carolina wren, and others spent the rest of the day grabbing bites of the crumbly stuff. Judging from the feeder activity it generated, "Castoff Combo No. 2" was a rousing success.

Vegetables

Although they love seeds and fruits, few birds are vegetarians in the sense of eating much of what we think of as vegetables. The more omnivorous bird species—those that naturally scavenge discarded foods—may gobble veggies along with other food scraps, but leftover salad and similar food may be ignored by most birds. As a general guide to serving vegetables, think about the foods birds normally eat and stick with vegetables that fall into the "seed" category: peas, beans, and corn. A bag of freezer-burned peas—thawed first—may meet with favor in the feeder, but go slow until you see if any birds will eat them.

Meat

Grease poured off ground beef or pork, bacon fat, drippings from the bottom of the roasting pan, fat trimmed from steaks and chops—all these make great binding agents to combine with dry crumbs to turn them into fatty, suetlike treats for the birds.

Pet Food

Obviously, seeds and treats made for pet birds will find favor among the wild birds at your feeders, but you'll quickly burn through your bird-food budget if you rely upon these items to keep your feeders filled. If a friend's parakeet passes on, gratefully accept any leftover supplies of food on behalf of your feeder visitors; otherwise stick to seeds sold in more economical quantities.

Dry pet foods meant for dogs and cats will also earn the attention of a few birds, although the portions (nuggets) tend to be too large for most backyard birds to manage. Jays, crows, and ravens are among the exceptions—these birds will grab a chunk or two from an outdoor dish whenever Fido's or Fluffy's absence gives them the chance. Inexpensive dog foods, in fact, are mostly cornmeal and fats, and so make a reasonably balanced meal for wild birds, just as they do for dogs. You can use dog food as a diversion to draw feeder bullies

A Note from Arlene

JAYS THINK PET FOOD IS THE CAT'S MEOW

I don't know anyone who regularly feeds their birds dry nuggets of dog or cat food, but I do know that jays will pick up as much of them as they can and fly away with them. We have house cats that are almost always indoors, because everyone knows how destructive cats can be on bird populations. But once when my husband and I were getting ready to go away for the day, one of the cats got outside, so I put a dish of food by the deck door for it to eat. No sooner had I walked back in and closed the door, than a blue jay landed on the dish and began picking up pieces. We then delayed our departure and made an extra effort to get the cat back inside, but after we did, I forgot to bring in the food dish. And when we got home after dark that night, the dish was completely empty. A raccoon or opossum could've found it, but I suspect it was all eaten by blue jays.

like crows and magpies away from your feeding station, but be careful about other critters that may also find this offering attractive.

Fruit

Windfalls or bruised, bug-nibbled, or wilted fruits don't repel birds the way they do most people. Overripe bananas, smushy peaches, even rotting fruit all have fans among wild birds. If you choose to put some out in a feeder, don't put it in a ground feeder, and make sure that you get rid of any that isn't eaten quickly; otherwise it will attract animals, especially raccoons.

Sometimes birds will come to decaying fruits, such as watermelons and cantaloupes, for the liquid they provide. But more often, they are drawn to past-prime fruit for the insects that collect around it. Although orioles usually prefer fresh, halved oranges, they will also eat oranges that have turned brown. And finches, especially the ubiquitous house finches, aren't picky about fruit's freshness—they'll eat just about anything. Sliced or rotting apples will attract northern mockingbirds, gray catbirds, and thrashers, and have been known to be visited by kinglets, warblers, and chickadees.

Dried watermelon and cantaloupe seeds can be put in bird feeders. Not a lot of stores sell them, but they're nutritious and birds will certainly eat them. Dry them on a sheet of newspaper after you clean a melon, then serve them in a feeder or stockpile them for future use.

Unexpected guests, like this cardinal, may come to a chunk of watermelon for a bite of its juicy flesh or for the insects the fruit attracts.

Skewers and strings are fun ways to serve fruits without gunking up your tray feeder or making fruit too easy for starlings to get to. Slide modest chunks or slices of produce like apples, pears, dried fruit, berries (whole), summer squash, or any other fresh fruits that you may have in your kitchen or growing in your garden onto bamboo or metal skewers and fasten a string at both ends to make a hanger. You can also make holes in the pieces of fruit and thread them onto a 2- to 4-foot length of twine, then tie the ends together and hang from a branch. Small, acrobatic birds will be able to cling to the skewered fruits to feed, but larger birds will be unable to hog these fruity kebabs.

FANCY FRUIT-NUT BLEND

This combo could be quite pricey if you bought all the ingredients at the supermarket, but it lends itself to substitutions of whatever items you have on hand and can include home-dried apples and bird food–grade peanuts in place of the more expensive nuts.

2 parts dried, chopped apples

2 parts raisins

2 parts chopped nuts and seeds (almonds, walnuts, peanuts, or shelled sunflower seeds)

1 part chopped prunes

1 part dried melon or squash seeds

Large mixing bowl or bucket

Paper bag

Mix the ingredients in the bowl or bucket. Start by adding small amounts of this blend to your feeder and store the rest in the paper bag in a cool, dry location. Offer more once the birds show an interest in this special treat.

Nuts

Birds will readily eat almost any nuts you care to share with them, and nut butters are a popular treat, too. But the price of serving birds nut products that have been manufactured for human consumption can be prohibitive, and birds are no more likely to eat rancid (spoiled) nuts or nut butters than you are. Salted nuts are not the best choice for birds, either, because birds may take in more salt than is good for them. At wild-bird specialty stores, you can find premium feeder mixes that contain all sorts of nuts, and birds certainly will gobble them up if you choose to provide such goodies. A downside of putting nuts out at your feeders, however, is that squirrels also find them irresistible and will become even more determined to get at the contents of any feeder that contains them.

Eggs and Eggshells

We don't like to think about it, but some birds eat eggs in the wild and will welcome cooked eggs served at the feeder. Eggshells are a valuable calcium source, as are crushed oyster shells sold as a poultry feed supplement by farm-supply stores.

Grit, usually in the form of soft sand or small pebbles, is used by birds in their stomach musculature or gizzards to help crush hard seeds, nuts, and grains. This is why you will often see a lot of birds pecking at dirt and alongside roadways. Crushed eggshells can be offered as grit and also given to increase calcium in birds' bodies, which is important all the time, but especially when eggs are being formed. Many references recommend baking eggshells before you feed them to birds, presumably to kill any disease pathogens that might be on the shells. The truth is that most pathogens that humans fear from raw eggs are not a concern for birds, and as mentioned above, birds rather often eat raw eggs in nature. Baking the eggshells does make them easier to crush into suitably small pieces for birds, and it keeps them from becoming smelly in the feeder, although the latter can be achieved by rinsing them thoroughly before you put them out. If you're making baked goods that include eggs in the ingredients, it's easy enough to rinse the shells and put them in the oven to bake along with your cake. The resulting shells will be dry and ready to crush up and serve in the feeder. If your egg dish du jour is scrambled eggs, how you handle the shells is up to you: Rinse, crush, and serve, or bake before serving—the birds will benefit either way.

How to Serve "People Foods"

When you have tidbits of food from your kitchen to offer the birds, putting them on a simple tray or platform usually is the easiest and most effective serving method. Feeders meant for holding seeds don't lend themselves to delivering "people foods" that are soft, moist, or irregularly shaped. Depending on what's on your menu, suet cages can offer an alternative to food placed in an open tray or tossed on the ground and can help to keep pests from devouring homemade goodies you prepared for the birds. Here are some other tips to help make "people foods" a success when you serve them at your feeders.

○ Start small: Offer only modest amounts of new foods.

○ Be patient: It may take time for birds to "discover" unfamiliar foods.

○ Consider demand: Serve new foods at times when natural food supplies are low.

The View from Deb's Window

Every year around the holidays, I make a snack mix of cereals, pretzels, and mixed nuts, using standard brands of mixed nuts that typically contain peanuts, cashews, almonds, pecans, filberts, and Brazil nuts. I don't like Brazil nuts, so I regularly pick them out and add them to my collection of seeds that eventually make their way to my bird feeders. Sometimes I just toss a Brazil nut out the door in the direction of the feeder. I don't know whether birds or squirrels more often enjoy this special treat, but I know it's a win-win. I don't feel bad about not eating the Brazil nut, and some wild creature gets a big nut to feast on.

○ Evaluate response: Watch to see which birds come to new foods and if or how quickly the food is eaten.

○ Prevent problems: Avoid leaving "people foods" out in feeders overnight, so you can limit interest from other wildlife.

○ Keep up with cleanup: "People foods" may spoil more quickly than foods normally served in bird feeders. Spoiled food is unlikely to sicken birds, because they're unlikely to eat it, but it may attract pests.

Be prompt about removing uneaten food before it becomes a nuisance.

Serving wild birds food meant for humans makes the most sense when you're saving money on birdseed by offering food that would go to waste. Otherwise, "people food" typically costs more than bird food and should be used to feed people, not birds. If you're buying a jar of peanut butter or a bag of cornmeal to turn into treats for your birds, consider buying two of that item and donating one to a food bank.

Making Peace with "Urban" Birds

Feeders in city settings may mainly host birds that some bird-watchers consider to be unwelcome pests. But it's not the fault of the birds, such as starlings and house sparrows, that humans brought them to places that put them in competition with native birds. And it's not the fault of birds like rock doves, better known as pigeons, that they're naturally

Dinner as Diversion

Besides helping to stretch your bird-feeding budget, serving food scraps to birds can work to your advantage by drawing bird bullies away from your seed and suet feeders. Because food scraps are most attractive to scavengers such as crows, jays, and starlings, serving them in a separate area away from your feeders can give smaller birds a chance to eat from the feeders in peace. Offer foods like cooked pasta, meat scraps, bits of sandwiches, cooked eggs, and similar items on the ground or on low trays or platforms to make them accessible to the greatest number of feeder hogs.

Of course, the diversion will only be successful if the birds you hope to lure away from your feeders actually take to their scavenger-friendly buffet. Along with any food scraps from your dinner table, you may need to serve some familiar and desirable foods, such as suet crumbles and unshelled peanuts, in the area where you want pests to gather. You'll also want to keep a close eye on what gets eaten and what is ignored, and be quick to clean up any leftovers. Depending on the menu, squirrels may take advantage of unsecured food offerings, and nocturnal guests also are likely to find them attractive. Skunks, opossums, mice, and rats all are a possible nighttime cleanup crew, and dogs and cats also may be drawn to the area. Because your goal is to distract pesky birds from bothering your feeders, be careful that your diversionary tactic doesn't bring new pests into your yard.

Starlings, pigeons, and house sparrows are a common presence in city settings where food is served outdoors. Try looking beyond their pesky behavior and developing an appreciation for their adaptability to urban conditions and their amusing antics as they squabble over cold French fries and other tidbits.

suited to living on the clifflike sills and ledges of tall buildings.

Not surprisingly, the most common birds found in cities are among those that readily gobble up "people food." If "urban" birds are the only ones that your city surroundings have to offer, enjoy their company and serve them the sort of urban fare they normally seek on the streets: Bits of bread and sandwiches, cracker crumbs, and tidbits of other baked goods will meet with favor. If you want to offer more traditional feeder foods, remember that pigeons, like other doves, are mainly ground feeders that seek small grains, like millet and cracked corn. Starlings and house sparrows will quickly clean up suet crumbled in a tray feeder, as well as black-oil sunflower seed and pretty much anything else you put out.

Once you change your outlook on city birds, you'll find that they can be very interesting to watch. Pigeons come in an array of different color combinations and many have iridescent plumage. Starlings' feathers also sparkle in sunlight, and their songs are pleasant to the ear. House sparrows may be the hardest to love, but they are active and often comical birds that chirp and bicker as they fight to get at any food. You may see one swipe food from another and then get to watch the ensuing battle for the purloined tidbit. House sparrows also eat plenty of insects, so they're good companions for urban gardeners.

Be a good neighbor if you're feeding birds in an urban environment or anyplace where many people live in close proximity. Be conscious of where droppings and seed hulls wind up beneath hanging or pole-mounted feeders, and make sure they're not falling through the slats of your balcony onto your neighbor's patio furniture below. Keep feeder areas clean to avoid attracting rats seeking spilled seed. If you scatter millet on the ground for doves and pigeons, avoid putting it anyplace where the small round seeds might create a slipping hazard for pedestrians.

Home Cooking for the Birds

Here are a few more recipes for bird-pleasing combos you can whip up in the kitchen and serve at your feeders.

HOMEMADE SEED BELLS

Like the bell-shaped treats you can buy at the store, these attractive, edible decorations make great gifts for bird-loving friends. Unlike store-bought seed bells, homemade bells can have customized seed content, avoiding filler seeds like wheat and milo that are likely to wind up uneaten on the ground.

INGREDIENTS AND SUPPLIES

Small clay pots (3- to 4-inch diameter)

Aluminum foil

Parchment paper or small oven-roasting bags

Pliers

Wire for making hangers (8- to 10-inch length for each bell)

2 egg whites per cup of birdseed

Birdseed of choice (roughly a cup of seed per bell)

Bowl

Fork or eggbeater

Wire cutters

Baking sheet

DIRECTIONS

1. Line each pot with foil, parchment paper, or an oven bag. Using the pliers, shape one end of each piece of wire into a closed loop, and bend it so the loop is at a right angle to the rest of the wire.

2. Beat the egg whites until they become fluffy but are still liquid. Combine the egg whites and birdseed in a bowl and stir until the seed is thoroughly coated. Fill each lined pot with the coated seeds, packing them in firmly. Stick the straight end of the wire into the center of the seed mix and out through the pot's drainage hole, and pull it through until the loop at the other end is slightly embedded in the seed mix.

Egg whites are the binding agent that holds the seeds together in these homemade bells. Use clay pots or any heat-resistant container to shape your own custom seed mixture into edible ornaments for the birds.

3. Bend the wire coming out of the drainage hole at a right angle against the bottom of each pot, and carefully set the pots on a baking sheet lined with foil. They'll be a little tippy, but the pan keeps egg whites from dripping out of the holes and onto the bottom of the oven.

4. Bake for 1 to 1½ hours at no more than 250°F. Extend the baking time if you're using larger pots, checking at regular intervals until the seed-egg mixture is set.

5. When your bells are set, slip them out of their pots and let them cool slightly before peeling away the liners while they're still warm. Be careful not to touch the wire while it's hot.

6. Once the bells have cooled, use pliers to bend the wire at the top of each bell into a loop or hook for hanging.

PINECONE GOODIES

These two recipes both lend themselves to being packed into the open scales of pine-cones, which then may be hung from branches like holiday ornaments for the birds. Both recipes call for the same supplies, but the ingredients differ.

INGREDIENTS AND SUPPLIES

4½ cups ground fresh suet

¾ cup crushed crackers

½ cup shelled sunflower seeds

¼ cup white millet

¼ cup dried chopped fruit or berries

Saucepan

Stirring spoon

Large mixing bowl

Wire, ribbon, or twine for hanging

Medium and large pinecones

Knife

DIRECTIONS

1. Melt suet in a saucepan over low heat, stirring to avoid scorching. Combine remaining ingredients in a large mixing bowl. Let the suet cool until it is slightly thickened, then add it to the bowl and mix thoroughly.

2. Tie a length of wire, ribbon, or twine securely to the narrow tip of each pinecone (so scales open upward like V's). With the knife, pack the mixture into the scales of the pinecones and store them in the refrigerator until you're ready to hang them outdoors.

INGREDIENTS

1 cup fresh suet*

1 cup peanut butter

3 cups cornmeal

½ cup flour

DIRECTIONS

1. Melt suet in a saucepan over low heat. Add peanut butter, stirring until melted and well blended.

2. Combine cornmeal and flour in a large bowl. Let the suet-peanut butter blend cool until slightly thickened, then stir it into the dry ingredients and mix thoroughly.

3. Pack, store, and hang the pinecones as described in the previous recipe.

*If you don't have access to suet or don't want to use it, you can substitute a cup of vegetable shortening in this recipe.

EASY SUET-FEEDER MIX-'N'-MATCH

INGREDIENTS AND SUPPLIES

1 cup fat, such as suet, lard, or vegetable shortening

1 cup creamy peanut butter

1 cup flour

1 cup berries, shelled seeds, nuts, and/or dried fruits

3 cups cornmeal

Saucepan or microwave-safe bowl

Baking pan or other container(s) to use as molds to fit suet feeder

Knife

DIRECTIONS

1. Melt the fat and peanut butter together in the saucepan or in the microwave. Once the liquid has cooled slightly, stir in flour and fruits/seeds/nuts and cornmeal and mix thoroughly.

2. Press/pour the mixture into the baking pan or other container(s) and chill in the refrigerator until solid. Cut into cakes to fit the size and shape of your suet feeder, or pop the suet out of the molds to fill your feeder.

BASIC BIRD-FRIENDLY QUICK BREAD

Not everyone is inclined to spend time and materials making baked goods for the birds, but if you enjoy baking and feel like experimenting, nearly any basic quick bread recipe can be customized for your friends at the feeders. Turn an overabundance of zucchini from your garden into birdworthy zucchini bread with shelled sunflower seed, or make overripe bananas into banana bread with peanuts in place of the pecans your family might prefer. If you're already baking for your own use, set aside one loaf for the birds and doctor it with birdseeds, cornmeal, raisins, bits of fruit, cereal crumbs, or other goodies your feeder birds will enjoy. Just remember, if you make loaves of bird bread along with bread for your family, be sure to keep track of which baked goods are which!

INGREDIENTS AND SUPPLIES

$3\frac{1}{2}$ cups sifted flour

$\frac{1}{2}$ teaspoon baking soda

1 cup sugar

4 eggs

2 cups mashed bananas

4 teaspoons baking powder

1 teaspoon salt

$\frac{2}{3}$ cup shortening

1 cup nuts or shelled sunflower seeds

2 large loaf pans, greased

DIRECTIONS

1. Preheat oven to 350 degrees. Combine dry ingredients, then add remaining ingredients and beat together for 1 minute. Pour batter into loaf pans and bake for 35 to 40 minutes, or until toothpick inserted in middle of loaf comes out clean.

2. Stockpile loaves of bird bread in your freezer to serve at times of the year when other foods are scarce. This banana bread will be especially welcomed at such times by robins and other fruit-lovers.

"People Foods" and the Birds That Seek Them

PEOPLE FOODS	BIRDS THAT SEEK THEM
Apples	Bluebirds, chickadees, jays, mockingbird, robin, starlings, thrashers, titmice, towhees, Carolina wren
Bacon	Bluebirds, crows, jays, ravens, woodpeckers, Carolina wren
Bread	Blackbirds, grackles, jays, magpies, mockingbird, robins, house and native sparrows, starlings, Carolina wren, many others
Cake and cookies	Blackbirds, bluebirds, chickadees, crows, jays, mockingbird, pigeons, robin, house and native sparrows, starlings, thrushes, titmice, Carolina wren
Cheese	Catbird, thrashers, Carolina wren
Cornmeal	Doves, other ground-feeding birds, juncos, native sparrows, wood thrush, towhees, yellow-rumped warbler
Crackers	Blackbirds, chickadees, crows, doves, jays, juncos, nuthatches, pigeons, sparrows, starlings, titmice, woodpeckers
Cranberries	Mockingbird, robin, waxwings, Carolina wren
Dog food	Blackbirds, crows, jays, mockingbird, robin, starlings, thrashers, thrushes, Carolina wren
Doughnuts	Chickadees, other feeder birds, jays, titmice
Eggs and eggshells	Chickadees, crows, game birds, grackles, jays, juncos, magpies, purple martin, ravens, house and native sparrows, starlings
Fruit	Red-winged blackbird, bluebird, catbird, dove, house finch, Steller's jay, mockingbird, orioles, robin, yellow-bellied sapsucker, fox sparrow, summer tanager, western tanager, hermit thrush, towhee, red-bellied woodpecker
Pasta, cooked	Crows, brown thrasher
Peanut butter	Bluebird, cardinal, chickadees, mockingbird, chipping sparrow, field sparrow, song sparrow, tree sparrow, summer tanager, wood thrush, titmice, yellow-rumped warbler, red-bellied woodpecker, Carolina wren
Pumpkin and squash seeds	Jays, nuthatches
Raisins	Red-winged blackbird, bluebirds, catbird, mockingbird, robin, thrasher, wood thrush
Melon seeds	Cardinal

eight

Feeding Station Features

Take your bird-feeding habit from feeder, to feeding station, to wild-bird-welcoming habitat. Once you get the hang of tending a feeder or two, you may want to expand your efforts to include more feeders as well as other elements that birds need to survive and thrive. Just as you can increase the variety of birds at your feeders by offering different kinds of food, you can also attract birds that don't normally turn up at feeders by adding features such as water and shelter to your landscape.

A feeder in a garden attracts multiple species of songbirds.

Creating a feeding station consisting of multiple feeders and water for drinking and bathing makes it easier for you to keep up with refilling and other basic maintenance, and it contains the mess of shells and spilled seeds to a limited area of your yard. But birds may find it less appealing—not every species takes to feeding in proximity to members of other species or even to other individuals of its own kind.

Managing Bird Feeders and Feeding Stations

If you group the feeders in your yard, you'll probably find that your feeding station seems wildly popular at certain times of the year and almost completely abandoned at others. In fall when birds are preparing for migration, and in winter when natural foods become scarce, a well-stocked group of feeders may bustle with birds from dawn to dusk, while those same feeders and foods may receive almost no visitors in late spring and through summer. As discussed in previous chapters, you'll want to adjust your feeding routines to match the activity level at your feeders at different times of year.

Put Feeders on the (Right) Level

Almost as important as what birds eat is the question of where they eat it. In natural settings, multiple species are able to live in the same area, because they occupy different niches within the broader habitat. Tanagers and warblers feed on insects high in the treetops; catbirds and wrens dine at shrub level on insects, seeds, and fruits; and robins hunt for worms and juncos for seeds at ground level.

When we put up feeders to invite birds into our yards, we ask the birds to ignore these instinctive protocols in favor of perching side by side at a tray of seeds. Not every species will adapt readily to dining in artificially arranged conditions, which is why only certain birds routinely visit feeders. The more you do to offer foods in situations similar to those in which birds feed in nature, the more birds will be attracted to your foods and feeders.

To appeal to the greatest variety of birds, place your feeders at different sites and arrange them at different heights. Place several feeding trays or platforms on the ground, then set up one or two feeders a few inches above ground level. Arrange some feeders a foot or two off the ground, and hang other feeders higher up in trees. (Place ground-level feeders in an open area away from bushes and plants, so that predators can't sneak up on the birds.)

When you create multiple feeding sites, you give ground-feeding birds all the room they need to eat in comfort. And by adding feeders at several different heights, you provide feeding options for birds that are too shy to feed directly on the ground. Make dining convenient for your feathered friends. A ground feeder makes eating easy for cardinals, while nuthatches prefer raised plat-form feeders. Titmice like any feeder that's set off the ground, and chickadees visit all kinds of feeders, including hanging types.

Feeder/Feeding Station Do's and Don'ts

When you're first setting up a backyard feed-ing area, or when you add a new feeder to an existing feeding station, be patient. Birds need to get used to a new feeder, even if they're already using other ones in your yard. They're wild creatures with natural feeding instincts, so if they choose berries, nuts, seeds, or other wild foods over the sunflower seeds you've just put out in a fancy new feeder, don't worry that your efforts have been wasted. Eventually that feeder will get plenty of use, as soon as the birds get used to it, when the seasons change, or both.

When you're setting up a feeding station, start out small and give the birds time to find and accept the new source of food. One seed feeder and one suet feeder are enough to start with. You can add more as time goes by, if you want. You may find that keeping even a few feeders filled and clean takes more of your time than you expected. Or you may be so happy with the birds you're seeing and learning about that you want to start adding more. Either way, be thoughtful about each feeder you install, and consider your own ability and willingness to main-tain it as well as the needs and preferences of the birds that will visit it.

Feeding-Station Success Whether you're putting up one feeder or several, you'll want to do everything you can to ensure that both you and the birds get the most out of your efforts. Here are some things to con-sider before you plant a post or mount a hanger.

Choose the right site. Location is so important. Even when feeders are in an open area, many birds use nearby trees and shrubs as cover from predators. Avoid plac-ing feeders in overly exposed sites like the

"Be sure to put your feeders up high enough so that when you mow under or around them, you don't hit them and spill everything—in addition to possibly hurting yourself. And be sure that you don't hang them from a rotting branch."

DAVE DEREAMUS, Easton, Pennsylvania

middle of a barren yard—birds will mostly ignore feeders placed out in the open, and the contents of the feeders will spoil more quickly as the sun heats them up.

Check the traffic. Pick a spot that's away from areas with a lot of people, pet, or vehi-cle activity. Birds won't feed at a spot where they are repeatedly disturbed.

Keep your eyes on the prize. While you're considering the exposure and activity levels of potential feeder locations, don't for-get to select a spot where you can see the feeder and its visitors, preferably from a window you look out of frequently from inside your home.

Choose the right height. Mount or hang feeders high enough so that cats can't easily jump onto them, and so you don't have to worry about bumping into them when you're mowing or taking care of your lawn. At the same time, keep reasonably easy access for cleaning and refilling in mind.

Mix things up. Vary the styles of feeders and place them at varying heights. A basic feeding station might have one high feeder (5 to 6 feet off the ground), one or two feeders at a few inches to 3 feet off the ground, and one feeder at ground level. Besides being at differing heights, these should vary in shape, size, content, and construction. Some birds prefer hanging tube or sock feeders, some prefer hopper feeders, some like platform feeders, others always come to ground feeders, and still others will use any and all of them.

Cater to different tastes. Although black-oil sunflower seed is popular with the greatest variety of birds, you'll enjoy more diversity at your feeders if you serve other foods, too. Think of your feeders as a sort of bird buffet, with one feeder of black-oil sunflower, one containing white millet, perhaps a tube of nyjer seed, and one or more feeders holding some form of suet.

Secure your investments. Buy or make feeders with covers that help shield their contents from the elements. Mount feeders so that ports and feeding trays are facing away from prevailing winds. Use swivel hooks to support hanging feeders, to keep them from swinging excessively in strong winds and spilling their contents or blowing down. Use sturdy poles for pole-mounted feeders and regularly check that the pole is firmly in the ground and that the feeders it holds are securely fastened to it.

Common Feeding-Station Pitfalls

Avoid these common mistakes when setting up a bird-feeding area in your yard.

⚪ Placement in open/exposed site where birds don't feel safe and exposure to elements causes rapid deterioration of foods and feeders

⚪ Heavily traveled site where birds are repeatedly disturbed

When Bigger Is Better

If your backyard feeders are emptying so quickly that keeping them filled is becoming a full-time job, it may be time to put out one or more large-capacity hopper feeders. A hopper feeder holds a quantity of seed and lets it drop into a feeding tray as birds feed and take seeds out. A hopper is ideal for holding lots of seed, because it protects most of its contents from exposure to the elements; only seed that is actually in the feeding tray is in danger of getting wet in rain or snow.

Choose a hopper that holds enough seed to keep your birds happy for a few days at a time. Look for sturdy construction that will keep the contents of the hopper from getting wet, as well as a secure closure mechanism to keep would-be feeder raiders from getting into the seeds. A weight-activated perch that closes the feeding tray is also useful for limiting access to seed-gobbling squirrels and other feeder hogs.

○ Multiple feeders close together and at same height

○ Difficult or complicated access that keeps you from maintaining feeders

○ Same seed in all feeders

○ No view of feeders: out of sight, out of mind

○ Hummingbird feeders too close to seed feeders—need to separate by at least 15 feet

○ Big feeder for small habitat—need to start small and size up if necessary

Features and Accessories to Make Feeding a Breeze

A visit to a wild-bird supply store or Web site gives the impression of an almost infinite variety of feeders and feeder accessories. During fall and winter months, this is reinforced at hardware stores and home centers that likewise stock their shelves with feeders and foods for wild birds. The appearance of variety can be overwhelming when you're trying to choose a new feeder for your yard, but the selection is not as vast as it appears. All those different styles and shapes of feeders are really just three basic types: hopper and tube configurations for seeds; trays for all sorts of foods; and suet feeders designed to hold rectangular cakes, rounded plugs, or softer spreadable suet.

When you're shopping for feeders, base your decision on the birds you reasonably expect to see, the foods that you plan to offer, and the features that will make it easy for you to fill and care for those feeders. If decorative feeders appeal to you, by all means factor aesthetics into the equation, too, but

recognize that bright colors and other adornments matter little to birds looking for a meal. Here are some things to consider when a new feeder is on your shopping list.

Durability. Feeder construction has improved dramatically over the past couple of decades. Newer models on the market make use of sturdy recycled plastic, antibacterial materials and coatings, and metal feeding ports to create feeders that last longer, resist squirrels better, and are less likely to spread diseases to visiting birds. All this quality comes at a price, of course, and you may suffer "sticker shock" when your eye is drawn to a large-capacity hopper or tube feeder with all the latest advancements in bird-feeding technology.

Only you can decide if a long-lasting feeder is worth the rather substantial investment compared to the price of flimsier feeders that may have to be replaced every year or two. Deluxe models are nice if your budget can bear them, but an inexpensive feeder may serve for a season or two and then be discarded without regret when it is beyond repair.

Ease of hanging or mounting. Questions of durability extend to the parts of a feeder intended for hanging or mounting it in your yard. Sturdy construction often results in extra weight and requires better mounting hardware, stronger poles, and longer screws and bolts to ensure that feeders stay where you put them. Even durable tubes and hoppers will suffer if they crash to the ground too often, and there's little point in hanging a high-priced feeder from a spindly support.

When you bring home a new feeder, you want to put it into use as quickly as possible, too. Check out the parts that are meant for hanging or mounting and make sure they'll work how and where you want them and that they are designed to let you install your feeder quickly and easily.

Ease of use for you. When a cold wind is blowing sleet down your collar and your feet are freezing in a foot of snow, you want to be able to quickly get the seeds into the feeder and get yourself back inside. To avoid rummaging in the snow for a dropped lid below the feeder, look for one with a lid that opens easily while remaining attached. Consider whether you can open a feeder and refill it while wearing gloves or mittens and whether features designed to thwart squirrels will likewise thwart you.

Also think about how latches, lids, and other parts will affect your ability to clean the feeder. Feeders that are meant to be disassembled—and easily reassembled—are easier to thoroughly clean and dry than

A Note from Arlene

WHAT TO DO ABOUT WINDOWS

A problem some people encounter when they set up a good feeding station is suddenly finding dead birds under or near the big windows of their home. Dr. Daniel Klem, the Sarkis Acopian professor of ornithology and conservation biology at Muhlenberg College in Allentown, Pennsylvania, and a nationally recognized expert on this problem, has been reporting for years that the number of birds killed by crashing into windows or other expanses of glass is staggering. It's not just a problem for homeowners, either. Countless numbers of birds are found dead daily during migration time below tall buildings that have huge glass windows or reflective siding on them. Through conservation efforts such as Lights Out Boston, Toronto's Fatal Light Awareness Program, and similar programs in cities across North America (see Resources in the back of this book), you can advocate for corporations to turn off building lights at night to protect birds.

At your own home, you can take more direct action to prevent window strikes. The best thing to do is to put a screen of some sort on your windows near your feeders. Screens such as the ones sold by the Bird Screen Company in Narvon, Pennsylvania, are made of fiberglass mesh that's soft, sturdy, and so easy to see through that it doesn't affect your view. I've had one like this for years on my big picture window in the living room, and I haven't had a bird die from hitting that window since I put it up.

Window decals meant to deter birds are sold widely and produce variable results. Silhouettes of birds of prey seem less effective than shiny stickers designed to be seen by birds and not by humans, but even these work only some of the time and only in some situations. Whatever you do, the goal is to break up the reflection on the window, so birds don't mistake it for clear flying space, while not obstructing the view the window was made to provide. To that end, fake owls seem particularly ineffective, and no more protect birds from crashing into windows than they protect gardens from hungry birds.

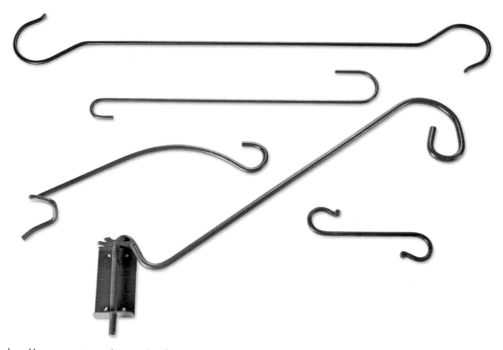

Hooks and hangers come in a wide range of configurations, so it's possible to hang feeders from all sorts of support. Choose sturdy hardware for hanging or mounting your feeders to prevent damage from falling to the ground.

those that are stapled, nailed, or glued together. A feeder that is hard to clean is a feeder that does not get cleaned.

Ease of use for birds. As mentioned previously, not all birds will use all types of feeders. Larger birds often have difficulty using the perches on tube feeders, and some species lack the agility necessary to use suet feeders designed for clinging rather than perching. Sometimes this is the point—to keep large or aggressive birds from dominating a feeder and driving away chickadees, titmice, and small finches. But you may enjoy bright red cardinals at your feeders or appreciate the sight of handsome blue jays, while small tubes with small perches tend to be inaccessible to these birds. Make sure the

feeder(s) you choose will welcome the birds you hope to see.

Security of contents. How well are the feeder's contents protected from the elements? How well are they protected from feeder raiders like squirrels or starlings? Both weatherproofing and pest-proofing can add features that make it harder for you to clean and refill a feeder, but they may be worthwhile if they save you the expense of replacing spoiled—or too quickly gobbled—seed.

Keeping Feeders Clean

Even the most avid and dedicated bird lovers count cleaning feeders among the tasks they'd love to do less. Features that make feeders better in other ways—more secure against the weather, more secure against pests, sturdier and longer lasting—make them harder to get and keep clean. And birds, for all the delights they bring us, are utterly unconcerned about hygiene at the dining table.

But keeping feeders clean is part of the implicit deal we make with birds when we invite them into our yards. You might won-der why it's necessary to clean feeders used by wild birds, when no one is going about swabbing bleach solution over the surfaces where those birds feed in nature. The reason is that our feeders are not natural, and they attract birds to feed in conditions that are unlike those they would choose in the wild.

Natural seed sources, for example, do not

Hate Cleaning Feeders? Try a Temporary Solution

An alternative to investing in and maintaining sturdy, well-made feeders is to serve seeds and other bird foods in temporary feeders that are destined to be discarded when they get dirty or begin to fall apart. This need not be as wasteful as it sounds, if you create short-term feeders from items that you can recycle after their feeder service is finished or from things that would be thrown out anyway.

Although temporary feeders rarely are as attractive or functional as their manufactured counterparts, they give you a chance to stretch your creativity as you consider the possibilities that may be found in your recycling bin or on the way to your trash can. Plastic jugs that held milk, juice, soda, or liquid detergent all are excellent candidates for conversion to feeders that ultimately may be recycled. Start by thoroughly rinsing out the original contents and letting the container dry completely.

A converted milk jug makes a serviceable bird feeder for short-term use. When it gets dirty or damaged by squirrels, toss it in your recycling bin and transform another jug for serving seeds or suet.

Determine how you will hang the finished feeder and what you will use for the hanger—repurposed wire clothes hangers work well for this task and can be reused for multiple temporary feeders.

Converting a gallon milk jug, for example, is quick and easy. Make a few small holes in the bottom of the jug for drainage, then use a utility knife to cut a rectangular feeding "port" (approximately 4 inches wide and 6 inches high) into each of the two sides opposite the handle. Leave at least an inch high rim at the bottom. Put seeds, suet crumbles, or other bird favorites in the bottom of the jug, and it's ready to hang or mount in your landscape. Use it as long or as little as you like—when it has outlived its usefulness, drop it in the recycling bin and convert a new jug for the birds. Although this type of feeder offers almost no resistance to seed-gobbling squirrels, it also will cause you almost no regret if squirrels chew it up.

replenish themselves on such a regular basis that birds are attracted to return to them over and over. Nor do natural food sources typically occur in the same concentration as a feeder, so birds don't naturally crowd together to feed repeatedly within the space of a few square inches. Similarly, species that flock together in winter and glean dropped seeds from the ground below feeders would not normally seek their food in a layer of decomposing shells and bird droppings.

And so we must clean, for the sake of the birds we enjoy and to keep our feeding areas from becoming eyesores in the landscape. For our own sakes, the best we can do is to

Don't stop with plastic jugs. Coated cardboard milk or juice cartons can be converted into feeders in a configuration similar to that of a plastic jug. A wooden or waxed cardboard tray that held tangerines can be made into a tray feeder that you can hang or mount on a deck railing. A liter-size plastic beverage bottle, hung upside down and fitted with perches below ¼-inch holes, makes a fine short-term feeder for serving nyjer or millet. You can make a small hole for dispensing these small seeds with the tip of a sharp knife. Then use the same knife to make a starter hole about 2 inches below the seed hole and push a bamboo skewer or chopstick through the bottle to form two perches. Let your imagination run wild: You'll find all sorts of objects that can fill the role of feeder for awhile and then go on their way to recycling or refuse—with no cleaning required

Temporary feeders made from repurposed items can be more than just a way to avoid feeder-cleaning chores. At times of the year when migration or winter weather brings more birds to your feeders, makeshift feeders let you expand your serving capacity to accommodate your extra guests without having to buy more feeders. When activity slows down, you can get rid of your homemade dining spaces and make new ones the next time the need arises.

Use temporary feeders made from repurposed items to expand your bird-feeding capacity at times of the year when natural foods are scarce and many birds are jockeying for positions at your feeders' perches.

choose feeders that are relatively easy to clean and to come up with tools and routines that make cleaning as quick and hassle-free as possible.

Routine Feeder Maintenance

Simple cleaning and maintenance each time you refill a feeder goes a long way toward keeping feeders in sanitary condition and good repair.

✺ Shake out tube feeders and knock out any clumped, wet, or old seeds before you refill the feeder.

✺ Dump seed residues from tray feeders, and use a whisk broom to sweep waste from platforms.

✺ An old spatula or similar repurposed kitchen tool makes a good scooper/scraper to dislodge caked seed in the bottom of a hopper feeder.

✺ A long-handled brush, such as one made for clearing snow from cars, can be useful in giving seed trays a quick dust-off.

✺ Clean up spilled seed and seed hulls beneath feeders regularly, before they kill grass below them or become moldy and unsightly. A leaf vacuum is useful for this task and gathers the mess for easy disposal.

✺ At least once each season and more frequently in wet or very humid weather, disinfect feeders with a mild bleach solution (1 part bleach to 9 parts warm water). Rinse thoroughly with plain water and let feeders dry completely before you refill them.

✺ When you're disinfecting feeders, take a moment to inspect them for damage and to make any repairs they may need.

A trip to the dollar store can supply you with basic tools for routine feeder maintenance. Stroll down the aisle of kitchen acces-

A Note from Arlene

SOMETIMES SEEDS SPROUT

No matter how good you are at maintaining and checking your feeders, occasionally during warm weather some of the seeds will sprout. It's not a good thing to look out at a feeder and see green shoots growing up from it, but it sometimes happens, particularly when activity at the feeder falls off and seeds go uneaten for a stretch. Things get warm and damp and then moldy inside the feeder, and soon seeds begin to sprout. Because they're not treated in the way that nyjer seed is, both sunflower seed and white millet can sprout in hot, humid weather. Some people go to the trouble of baking their birdseed before they put it in feeders to prevent it from sprouting. While I'm sure that works, it's also an incredible amount of work. If seeds begin to sprout in a feeder—and it has happened to me at times through the years—cut back on how much seed you're putting in that particular feeder, or even take it down for a short time and use the opportunity to clean it thoroughly while it's out of the bird-dining rotation.

sories and consider metal spatulas and rigid plastic scrapers that are just as handy for clearing the residue from the bottom of a hopper feeder as they are for flipping a pancake or scraping out a bowl.

While you're there, check out the items in the cleaning supplies area and pick up an inexpensive brush or two. A whisk broom or a scrub brush is helpful for breaking up and brushing away caked seed and hulls; pick a long-handled brush for reaching the tray of a high-hanging hopper. Look for round bottle brushes to fit into your tube feeders; if you have a large-diameter tube, a round toilet brush might be just the right size.

Yard sales and restaurant-supply stores are other good places to shop for tools that will lend themselves to the task of keeping your feeders tidy. Repurposed hand tools meant for gardening or heavy-duty kitchen tools are durable enough to provide years of service on the feeder-cleaning detail.

Ground (Mess) Control. Seeds and shells are bound to fall or be dropped as the birds eat at the perches or fly away from the feeder. Most of the debris will end up on the ground, unless you put a tray of some sort under a feeder to catch what drops. Some feeders come with trays attached, or you can buy separate trays to attach to a pole or to hang beneath a tube or hopper. You can even fashion your own hanging tray out of a plastic garbage-can lid or similar item. Just drill a few small holes in it for drainage and add cords or chains to hang it. A tray like this will become a de facto feeder for birds that can't get seed from the tube or hopper above it, so

A mesh tray hanging beneath a feeder will catch dropped seeds and shells and cut down on your feeder area cleanup chores, but you will need to clean the tray itself because some birds will dine from it.

you'll need to treat the tray as such and keep it clean. When you refill the hanging feeder, take the opportunity to empty out the tray below it and brush it for good measure.

Down on the ground, you have other options for controlling and containing the fallout from a feeder. You can set a tray (or trays) on the ground to catch most of what falls, or put down a lightweight mat that can be swept off or lifted and emptied regularly. Pavers on the ground beneath your seed feeders are another way to solve the cleanup problem. Instead of patchy-looking grass and weeds, a few square feet of paving is easily swept clean and can be dressed up with potted plants or masked with plantings around the edges. A seasonal application of mulch below the feeder is another way to catch fallen seeds and shells while avoiding sickly grass; you can refresh the mulch now and then by stirring it with a garden rake or hoe.

In any of these arrangements, a leaf vac or a handheld vacuum can make quick work of lightweight seed detritus. The key is to ply your vacuum regularly and while the waste material is dry—once it gets rained or snowed on, the layer of seeds and shells is much harder to clean up by any method.

Seed-Storage Techniques Keeping multiple feeders filled usually means keeping a supply of seed on hand. Feeder activity typically increases both before and after a winter weather "event," and this is no time to find that you're out of sunflower seed. You'll want to store your seed supplies where you can keep them cool and dry to prevent spoilage and also secure them against insect infestation and rodent raids. The high oil content of bird favorites like nyjer and sunflower seed makes them prone to spoiling in warm conditions, while moisture promotes mold growth. Watch your seed supplies for signs of spoilage, like clumping or "off" rancid odors.

Metal containers with snug-fitting lids work best for keeping mice out of your birdseed supply. Even heavy-duty plastic presents little obstacle to rodents intent on feasting on the food you've stockpiled for filling your bird feeders. Chipmunks and squirrels also will seek out birdseed stashed in a garage or shed and can do substantial damage in getting to and depleting your supply.

Preventing insect infestations can be more difficult. Although tightly sealed containers help to block grain moths and weevils from getting to your seed stocks, your first line of defense is to avoid bringing pests home in seed that you buy. Shop for seed at stores that do a brisk business in it, so that you buy fresh seed that hasn't been sitting on a shelf for months. Be on the lookout for webbing, small brownish moths, or pupal cases near the seams of seed bags, and reject any in which those signs of insects are present. If you do wind up with infested seed, discard it promptly, thoroughly clean your storage containers, and vacuum the area where you keep your birdseed supply. Pheromone traps are available that can help you monitor the presence of grain moths.

A metal garbage can with a tightly fitted lid is a good solution for securing sunflower seed or other foods you buy in bulk quantities. Tins like those in which popcorn is sold work well for smaller amounts of seed. Decorative storage tins often appear in catalogs of bird-feeding supplies, but you often can find similar-size containers filled with snack foods (for people) at more reasonable prices than those charged for the empty tins. After you and your family have enjoyed the contents, the tins can be put to use to hold seeds and seed mixes. Put a small amount of uncooked rice or a silica packet (like those included in the packaging of leather goods and electronics) in the bottom of a tin before you fill it with seeds, to prevent moisture from spoiling the contents.

Scoops and Funnels When you're gathering feeders and tools for tending them, don't forget to add a few scoops and funnels to your shopping list. Scoop/funnel combina-

Scoops help you get seeds into your feeders without wasteful spills. A "fancy" scoop (top and left) with a built-in trigger in its handle makes it easy to pour seed into a tube feeder, but even a repurposed plastic cup works better than precariously pouring straight from the bag.

tions that let you take a feeder's worth of seed from a bag and pour it easily into a tube are especially handy and can save you from lugging a heavy bag around your yard. If you're saving money on seed by buying in bulk, scoops help you move the smaller amounts you need for feeder refills. Bird-feeding supply stores and Web sites offer an array of nifty gadgets to make it easier to get seed into your feeders without spills, but even a large-size plastic cup saved from a trip to the movies will do the job.

Welcome Birds with Water

A good feeding area can be made great with the addition of water. It's one of the most important things you can add to a feeding station, but it's often the last thing people think of including in their efforts to attract birds. Providing a source of water can be as easy as putting out a birdbath or as involved as building a natural-looking waterfall, digging a pond, installing a recirculating pump, and then making a streambed to connect the waterfall and the pond.

Water is important not just because birds drink it, but also because they regularly take baths, even in winter when it's freezing cold outside. They have to keep their feathers in top shape, and bathing and preening are critical elements in birds' feather-care routines. Some birds use water for purposes other than for drinking and bathing. For example, grackles will bring food to water, dip it in, and then eat it. They also will drop eggshells or the fecal sacs from their nestlings in water, which can make a mess in a birdbath or pond. If this happens, just clean them out. This behavior

A water source will attract birds to drink and bathe that don't regularly visit feeders. Even in cold weather, birds need to maintain their feathers, and an unfrozen bird bath may be almost as popular as a well-stocked feeder.

will stop when the young birds leave the nest.

Although birdbaths, fountains, and ponds tend to be more common in home landscapes in places where temperatures remain above freezing all or most of the time, it's not terribly difficult to maintain clean, open water for birds through winter even in northern regions. The birds certainly appreciate having a place to drink and bathe, and you may find that a heated bath is nearly as popular as a feeder full of sunflower seed. Some people maintain backyard birding habitats that have water but no feeders!

If you want to provide water, but you live where the seasons change and get cold, you can still manage year-round by putting water heaters in birdbaths or ponds. Fountains and waterfalls usually have to be shut down during winter months in cold-weather regions, but a bath or two may be kept in operation by using a submersible heater or by choosing a birdbath model with a built-in heating unit. Solar baths that are designed to collect enough warmth from the sun to keep their contents from

freezing will work if your winter weather typically is cold but sunny. Another non-electric solution is to simply put out one or two shallow containers of fresh water each day, swapping them with the previous day's frozen water dishes and bringing those indoors to thaw. Use flexible rubber or plastic containers, like pet-watering bowls or garbage-can lids, that won't be damaged by repeated freezing and thawing. If you put out fresh water at the same time each day, the birds will quickly adjust to your schedule and will be waiting for a chance to drink and bathe when you appear.

All birds need water to survive, but some species find it particularly attractive. The vigorous bathing habits of catbirds, goldfinches, and towhees make fine entertainment on a summer day when the perches at your feeders may be empty. Chickadees, crossbills, mourning doves, orioles, titmice, and waxwings are among other species that frequent backyard water features, and hummingbirds are well known for their love of sprinklers and other fine sprays of water.

Choosing and Tending a Birdbath

Commercially available birdbaths may be made of ceramic, metal, concrete, plastic, or another nonporous material and may be designed to sit atop a base of some sort or to mount on a deck or porch railing. You can also make a bath out of repurposed household items or garage sale treasures, as long as you keep birds' needs in mind. A suitable birdbath should be shallow, preferably with a gradual slope from the edge into the water, and have a rough bottom. If your bath lacks these features, rest a sturdy stick or two across the water to serve as a perch from which birds can drink. Use sandpaper to roughen a smooth-bottomed bath or add a large flat stone for birds to stand on. A layer of gravel or small stones makes the bath more accessible to birds, but also makes cleaning much more difficult.

As with feeders, birdbaths require a modest amount of maintenance to safeguard the health of the birds that use them. Leaves and other debris collect in birdbaths, and birds drop food and feathers and occasionally defecate in them. In warm weather, the water gets cloudy, and algae grows in it. Keep a stiff-bristled brush handy and use it to brush out the bath on a regular basis—ideally every couple of days when you change the water. In addition to keeping the water clean for the birds that use it, refreshing a bath frequently keeps it from becoming a breeding

A Note from **Arlene**

WHETHER PUDDLE OR POND, WATER BRINGS IN THE BIRDS

I started with a small depression in the ground that I filled with water every so often. Almost immediately birds began coming to the water, and I could see the difference it made in my feeding area right away, even when I only had a small puddle. As the years passed, I eventually graduated to a waterfall/streambed/pond setup.

I also have several birdbaths, so I can pick and choose which ones to use in different seasons. I put heaters in some during winter, because they're near the feeders I concentrate on then. In summer, I let some of these dry out and let nearby flowers grow up and over them. Except in periods of extended drought, natural water is usually more available in summer, even if it's only in the form of liquid from berries and fruits.

"There's no such thing as a [completely] squirrel-proof bird feeder. However, there's a battery-operated one on the market that comes close. It's activated by the weight of the squirrel, and throughout all the years I had the [wild-bird supply] store, only one customer ever said that her squirrels managed to figure it out."

AL GUARENTE, Media, Pennsylvania

site for mosquitoes in your yard. A strong stream of water from a hose can save you the need to brush out a birdbath; you may want to place your birdbath where you can reach it with a hose just for that reason.

Give each bath a more thorough cleaning every week or so. Scrub out dirt and algae and wash with a 10-percent bleach solution (1 part bleach to 9 parts water), a water/vinegar solution, or dishwashing liquid. Rinse completely before refilling with clean water.

The Sound of Running Water

Birds will be quick to find any water features you include in your landscape, but the sound of moving water is like a magnet to them. Moving water also reduces algae growth and prevents mosquito problems, too. Simple battery-powered devices and small electric pumps are made specifically for use in birdbaths, or you can use equipment designed for use with fish tanks. A small, solar-powered fountain is another option for enhancing the bird appeal of a garden pond. Whatever you choose, bear in mind that these devices will also require

occasional care. Most have filters that will need cleaning, and parts in contact with the water will need to be wiped with the same cleaning solution you use for your baths.

An easy, albeit short-term, technique for adding the sound of water to a stationary birdbath is to make a simple dripper. Fill a gallon plastic jug or similar container with water and hang it above the bath from a branch or from a shepherd's crook or similar support. Make a very small hole in the bottom of the jug and loosen the lid just enough to allow water to drip out very slowly into the bath below. While this approach is low-tech compared with solar fountains and recirculating pumps, it costs almost nothing to put in place, and a single jug can provide the sound of dripping water for a full day of bird-bathing pleasure.

Safety for Birds, Food, and Feeders

When you put food and feeders out for the birds, chances are good that a few other animals—both wild and tame—also will be attracted to your yard. Part of your obligation to the birds is to do what you can to keep them safe when they are drawn into your landscape. You also owe it to yourself and to your neighbors to avoid creating a nuisance by attracting potentially dangerous or destructive wildlife into the area around your home.

Squirrel Deterrence Check out the catalog or visit the Web site of any company that sells supplies for bird feeding and housing, and you'll see just how much money and effort is devoted to fending off squirrels. Many wild animals may be drawn to bird feeders, but squirrels tend to be the most persistent, the most numerous, and the most obvious of the nonbird feeder visitors. Because they are active during daytime, we get to see squirrels as they raid our feeders, scoffing down seed at an alarming rate. We can also watch as they gnaw through wood or plastic to get at seeds or as they pull feeders from hooks and hangers and then feast on the spills that result when everything crashes to the ground.

Keeping squirrels out of your bird feeders can become a full-time job—and even an obsession. They are intelligent creatures, adept at outsmarting your latest squirrel-blocking device, and single-minded in their intent to reach the contents of a feeder. Even at times of the year when natural food is plentiful, squirrels will choose the delicacies contained in a bird feeder over acorns strewn openly on the ground. In winter, when nature's bounty grows scarce, there's almost nothing that will stop them from raiding your feeders.

While the advertising may claim otherwise, there's almost no feeder that squirrels can't eventually get into. If squirrels live in your neighborhood, the best you can do is minimize the damage they cause to your feeders and limit the amount of birdseed they eat. Then declare a truce and go back to enjoying the birds. Remember that no matter how it may appear to you, squirrels are just being squirrels and do not have any particular vendetta against you. Try these techniques to keep the peace between you and your local "bushy-tailed rats."

◯ Offer squirrels a feeder or feeders of their own, stocked with treats like whole peanuts or whole ears of corn.

"Try giving squirrels their own feeder stocked with their favorite food. They're nearly impossible to outwit, so give them a place of their own. Squirrels in my yard love striped sunflower seed, so I fill a large feeder for them and put it on the ground. You can hang it, if you prefer. The squirrels concentrate at this feeder, and placing it on the ground makes it easy for them to get to the seed. It's not 100 percent foolproof, but they spend the majority of their time away from the other feeders."

MIKE FIALKOVITCH, Pittsburgh, Pennsylvania

◯ Choose squirrel feeders that entertain you—a spinner that holds three or four ears of corn and turns when squirrels go after the treat is a good source of harmless amusement.

◯ Put baffles on poles below pole-mounted feeders or above hanging feeders to make it more difficult for squirrels to shinny up or down to get to the birdseed.

◌ Leave enough space between feeders and branches of nearby shrubs or trees to make it difficult for squirrels to jump from the branches onto the feeders.

◌ Use a feeder with a weight-activated barrier that closes the feeding port when something heavier than a songbird lands on the adjoining perch. These feeders are useful for stopping raids by larger birds and other mammals, too.

◌ Buy tube feeders with metal fittings around the feeding ports. Squirrels are remarkably adept at chewing through wood and plastic and will damage a tube feeder by enlarging the feeding ports until the contents spill out.

◌ Use carabiners or other locking clips to secure hanging feeders to their hangers. In their efforts to get to a feeder, squirrels often knock them off their hooks and then enjoy the resulting spillage on the ground. Even the sturdiest feeders are prone to breaking when dropped repeatedly.

◌ Even if you're tolerant of squirrel activity at your feeders, most birds will not be. Squirrels do raid birds' nests and will eat eggs and nestlings when they get the chance.

Pest Birds at the Feeder Not every bird that comes to your feeders will be a beautiful songbird. Nonnative "introduced" species such as European starlings and English, or house, sparrows are widespread and well adapted to conditions across most of North America. Crows sometimes show up in noisy groups and disturb the peace while

trying to get at food in feeders designed for much smaller birds. Large flocks of blackbirds may descend on your feeders in winter and stick around until every morsel has been eaten. Even natives, like jays and mockingbirds, can create discord at your feeders when these big birds claim an area for their own and bully any other birds that try to fly in for a meal.

When birds of any species become pests at your feeders, keep in mind that they are simply following their natural instincts. It's dismaying that starlings and house sparrows displace native cavity nesters like bluebirds and woodpeckers, and also that brown-headed cowbirds lay their own eggs in songbird nests and push the songbird eggs out of them. But there is no malice in these actions; the birds are only doing what they instinctively do to survive.

While you are unlikely to rid your yard completely of less desirable species, you can manage their numbers and discourage their visits through your choices of feeders and the foods you put out in your yard. Starlings, for example, are fond of suet, but are poorly adapted to clinging to vertical surfaces the way woodpeckers can. If you limit suet servings to wire cages that hang vertically or to starling-resistant feeders that only give access to birds that can cling to the feeder's underside, you will effectively stop starlings from getting to the suet.

Starlings and house sparrows both are attracted more than most songbirds to "people foods." Jays and crows are also omnivorous and are more likely to frequent your feeders if kitchen scraps are on the menu. If

In winter, blackbirds and other similar species form large flocks that feed and roost together. If such a flock targets your feeders, they may persist until the food runs out, while their presence will discourage most other birds from visiting your yard.

pest birds are a problem where you live, avoid offering bread and other tidbits from your table to keep from encouraging the pests to stick around. Or you can draw pest birds away from your seed and suet feeders by creating a separate feeding area for less desirable birds and serving bread and other kitchen odds and ends only in that spot. This can be a solution if you find yourself hosting a large and hungry flock of blackbirds. Spread inexpensive cracked corn or chicken scratch on the ground as far away from your regular bird feeders as possible. If necessary, take down your usual feeders until the crowd moves on, as it will within a few days, if there's not much to eat.

Don't be discouraged when some of these less-than-elegant guests turn up at your feeders. Do your best to be patient and use pre-ferred foods, alternate feeders, and more accessible feeding spots to convince them to dine in places other than the feeders you've filled for songbirds.

Cats and Bird Feeders Very few things—habitat loss and plate-glass windows, primarily—threaten wild birds' lives as much as cats. Whether they are well-fed pets or scrawny feral animals, cats are remarkably adept at hunting birds and will hunt them instinctively. Even when its belly is full, a cat will take advantage of unsuspecting prey at a feeder simply because it can. When you put out feeders for birds, you must also take steps to prevent those bird feeders from becoming cat feeders.

First and foremost, keep pet cats indoors. Their lives will be longer and healthier as a result, and there will be no question of them going after wild birds. Once Muffin and Fluffy are contained, take these steps to keep feeder birds safe from any cats that roam freely in your neighborhood.

◯ Mount freestanding feeders on poles that cats can't climb.

◯ Place hanging feeders so cats are unable to climb up to them.

◯ Site low tray feeders or ground-feeding areas in open spots that don't give cats places to hide.

◯ Place baths and other water sources in open areas.

◯ Keep cats and dogs indoors when you know young birds are starting to leave the nest.

◯ Deter cats you see lurking around your feeders with a strong spray of water from a

hose or a powerful squirt gun. This won't hurt them, but it will discourage them.

◯ Support programs that spay and neuter cats to diminish the population of strays.

Bears and Bird Feeders At the southern edge of Pennsylvania's Pocono Mountains, Gene Durigan of Lehighton lives in a spot that's ideal for feeding and watching a wide variety of wild birds. With acres of woodlands bordering his property and two streams nearby, habitat is abundant and welcoming for birds and other wildlife. In fact, it's so welcoming that Gene sometimes has to take down his bird feeders, because other wildlife in the area includes black bears that may pass within a few yards of his house as often as a dozen times a year.

Bears have raided his garbage cans. Bears have split open his compost bin. And, yes, bears have feasted on the seeds from his bird feeders. While the video Gene shot of a mother bear and three cubs gathered around his seed feeder is cute as can be—with the cubs begging for a morsel while the mother holds the feeder in her front paws and stuffs her snout into its hopper to lick out every single seed—he would rather the bears remain a little farther away from his back door.

"Once during the night, I heard a racket outside the window where there was a bird feeder encased in wire to keep squirrels from getting the sunflower seed. Using a flashlight, I saw that there was a full-grown raccoon inside the feeder, although I couldn't imagine how he had gotten in there. He was very upset, and I wasn't sure what to do. So I gently lifted the feeder from the tree to the ground using a big stick, and I saw that the wire holding the top of the cage together had rotted and created a chute. The raccoon had fallen through, and the two halves of the cage sprang back into place, trapping the raccoon. I, of course, let the raccoon out and made a mental note to remember to check wire cages around feeders more often."

RON FRENCH, Chalfont, Pennsylvania

He notes that despite the bears' size and strength, none have yet damaged a feeder beyond repair. "I find that the more expensive and well-built the feeder is, the more likely it is to be gone," Gene says, explaining that the bears sometimes carry off a feeder they can't readily open and empty. He has followed bear tracks in the snow to find some feeders, while other feeders have been gone for weeks or months before he finds them in the woods. "The cheesy basic feeder with the roof that lifts on two wires—that bears can easily get open—has suffered the least bear damage," Gene says. "Squirrels did more damage to it."

His hummingbird feeder has gone undisturbed even when bears have been in the yard and emptied the seed feeder. He has straightened the feeder's wrought-iron shepherd's-crook pole a number of times and now uses a pole with a single foot brace. By positioning the pole so the brace is pointed away from the direction the bears usually pull on the feeder, the pole comes out of the ground rather than bending.

Gene has learned to use the smell of used cat litter to make the garbage cans unappealing and to deeply bury anything remotely edible in the compost pile. He no longer puts out suet for the birds, because it was rare that they would get through an entire suet cake before a bear took the block. And when bears begin making regular visits to the seed feeder, he takes it down for a couple of weeks to give them time to forget it and seek their meals elsewhere.

"We like the bears," he says, "but we don't like them to feel welcome. We still want them to run when they see us." He explains that the local black bears generally run away as fast or faster than the white-tailed deer that are also common in his area.

The View from Deb's Window

Kestrels, red-tailed hawks, and a red-shouldered hawk are among the raptors I have seen perched in my yard, obviously attracted by birds visiting my feeders. The speed with which these large birds move is awe-inspiring and leaves me little doubt that they could have any songbird they set their sights on, given a clear shot at their prey. Fortunately, my landscape offers plenty of brushy hiding places near enough to the feeders to let the smaller birds escape to safety. One winter day, I saw a kestrel land atop a bare but twiggy Japanese maple whose branches are a popular roosting site for feeder birds. I could see a few small birds on the ground below the maple's branches—as could the kestrel. After a few minutes, the kestrel dove into the branches in pursuit of a meal, but was slowed just enough by the twigs that it was unsuccessful and soon left the yard to hunt elsewhere.

Birds of Prey versus Birds at the Feeder Varying the height of feeders in your yard is another way to protect feeder birds from predators like hawks. Don't put your feeders close together or all at the same height. Give the birds room to fly in, fly out, and move around at will among the feeders. Having your feeders hanging or mounted at varying heights gives the feeder birds a chance to get away when a bird of prey flies into the feeding area, which is perfectly nor-

mal and will happen probably more than you'd like. Hawks usually take the weak, sick, or old birds, and that's how nature intended it.

Your backyard feeding station is an artificial feeding area that gathers a lot of birds in one place. Hawks in your area will quickly learn this, and there's not much you can do about it. If all the feeders are at the same level, a hawk can just make a straight bee-line for them and chances are greater that it will get what it came for. But if the feeders

Once you've become adept at offering food and water to birds, you may want to add shelter to the list of amenities in your landscape. Provide nest boxes that are the recommended size for the birds you hope to host and that have features designed to deter predators.

are hung at different heights, the birds will scatter in all directions, making it harder for the hawk to get any of them.

Feeders that hang from branches sheltered by a canopy of trees and feeders placed within 10 feet of trees and shrubs also give your feeder guests a flying chance at escaping a hungry raptor. Sparrows, juncos, chickadees, titmice, and other small birds will take cover in the twiggy branches of bushes and small trees where most hawks find it difficult to pursue them.

Keeping Feeder Birds Healthy

Just like all wild creatures, birds can get sick. If you see any sign of diseased birds at your feeders, it's best to stop feeding for awhile. Most of the diseases birds get are picked up away from your feeders, but an infected bird can easily spread germs around when it comes in to feed. Stopping feeding for a week or two keeps healthy birds from coming to your feeders and encountering diseased birds.

The disease most commonly encountered is mycoplasmal conjunctivitis in house finches. It's most prevalent in the East, but is likely to make its way across the entire country. It's a respiratory disease whose outward symptom is swollen, red, and closed eyes. If you see a bird in this condition, remove the feeder it was using, disinfect it thoroughly, and wait a couple of weeks before putting it back out. Watch for finches at your feeders and use binoculars, if necessary, to look for birds displaying characteristic symptoms.

West Nile virus is a communicable avian disease that's gotten a lot of press because it can be spread to humans. It's usually found in the larger birds, such as crows, jays, and

The View from Deb's Window

For many years, we had a rectangular, flat-topped porch light that was mounted directly over our front door. Each spring, it seemed, robins would choose the top of that light as a location for their messy mud, twig, and grass nest, and the obvious difficulties would ensue. The birds were quick with their building efforts, so we would leave our house in the morning and return home by the end of the day to find a completed nest atop the porch light. Removal required a stepladder as well as a bit of cleaning to remove residual mud from the light and the wall behind it. Keeping the birds from building anew the next day was tricky—we eventually found that we could tilt the light to the side so its flat top was angled toward the ground and no longer presented a tempting shelf for would-be nest makers. When we grew tired of looking at our rakishly askew entry light, we took it down and replaced it with one that has a pointy finial on top and no place for building a nest.

"Tom and I mostly photograph our favorite birds of prey, but since we have many smaller birds in the yard now, we sit out back with a camera often. It is soothing to watch them and learn their habits."

DONNA CHIARELLI, Kutztown, Pennsylvania

raptors, but it affects other species, too. The only way to know if a bird has West Nile virus is to have its dead body tested. Most birds, however, die from natural causes, accidents, or predators—don't automatically assume if you find a dead bird that it had West Nile virus.

Avian pox, another infection that occasionally afflicts wild birds, can be visually diagnosed, because warty lesions are present on a bird's head, legs, or feet. Some people mistake the lack of feathers on a bird's head for a disease, but it usually isn't. A bird may be partially or almost completely bald, but the cause normally is a mite infestation or natural molting. In both cases, the feathers will eventually grow back in.

After a feeding break to allow diseased birds to leave the area, consider adding a new feeder or two to your yard to reduce crowding at all your feeding areas. Many wild birds would rather have more distance between themselves and other feeder birds, and the extra space helps to keep diseases from spreading so easily from one bird to others.

Housing and Nesting

Bluebirds, wrens, woodpeckers, and other birds that naturally nest in cavities will make use of birdhouses placed in suitable locations in your landscape. As with feeders, houses for birds need to be well constructed and designed to give birds access, while excluding predators. Fancy paint jobs and decorative features are for human enjoyment and do nothing for the birds the houses are meant to shelter. Bright paint jobs simply make houses visible to predators; decorations trap dirt and make it harder to keep houses clean, while giving predators footholds for raiding nests. Unfortunately, putting up a poorly constructed house often is worse than not putting up any birdhouse at all, because you may attract desirable species to nest in conditions that put them in danger from predators or that risk the health of their nestlings.

Other birds, such as robins and house finches, will take advantage of all sorts of outdoor décor to create nesting sites. Decorative wreaths and hanging baskets are particularly favored by many species of birds. The trick is to convince them to choose other locations that are not too close to places where you and your family spend time outdoors, to minimize conflicts between unsuspecting humans and agitated bird parents.

If you want to add birdhouses to your landscape, get the recommended specifications for dimensions and mounting heights from a reliable source, such as the National Audubon Society, the Cornell Lab of Ornithology, or the North American Bluebird Society (www.nabluebirdsociety.org). These organizations can give you the best practices for offering birds housing that meets their particular needs, while keeping them safe from predators and excluding their competition.

Enjoying the Birds at Your Feeders

While you're dutifully filling and cleaning and otherwise tending feeders and bird-baths in your yard, be sure to take time to enjoy the results: the sights and sounds of wild birds. Most of us start by simply appreciating their beauty, but as time goes on, you may want to learn more about their habits, behaviors, and life cycles. Here are some ideas of ways to increase the pleasure you get from inviting birds into your sur-roundings.

○ Keep a list of birds and where and when you see them.

○ Take part in local or national bird counts to further scientific study of bird populations.

○ Use recordings to learn to identify birds by their songs and calls.

○ Start a nature journal and include sketches of feeder birds along with notes about their behavior and appearance.

○ Sit quietly near your feeders with a camera and capture close-ups as the birds grow accustomed to your presence.

The View from Deb's Window

While some people frown on the practice of hand-feeding wild birds, because they see it as interfering too much with nature and breaking down birds' natural wariness of potential predators, it is a remarkable experience that can turn a casual bird-watcher into a committed bird lover. Typically, working up to hand-feeding a wild bird is a slow process that requires patiently establishing oneself in the landscape and gradually getting to the point at which a bird will come to food in your hand.

I had my first experience hand-feeding a wild bird courtesy of the patience of others—birders at a local park who had already done the work of convincing the birds there that landing on someone's outstretched hand to grab a peanut was a perfectly safe thing to do. The bird, of course, was a black-capped chick-adee, and I had to do little more than stand still for a few minutes with my hand out with a shelled peanut promi-nently resting on my fingers, before it alighted on my palm, picked up the peanut, and flew off with it.

I was amazed then and I remain so, even years later. The surprisingly slight weight of the bird on my hand and the delicate pressure of its tiny feet made an outsize impression. I have since convinced other chickadees in my own yard to take seeds from my hand, and once, a tufted titmouse paused ever so briefly to grab a sun-flower seed. Even without the patient process of building the birds' confidence, I find that the "regulars" around my yard—especially the hyper-friendly chickadees—grow accustomed to my feeder-filling routine and stay close by when I come outside to replenish their food supply. A new feeder supplied my most recent "close encounter": As I was filling its clear globe with sunflower seed and millet, I heard a whir of wings and watched a chickadee land in one of the feeding ports and grab a seed, even while I held the feeder in my hands.

nine

—

Bird Favorites for Your Garden

By far the easiest, most cost-effective, and surefire successful way to attract birds to your yard and to encourage them to stay is to grow bird-friendly plants and plant groupings. No matter how many feeders you maintain and how often you fill them, the birds that visit them (and the birds that never come to a feeder) still get nearly all of their nutrition nearly all the time from natural food sources—from weeds that produce thousands of seeds, to fruiting shrubs, to trees that harbor leaf-eating caterpillars. While a well-stocked feeder provides visiting birds with something to eat, plants that supply birds with seeds, fruits, or insects also may offer them shelter, nest-building materials, and places to build their nests.

Bohemian waxwings feasting on mountain ash fruits

In human terms, a feeder is like a restaurant. You might take a meal there now and then, but you wouldn't make it your home or raise your family in it. Birds will come to your yard for seeds, suet, and other feeder foods. Some of them may stay if they also find natural food sources—including insects to eat and to feed their young, water for drinking and bathing, places to take shelter from the elements or from predators, secure roosting spots, and places to nest.

Don't be discouraged if you have only limited space, or if the idea of providing everything birds need seems beyond your abilities or your resources. You don't have to completely overhaul your landscape to make it more welcoming to birds. Do just as much as you are willing and able to do. Start small—a single pot of red salvia on your balcony, a bed of birdseed plants like sunflowers and millet, or a clematis vine growing over the porch railing—and see how it goes.

If you're already filling and maintaining a feeder or two (or several), you may be thrilled when a hummingbird stakes out your morning glory vine or when goldfinches begin harvesting seeds from the drying heads of sunflowers standing in your garden. From there you can expand your efforts—grow a greater variety of seed-producing plants or add a fruiting shrub or two. Gardening for the birds starts out much like maintaining feeders, except that many of these "feeders" are self-filling. And as with feeders, if you like the results, you can always do more. Give birds a dedicated garden bed planted with their seed-yielding favorites, or give them a corner of the yard that includes a water feature and a few convenient bushes for perching and preening. Your bird garden may grow to encompass your entire landscape, or it may remain a small but inviting patch of bird-attracting flowers next to a feeder and a birdbath. Either way, you'll find that including plants and plantings in your bird-feeding efforts can bring in the birds as readily as a hopper full of high-priced seed.

Invest in Habitat

When you're looking for ways to make your yard more inviting to birds, it helps to stop thinking in terms of landscape specimens—individual trees or shrubs plopped in the middle of a lawn—and to start thinking of, planning, and installing plant communities. Different birds feed, mate, and nest on different levels of a natural habitat. Some occupy treetops and rarely venture down to feeder level, some live mainly in the understory of shrubs and small trees, and some remain on or close to the ground. Creating plantings that offer these different levels takes more planning and preparation than simply putting up a feeder and installing a birdbath, but it results in much more natural conditions that welcome greater numbers and different species of birds than any feeder or feeding station could.

Think about what kinds of plant communities naturally occur in the area where you live, because those will be most attractive to your native birds. Visit local parks and nature preserves and take note of where you see bird activity. Consult with local nurseries or landscaping companies to find out what plants are well suited to your home landscape. While a diverse landscape will attract the greatest variety of birds, don't go overboard adding one of everything you see. Develop a plan that fits the scale of your yard to make an environment that both you and the birds can enjoy.

Information on how to create a good backyard habitat is available from many conservation organizations. The National Audubon Society and the National Wildlife Federation

"We see dozens of different bird species in our landscape because we have created a habitat that provides shelter and places to nest as well as water and food. We put out seeds, suet, and nectar for hummingbirds, and fruit and jelly for orioles and catbirds. But native trees and shrubs, the pond, and even a few dead branches are the features that keep the birds around to mate and build nests and raise their young here."

THOMAS LECKEY, Bucks County, Pennsylvania

both offer online checklists and guidelines that are loaded with ideas to help you increase your landscape's bird appeal. These organizations also have backyard habitat designation and certification programs that recognize individual landscapes that are maintained for the benefit of birds and other wildlife. Other conservation groups offer similar programs, although not on a national scale.

Cut the Grass

To most birds looking for promising places to find food and shelter, a large expanse of close-cropped lawn is the opposite of inviting. A few species—mainly robins, flickers, and starlings—will reliably show up to hunt for grubs, ants, and earthworms in a lawn area. But other birds will shy away from wide open space that leaves them exposed to hawks hunting overhead, and no birds will find cause to frequent a lawn that's been treated with chemicals to rid it of insects and/or weeds.

You don't have to eliminate turf entirely to make birds welcome in your yard, but you can certainly reduce lawn areas to make your landscape more bird friendly. Add shrubs, hedgerows, and flowerbeds around the edges of a lawn, so birds have places to take cover from predators and to find nectar, seeds, and insects to eat. The usual birds of the lawn will find plenty to eat in a smaller grassy space and will also seek their meals in leaf litter or mulch. As an added benefit, a smaller lawn area will demand much less of your time and resources to tend it, leaving you more time to sit and watch the birds.

Choosing Bird-Friendly Plants

In making the transition from attracting birds with a few feeders to creating an inviting habitat for birds, it makes sense to start with plants that produce food for birds. We may think of these plants as "living feeders." Because birds eat the seeds and fruits of all sorts of plants, from lowly weeds to lofty oaks, it's fairly easy to enhance your landscape with a variety of these menu options for birds.

When focusing on plants that produce berries, seeds, and nuts for the birds, however, we often overlook plants that support insects. Because insects (as well as arachnids, such as spiders, and other arthropods) are the food of choice for the vast majority of wild birds—and the food that nearly all birds feed to their nestlings—allowing insects to occupy their natural niches in your landscape will bring you far more birds than fruits, seeds, nuts, and feeders combined.

Accepting insects as a way of welcoming birds may take some getting used to, but it's not as hard as you might think. Allowing the bugs that birds enjoy does not mean surrendering your yard and gardens to an army of creepy-crawlies. On the contrary, many of the insects that birds find tasty exist without our awareness. Leaf-eating caterpillars that live high in the treetops, for example, rarely register their presence with humans on the ground.

To increase your landscape's IQ (insect quotient) on birds' behalf, take these simple actions—two of which are actually *in*actions.

Accept Imperfection

We've come to expect only perfect flowers, unblemished fruits, and weed-free lawns without recognizing the cost of all this pristine beauty: the loss of other natural beauty. Without insects to feed their young, birds will go elsewhere to breed and nest. Without the very specific food plants used by their caterpillars, butterflies will go elsewhere to lay their eggs. When we refuse to allow a few nibbled leaves or an occasional spoiled blossom, we are effectively banishing birds and butterflies from our yards.

Put Away the Pesticides

In pursuit of our love affair with unblemished beauty, we've gotten carried away with sprays and powders, granules and dusts that we wield at the first sign of a bug on the roses or a dandelion in the lawn. In addition to eliminating food sources for birds, insecticides may introduce toxins into the environment that harm birds directly—and they sometimes turn out to be not so good for people, either. Instead of reaching for the sprayer at the first sign of pests on your plants, try a wait-and-see approach. Give nature time to take its course, and you may find the problem resolved without any effort on your part. If you have to take action, try a nontoxic method, such as a strong spray of water to wash away aphids or mites or selective pruning to remove tent caterpillars.

Choose Native Plants

Besides spraying to eradicate every insect we see, we've also built our unsustainably pest-free landscapes on a foundation of nonnative, or introduced, plant species. One of the things we love about those showy beauties from Europe and Asia is that *they don't get bugs!* But 90 percent of plant-eating insects are specialists, says University of Delaware entomology professor Douglas Tallamy, author of *Bringing Nature Home.* This means they eat only one kind of plant or a limited group of closely related plants. When the insects at the bottom of the food web can't find the specific plant food they need to survive (because it's been replaced by nonnative species), those insects disappear and no longer fulfill their role of becoming food for

MORE ABOUT CHOOSING NATIVES AND AVOIDING INVASIVES

Berry- and fruit-producing plants native to the part of the country in which you live are almost always better choices than most nonnative plants, even if the nonnatives also provide natural food. Natives are desirable because they don't have to struggle much to live or adapt to a new climate, they establish quickly but aren't invasive, and they support insects that birds feed on. The birds in your area are used to them and instinctively know when, where, and how to get the food they provide.

Although exotic shrubs and trees may produce fruit or berry crops that birds will eat, some of them should be avoided. Two of the best examples of this are the invasive exotic autumn olive (*Elaeagnus umbellata*) and its relative, the Russian olive (*E. angustifolia*), even though these trees produce copious crops of berries that just about all the berry-loving birds readily eat. At one time, autumn olive was thought to be great for wildlife and was widely planted. More than 30 years ago, when we had just started landscaping our property, the Pennsylvania Game Commission gave my husband and me autumn olive trees to plant. We planted them all, and they all grew well and fast. Several years later, they began producing lots of berries, and I was thrilled to see all kinds of birds on them. In 1997, the first documented ash-throated flycatcher, a western species that sometimes wanders east in fall, appeared on our property, and its favorite food was the autumn olive berries. But by then, autumn olive had been placed on the invasive species list, and some of the many people who came to see the flycatcher looked at me oddly and asked me why I had planted them. Frankly, I got tired of giving the explanation.

Because autumn olive berries are so abundant, and so many different birds eat them, they have been known to completely annihilate native species that used to grow in fields where they've established themselves. Another reason that autumn olives are considered to be so bad for the native habitat is that no native ground plants are able to grow under them. Even though birds love their berries, the limited benefit of that one source of food comes at the detriment of the overall environment and with the loss of [other] food and shelter for many kinds of wildlife, including birds.

birds, other insects, reptiles and amphibians, and small mammals. Those creatures, in turn, must seek their meals elsewhere, and so on. Widespread use of nonnative plants carries other consequences as well, but perhaps the biggest cost to birds is the loss of insect populations that rely on native plant species.

Why Native Plants Matter to Birds

Simply put, native plants feed native insects, and those insects feed birds—especially baby birds. No insects, to a large extent, mean no birds.

Because most plant-eating insects feed exclusively on certain species of plants or on a few closely related plants, those insects disappear from areas where their host plants no longer exist. They do not make the switch to feeding on whatever introduced plant species have replaced their native hosts, because only a small percentage of insects generally feed on different kinds of plants, and these insects are not widely eaten by birds. For example, one of the most troublesome generalists from a gardener's perspective is the Japanese beetle, an introduced pest that arrived on a shipment of introduced plants. Some birds feed on Japanese beetle larvae (grubs) that thrive in our lawns, but few eat the voracious adult beetles.

The example of Japanese beetles highlights another cost of nonnative plants: They often serve as an entry point for nonnative pests and diseases. Nearly all of the most devastating pest and disease epidemics that have affected North American landscapes over the past two centuries can be traced to plants and plant materials brought from overseas. American elms and American chestnuts are two of the best-known casualties of these unintended invasions. And largely gone with them are the species of insects that relied on them for food and the wildlife that relied on those insects.

A third downside of introduced plant species from the birds' perspective is that nonnative plants often escape cultivation and displace native plants. Birds may even contribute to this problem by feeding on fruits or seeds produced by nonnative plant species and sowing those seeds in their droppings wherever they go. A great many plants you now find on lists of invasives were once welcomed and widely planted for their ornamental and environmental benefits—autumn olive and kudzu are just two examples. Without natural insect enemies to keep them in check, introduced plants chosen for their vigorous habits are free to range far and wide, crowding out native plants as they grow. Birds may eat seeds or fruits of these introduced plants, but they don't find insects on them to feed their young, and so are unlikely to breed and nest in areas overrun by them.

These examples make it clear why birds will benefit when you choose to add native plants to your landscape. The benefits extend beyond the borders of your property, as well. When you buy native plants, you support stores that sell them and nurseries that grow them, and you reinforce the demand for native species throughout the green industry. When your neighbors admire the increased bird activity in your yard and follow suit with native plantings of their own, the positive effects can ripple throughout your region.

Shopping for Bird-Worthy Plants

Choosing native plants to make your yard more inviting to birds is much like shopping for any landscape plants. You may have to seek out a nursery that specializes in natives for your area to get the best selection, but the same commonsense rules apply wherever you shop.

A bed of sunflowers will brighten your garden and grow into living feeders for goldfinches and other seed-eating birds. Let birds dine straight from the flowers or harvest the seed-filled heads and dry them to serve later.

Choose plants that are appropriate for the site where you want them to grow. Take into account the mature size of shrubs and trees, and make sure that today's slender sapling has room to reach its full potential in years to come. Consider sun, shade, and exposure to prevailing winds, as well as soil moisture. Look for healthy plants that are free of signs of pests or diseases. If possible, check to see that any potential purchases have healthy roots that are not cramped and tightly circled in the container—plants that are severely rootbound may never fully recover.

Annuals and Perennials with Bird Appeal

If you're trying out bird-friendly gardening for the first time, or if you have a limited space or budget for new plantings, choose annuals and perennials: They offer speedy results, inexpensive planting options (seeds

A Note from **Arlene**

PLAN FOR GROWTH

A big mistake people make when they plant berry or fruit plants for birds is not taking into account how much those plants will grow in the coming years. I've made this mistake more than a few times myself. Once I became enthralled with a picture of snow buntings eating the berries of a snowberry bush (*Symphoricarpos albus*), and knew I had to have one. I also knew that a snowberry bush would grow well in my climate, so I planted one in a bed alongside the house close to the kitchen door. It didn't take long to realize I had made a big mistake. It grew so well that soon its branches began hitting me when I walked out the door. So I dug it up and replanted it far away from the house, where it's now 10 feet tall and wide years later. But I had to dig the remnants of its roots out from that bed many times in the following years. So make sure you do your homework before you plant anything, no matter how bird friendly it may be.

versus plants), and greater adaptability to different planting conditions than most woody plants do. If you decide you don't like the location of a bed of bird-attracting annual flowers, you can simply sow them in a different site next season, and most perennials are easily relocated if you decide you or the birds would prefer them elsewhere.

Seeds Galore and More! When it comes to providing seeds for the birds, you can't beat Mother Nature. You can, however, help her along by planting year-round seed sources. Many herbaceous perennials produce seedheads that supply birds with food even during winter months when the plants themselves may be dormant. A garden of annuals, perennials, and ornamental grasses can brighten your landscape through the growing season and supply copious quantities of seeds for birds to enjoy from late summer through the following spring.

Annual Flowers for the Birds

Annuals complete their life cycle in a year's time, and for that reason, they typically produce abundant quantities of seed to ensure that others like them will grow the next season. One of the easiest ways to see which heavily seed-producing annuals you already may have planted is to check your gardens or containers closely in spring, when new plants are just emerging. Look for familiar foliage among the sprouts. Annuals that reliably "return" from year to year do so by sowing plenty of seeds ready to sprout in this way. Planted in a sunny spot, a bed of these annuals will produce an abundance of seeds for the birds in your yard. Watch for end-of-season sales on packets of seeds at your local garden center, hardware store, or home center, and for a song you may pick up bird favorites to sow next spring.

ANNUAL PLANT	DESCRIPTION	BIRDS ATTRACTED
Love-lies-bleeding (*Amaranthus caudatus*)	Drooping deep-pink flower heads look like 10-inch strands of fuzzy yarn and produce oodles of tiny seeds; plants are bushy and 3 to 4 feet tall with magenta stems.	Finches, juncos, tree sparrows
Tickseed sunflower (*Bidens aristosa*)	Fragrant yellow daisies bloom in masses on plants 4 feet tall and wide, with ferny foliage.	Buntings, cardinals, chickadees, finches, game birds, goldfinches, redpolls, pine siskins, titmice
China aster (*Callistephus chinensis*)	Blue, rose, or white blooms are 2½ inches wide; plants grow 2 feet tall.	Buntings, finches, goldfinches, sparrows
Bachelor's buttons (*Centaurea cyanus*)	Blue, pink, purple, red, or white blooms grow 1 to 2 inches wide on 1- to 3-foot-tall plants.	Buntings, finches, goldfinches, sparrows
Calliopsis (*Coreopsis tinctoria*)	Bright yellow daisylike flowers with dark red-brown centers attract butterflies; plants grow to 4 feet tall.	Finches and sparrows

A Garden for Game Birds and Others Seeds that attract game birds like doves and grouse are also tempting to dozens of smaller seed-eating birds. By planting a mixed patch of perennial and annual seed plants, you can create a birdseed garden that will welcome seed-eating species from wild turkeys and quail to finches and native sparrows. Start with clovers, such as bird's-foot trefoil (*Lotus corniculatus*), which sports clusters of sunny yellow blossoms, and bush clo-

vers (*Lespedeza* spp.), which have small pink or purple pealike flowers. For a fast payoff, include annuals, like sorghum, buckwheat, and small-seeded soybeans and peas. Prepare a small planting bed, mix together a handful of seeds, and sow the seeds over the bed. Water generously until the seeds germinate, then take the low-maintenance approach—just wait for your bird visitors to arrive. Businesses that sell foods and products for attracting wild game are good places to find seeds of

ANNUAL PLANT	DESCRIPTION	BIRDS ATTRACTED
Cosmos (*Cosmos bipinnatus* and *C. sulphureus*)	Blooms are 1 to 2 inches wide; *C. bipinnatus* has pink, white, or crimson ray flowers with a yellow center; plants grow 4 to 6 feet tall; *C. sulphureus* has yellow, red, or orange daisylike blooms on 2- to 3-foot-tall stems.	Buntings, cardinals, doves, goldfinches, house finches, juncos, redpolls, siskins, sparrows
Annual sunflowers (*Helianthus annuus, H. debilis*)	Yellow, red, and rust-colored blooms grow 3 to 12 inches wide on plants that are 1 to 12 feet tall (size depends on the variety).	Cardinals, chickadees, finches, jays, titmice, woodpeckers
Garden balsam and impatiens (*Impatiens balsamina, I. wallerana*)	Short, bushy plants grow to 2 feet tall with pastel, white, or jewel-toned flowers that attract hummingbirds.	Cardinals, grosbeaks, towhees
Flax (*Linum* spp.)	Blue or white delicate ½-inch-wide blooms grow on 3- to 4-foot-tall stems.	Doves, sparrows, towhees
Black-eyed Susan (*Rudbeckia hirta*)	Daisylike yellow blooms have brown centers and grow 2 to 3 inches wide; plants grow 1 to 3 feet tall.	Buntings, cardinals, finches, juncos, siskins, sparrows, towhees
Marigolds (*Tagetes* spp.)	Ruffled, double, or single flowers in yellows, oranges, and reds grow on stems from 6 inches to 3 feet tall, with ferny foliage.	Juncos, siskins, sparrows
Mexican sunflower (*Tithonia rotundifolia*)	Bright orange-red daisy flowers attract hummingbirds and butterflies; large-leaved plants grow 4 to 8 feet tall.	Buntings, cardinals, chickadees, finches, jays, nuthatches, sparrows, titmice, towhees
Zinnias (*Zinnia* spp.)	With a wide range of flower colors, including pastels and brights, bushy plants grow from a few inches tall to 3 to 4 feet.	Buntings, cardinals, chickadees, finches, goldfinches, redpolls, siskins, sparrows, titmice

> *"Every year we usually have a few nests of sparrows in our Virginia creeper awning over the front porch. I usually hang a feeder in there, too. The cats love to watch that from the front window."*
>
> **DONNA CHIARELLI,** Kutztown, Pennsylvania

annual and perennial seed plants that many game birds will find attractive.

Perennials for Beauty and Bird Food While the benefits to birds of annual plants derive mainly from their seed-producing abilities, perennials' contributions to birds may be more subtle, although no less worthwhile. Some perennials (those plants that persist for several years or more), mostly those of the aster family, produce seeds favored by many birds, and others are nectar sources sought by hummingbirds. A bountiful perennial garden can provide plenty of bird-friendly advantages, even if it includes only a few sources of seeds, fruits, or nectar.

A healthy, diverse garden of flowering perennials is a magnet for insects, and these, in turn, will attract the birds that dine on them. Colorful flowers too small to serve as nectar sources for hummingbirds are just right for small flying insects that also are part of the hummers' diet. Butterflies are drawn to perennial gardens, too, to drink nectar and to lay eggs on the host plants that feed their caterpillars. The caterpillars, in turn, may become food for songbird nestlings. From fall right through winter, coneflowers (*Echinacea*, *Rudbeckia*, and *Ratibida* spp.), native asters (*Symphyotrichum* and *Eurybia* spp.), Joe Pye weed (*Eupatorium* spp.), and goldenrods (*Solidago* spp.) hold up sturdy stems that support birds foraging for seeds and overwintering insects.

Whatever the style or color scheme of your perennial garden, chances are good that it

Surviving versus Thriving

Several factors beyond the ability to withstand a region's average minimum temperature determine whether a plant will thrive or just survive there. While hardiness zone information (see USDA Hardiness Zone Map on page 304) is useful in ruling out plants that almost certainly cannot survive temperatures below a certain point, it doesn't address other climate issues that affect plant health. A perennial that is native to the American Southwest, for example, may be able to withstand the low temperatures found in southern New England in winter, but not the humidity of summers there. To ensure that you fill your landscape with plants that will thrive instead of barely manage, your best bets are those that are native—not just to the same continent or country, but also to the region in which you live.

Considering a plant's regional origins is especially important when you are planning a garden to attract birds. Plants that are native in one region of North America may not support wildlife—from insects on up through the food web—in another part of the continent. Birds in the Pacific Northwest may not recognize a plant that's native to the Mid-Atlantic region as a viable food source, even if it is hardy 3,000 miles from its natural origins.

25 Perennials with Bird Benefits

The list includes plants for sun and shade, for dry sites and wet, and for mild climates and cold-winter regions. Choose perennials that suit your site and preferred style of gardening, and the birds will enjoy it, too.

PERENNIAL PLANT	BENEFITS FOR BIRDS
Yarrows (*Achillea* spp.)	Heads of small flowers attract insects
Agapanthus (*Agapanthus* spp.)	Nectar
Anise hyssop (*Agastache foeniculum*)	Nectar, seeds
Agaves (*Agave* spp.)	Nectar
Columbines (*Aquilegia* spp.)	Nectar
Coreopsis (*Coreopsis lanceolata*)	Seeds
Crocosmias (*Crocosmia* spp.)	Nectar
Purple coneflower (*Echinacea purpurea*)	Seeds
Asters (*Eucephalus, Eurybia,* and *Symphyotrichum* spp., formerly *Aster* spp.)	Seeds, overwintering sites for insects
Joe Pye weed (*Eupatorium purpureum*)	Seeds, overwintering sites for insects
Indian blanket (*Gaillardia pulchella*)	Seeds
Perennial sunflowers (*Helianthus* spp.)	Seeds, overwintering sites for insects
Blue flax (*Linum perenne*)	Seeds
Liriopes (*Liriope* spp.)	Fruits
Cardinal flower (*Lobelia cardinalis*)	Nectar
Lupines (*Lupinus* spp.)	Seeds
Bee balms (*Monarda* spp.)	Nectar, seeds
Garden phlox (*Phlox paniculata*)	Flowers attract butterflies, other insects
Buttercups (*Ranunculus* spp.)	Seeds
Gloriosa daisy (*Rudbeckia hirta* 'Gloriosa')	Seeds, overwintering sites for insects
Salvias (*Salvia* spp.)	Nectar
Compass plant (*Silphium laciniatum*)	Seeds
Goldenrods (*Solidago* spp.)	Seeds, overwintering sites for insects
Violets (*Viola* spp.)	Seeds, roots for wild turkeys to eat
Yuccas (*Yucca* spp.)	Nectar

will naturally include plants that have something to offer birds. Even the layer of mulch and plant debris beneath the bright flowers and handsome foliage can benefit birds— species like towhees and wood thrushes will hunt for earthworms and insects there. Other birds will welcome the shelter that the plants provide.

Vines, Groundcovers, and Grasses

In addition to any fruits, seeds, nectar, or insects that birds might glean from vines, groundcovers, and grasses, these types of plants can provide birds with cover from predators, sheltered sites for roosting, materials for nest building, and places to build those nests. Vines typically clamber up into places that are more accessible to birds than

Bird-Worthy Vines

Try some of these bird-approved vines to see which birds pay them a visit. Some vines benefit birds three ways: with food, shelter, and nest sites. Watch out for the ones noted as "vigorous"—these plants may be invasive in growing conditions they find favorable. Check with your local Cooperative Extension office or your state or regional Department of Natural Resources or similar agency to see if there are vines you should avoid planting in your area.

VINE	DESCRIPTION	BIRD-WORTHY FEATURES	HARDY IN
Porcelain berry (*Ampelopsis brevipedunculata*)	Vigorous with dark green, lobed leaves; round berries mature to shades of blue and purple; to 15 feet	Cover, fruit	Zones 5–8
Rattan vine (*Berchemia scandens*)	Vigorous woody vine produces blue-black fruits; to 15 feet	Fruit	Zones 6–9
Trumpet creeper (*Campsis radicans*)	Vigorous climber bears clusters of orange-red trumpet-shaped flowers beloved by hummingbirds; to 30 feet	Cover, nectar	Zones 5–9
American bittersweet (*Celastrus scandens*)	Woody vine produces clusters of seedy orange-yellow fruit; to 30 feet	Cover, seeds	Zones 3–8
Western white clematis (*Clematis ligusticifolia*)	Deciduous perennial vine bears abundant small white flowers through summer; showy downy seedheads follow; to 20 feet	Seeds, cover	Zones 5–7
Anemone clematis (*Clematis montana* and hybrids)	Deciduous perennial blooms in late spring and early summer, bearing plentiful large single flowers; to 30 feet	Seeds, cover	Zones 6–9

to predators, while birds that seek food and make their nests at ground level benefit from dense clumps of grasses and continuous swaths of groundcovers that let them move about undetected.

Vines for Good Bird Viewing

With their tangle of stems and often luxuriant leaves, vines are favorite hiding places and nesting sites for many songbirds. Look in vines such as Boston ivy (*Parthenocissus tricuspidata*) and you'll discover lots of bird nests. Wrens, sparrows, and robins are among the birds that often roost in Boston ivy at night, and its thick growth also provides a home for catbirds. The best part of having ivy-covered nests is that you don't know there are any birds in there. But at night, just before dark, you may hear them twittering as they settle down to sleep. And you can watch the catbirds coming and going with food for their babies.

VINE	DESCRIPTION	BIRD-WORTHY FEATURES	HARDY IN
Autumn clematis (*Clematis terniflora*)	Deciduous perennial vine bears clouds of fragrant white flowers in late summer into fall; to 20 feet	Seeds, cover	Zones 5–9
Morning glories (*Ipomoea* spp.)	Mostly annual vines bear showy, funnel-shaped flowers convenient for hummingbird dining; to 10 feet	Nectar	Annual
Cardinal climber (*Ipomoea* x *multifida*)	Bright red, funnel-shaped blooms beckon hummingbirds to visit; to 6 feet	Nectar	Annual
Coral honeysuckle (*Lonicera sempervirens*)	Woody, deciduous or evergreen climber with tubular red-orange flowers that appeal to hummingbirds; to 12 feet	Cover, nectar	Zones 4–9
Virginia creeper (*Parthenocissus quinquefolia*) and Boston ivy (*P. tricuspidata*)	Vigorous woody climbers need sturdy support; red fall color; to 50 feet or more	Cover, nest sites	Zones 3–9
Climbing roses (*Rosa* spp.)	Woody; often very thorny and in need of training to supporting structures; showy flowers may yield bright red hips; to 12 feet	Cover, nest sites, sometimes fruit (hips)	Zones 5–9
Greenbriers (*Smilax* spp.)	Woody, deciduous or evergreen, and sometimes prickly vines produce yellow, black, blue, or green berries; to 15 feet	Fruit	Zones 4–9
Grapes (*Vitis* spp.)	Woody vines need sturdy support, but provide habitat and food; to 25 feet	Cover, fruit, seeds	Zones 5–9

Other vines favored by birds include: Virginia creeper (*Parthenocissus quinquefolia*), autumn clematis (*Clematis terniflora*), anemone clematis (*C. montana*), and grapevines. All are excellent bird homes and hideouts.

Good Groundcovers for Birds

From a bird's point of view, good groundcovers are those that create a low, fairly dense canopy that they can travel beneath, much in the same way that we walk beneath the trees in a wooded area. Hidden from the view of potential predators, birds such as towhees and thrushes will rustle in the leaf litter, looking for seeds and insects. Groundcovers that are too low and tangly—like periwinkle (*Vinca minor*) or English ivy (*Hedera helix*)—don't give birds the space they need to move easily below sheltering leaves, and those that are too short—like most lawn grasses—don't provide shelter. The best groundcovers also produce fruits or seeds for birds to eat.

Grasses for Birds and Beauty

Thick-growing prairie grasses or other ornamental grasses planted here and there in the landscape provide a safe haven for birds that

Bird-Worthy Groundcovers

A few inches of space to move about beneath a sheltering canopy of foliage is a bird's idea of a welcoming groundcover. If there are also berries to eat and places to nest, so much the better!

GROUNDCOVER	BIRD BENEFITS
Bearberry (*Arctostaphylos uva-ursi*)	Cover, berries
Bunchberry (*Cornus canadensis*)	Cover, berries
Strawberries (*Fragaria* spp.)	Cover, nest sites, berries
Wintergreen (*Gaultheria procumbens*)	Cover, berries
Huckleberries (*Gaylussacia* spp.)	Cover, berries, nest sites
Liriope (*Liriope spicata*)	Berries
Partridgeberry (*Mitchella repens*)	Berries
Allegheny spurge (*Pachysandra procumbens*)	Cover, nest sites
Mayapple (*Podophyllum peltatum*)	Berries
Blueberries (*Vaccinium* spp.)	Berries, nest sites
Ferns, such as maidenhair fern (*Adiantum pedatum*), cinnamon fern (*Osmunda cinnamomea*), interrupted fern (*O. claytonia*), polypody ferns (*Polypodium* spp.), Christmas fern (*Polystichum acrostichoides*)	Nest sites

need to make a quick dash to safety. Grasses grow quickly, too, making them useful to birds soon after they're established in your yard. And most stay useful over winter, offering birds a tangle of sheltering stems, not to mention a bounty of nutritious seeds and nesting material in spring.

In the landscape, ornamental grasses offer a combination of bird habitat and natural beauty. You can use them to add vertical accents to a bed of mound-shaped perennials or to soften hard lines in your yard. Grasses also make excellent foils for bold flower colors. For the birds' enjoyment and your own, try one or more of these easy-growing prairie natives: big bluestem (*Andropogon gerardii*), switchgrass (*Panicum virgatum*), or Indian grass (*Sorghastrum nutans*).

Good Grasses for Birds

Grasses produce abundant crops of seeds that are attractive to many birds, including buntings, doves, finches, game birds, juncos, and native sparrows. Blackbirds eat the seeds of larger grasses such as common cattail *(Typha latifolia),* and wrens and chickadees pluck fluff from its seedheads to line their nests. Some birds gather dried grass to use in nest building, while others simply make their nests in clumps of grass.

Here are some grasses that are both ornamental and appealing to birds.

Big bluestem (*Andropogon gerardii*)
Blue grama grass (*Bouteloua gracilis*)
Fescues (*Festuca* spp.)
Deer-tongue grass (*Panicum clandestinum*)
Switchgrass (*Panicum virgatum*)
Little bluestem (*Schizachyrium scoparium*)

Indian grass (*Sorghastrum nutans*)
Prairie dropseed (*Sporobolus heterolepsis*)

Weedy Grasses for Birds

You may prefer only elegant ornamental grasses in your landscape, but birds are more interested in what's to eat than in aesthetics. Seed-eating birds will gladly dine on seeds of weedy grasses such as foxtails (*Setaria* spp.) and crabgrass (*Digitaria* spp.), as well as on annuals like millet (*Panicum miliaceum*), milo (*Sorghum bicolor*), and annual ryegrass (*Lolium multiflorum*). You probably won't choose to sow crabgrass for your birds, but a bed of millet and milo combined with annual flowers like amaranths and zinnias can make a lovely edible seed patch for native sparrows, finches, and other small birds.

Bohemian waxwings rarely visit feeders but may arrive in a flock in late winter to pluck every last fruit from a tree or shrub that's to their liking.

Shrubs and Trees for Birds

The most well-stocked feeding area cannot begin to compete for birds' attention when compared with a yard that offers the natural shelter, perch space, roosts, nest sites, and foods provided by a variety of shrubs and trees. Just as woody plants give structure to our landscapes and create shade and privacy around our homes, so do they offer similar benefits to birds. From places to rest and hide from danger, to cavities for nesting, to meals of leaf-eating insects, these plants fill a host of roles in birds' lives.

Because they are so essential—and so permanent—it can feel overwhelming to choose bird-friendly woody plants to add to your landscape. Start by narrowing your choices based on the plant species that are suited to the climate where you live and to the soil conditions, exposure, and size of the site you want to plant. For maximum bird appeal, consider native species, and if possible, plant a mixture of deciduous and evergreen trees or shrubs. Deciduous trees produce the most food for birds, and evergreens give the most shelter. Keep in mind that even landscape plants that don't produce seeds or fruits for birds may still provide them with valuable natural food in the form of insects. Not every plant has to yield a crop of berries to be attractive to birds.

The good news is that many of the best native North American plants for attracting birds occur as different species in different regions. This makes it relatively easy to find the one that's right for your growing conditions and for the birds in your area. For instance, there are 16 native dogwood species in North America, but in the East the most common one you'll find is the flowering dogwood (*Cornus florida*), while in the coastal areas of California north through Washington, the one most commonly found is the Pacific dogwood (*C. nuttallii*). There are also several dogwood species that like to grow in moist or swampy ground, and others that only get to be as big as shrubs.

Similar regional differentiation exists in several other excellent bird plants. Maples (*Acer* spp.), serviceberries (*Amelanchier* spp.), hollies (*Ilex* spp.), junipers (*Juniperus* spp.), pines (*Pinus* spp.), oaks (*Quercus* spp.), and viburnums (*Viburnum* spp.) all occur in different forms that are well suited to the

Eye-Pleasing Berries Become Food for Birds

Horticulturist and garden coach Pam Ruch of Emmaus, Pennsylvania, likes to include plants in her designs that both birds and people can enjoy. One of her favorites is tea viburnum (*Viburnum setigerum*), an 8- to 12-foot-tall shrub with flat clusters of white flowers in spring that produce an abundance of bright red berries in fall. The birds like the berries, she explains, but not so much or so soon that the birds gobble them all up shortly after they ripen. Unlike inkberry hollies, which seem to be stripped of their fruits in a matter of days, tea viburnum keeps its fruit through winter, and birds visit in spring to enjoy the berries that have been weathered by freezing and thawing.

Top-Notch Fruiting Shrubs for Birds

The line between shrubs and small trees is an arbitrary one, and the distinction matters not one bit to the birds. Many of the plants listed below have some species that are treelike and tree size and others that are shrubbier in shape and stature. Use this list of fruiting shrubs favored by birds to get an idea of the many possibilities available to you, then talk with local gardeners, growers, and bird lovers to identify shrub species that are appropriate for your landscape.

SHRUB	BIRDS ATTRACTED
Serviceberries (*Amelanchier* spp.)	Bluebirds, waxwings, many others
White fringetree (*Chionanthus virginicus*)	Bluebirds, catbirds, mockingbirds, orioles, robins, tanagers, thrashers, thrushes, waxwings
Gray dogwood (*Cornus racemosa*)	Many
Red osier dogwood (*Cornus sericea*)	Many
Cotoneasters (*Cotoneaster* spp.)	Many
Downy hawthorn (*Crataegus mollis*)	Many
Eastern red cedar (*Juniperus virginiana*)	Many
Box huckleberry (*Gaylussacia brachycera*)	Catbirds, jays, thrushes, waxwings
Possumhaw (*Ilex decidua*)	Many
Winterberry (*Ilex verticillata*)	Many
Oregon grape holly (*Mahonia aquifolium*)	Many
Northern bayberry (*Morella pensylvanica*, formerly *Myrica pensylvanica*)	Bluebirds, flickers, tree swallow, thrushes, yellow-rumped warbler, woodpeckers
Black currant (*Ribes nigrum*)	Robins, jays, mockingbirds, many others
Elderberries (*Sambucus* spp.)	Many
Snowberry (*Symphoricarpos albus* var. *laevigatus*)	Evening and pine grosbeaks, many others
Arrowwood (*Viburnum dentatum*)	Many
Nannyberry (*Viburnum lentago*)	Flickers, robins, waxwings
American cranberrybush (*Viburnum trilobum*)	Bluebirds, ruffed grouse, robins, brown thrasher, thrushes, wild turkey, cedar waxwing, many others

regions to which they are native. From that list alone you could find trees and shrubs that are evergreen or deciduous, coniferous or flowering, and seed- or fruit-bearing for almost any area of the continent.

In unique climate areas, such as deserts or seacoasts, the number of plants that are adapted to the local growing conditions will be fewer than in more moderate climates. But wherever you choose to make your bird-attracting garden, selecting native plants will give you the greatest odds of success both in creating a healthy, beautiful garden and in bringing in the birds.

Trees for Seeds

While small birds, such as sparrows and finches, feast on seeds of grasses, larger birds turn to trees for their seeds. Some birds even have specialized beaks that allow them to feed on a particular seed or seed type, such as nuts. Crossbills, for example, have uniquely crossed bills that enable them to get to the seeds within the cones of pines and other conifers. No matter where you live, even in the desert, you will find trees that produce some kinds of seeds that the birds in that area will eat. A short list of good wild seed or nut producers includes

Seeds and fruits that don't look the least bit tempting to us are still very attractive to birds like this redpoll, which is going to acrobatic lengths to eat catkins from a birch tree.

Tree Seeds Favored by Birds

Where there are trees, there are also birds that feed on their seeds. Not surprisingly, the size of the seed and the ease or difficulty with which it can be separated from its shell or coating affects which birds are able to eat it.

TREE	BIRDS THAT EAT ITS SEEDS
Firs (*Abies* spp.)	Finches, nuthatches, game birds, grosbeaks, chickadees, crossbills, Clark's nutcracker, grouse, magpies
Maples (*Acer* spp.)	Evening grosbeak, purple finch, pine siskin
Box elder (*Acer negundo*)	Evening grosbeak
Alders (*Alnus* spp.)	Fox sparrow, goldfinches
Birches (*Betula* spp.)	Cardinal, crossbills, finches, grouse, nuthatches, chickadees
American beech (*Fagus grandifolia*)	Game birds, crows, grackles, jays, woodpeckers, crossbills, grosbeaks, finches
White ash (*Fraxinus americana*)	Game birds, finches, grosbeaks, cardinal
Western larch (*Larix occidentalis*)	Goldfinches
Black gum (*Nyssa sylvatica*)	Bluebirds, catbirds, kingbirds, flickers, mockingbirds, robins, thrashers, tanagers
Spruces (*Picea* spp.)	Finches, chickadees, crossbills, pine grosbeak, grouse, red-breasted nuthatch, pine siskin, cedar waxwing
Pines (*Pinus* spp.)	Crossbills, goldfinches, towhees, tanagers, chickadees
Cottonwoods (*Populus* spp.)	Ruffed grouse, evening grosbeaks
Mesquites (*Prosopis* spp.)	Mourning doves, cardinals, pyrrhuloxia
Oaks (*Quercus* spp.)	Chickadees, jays, nuthatches, quail, titmice, wild turkey, woodpeckers
Hemlocks (*Tsuga* spp.)	Chickadees, titmice

black gum, oaks, elms, maples, birches, beeches, hickories, walnuts, sassafras, sycamores, hackberries, and many more deciduous trees.

All conifers, as their name says, produce cones with seeds in them. Check to see which grow in your area. In winter or when the cones are ripe, you will almost always find birds among the branches of pines, firs, spruces, and other evergreens. In parts of the West, the lodgepole pine is one that attracts a lot of seed- and nut-eating species.

Allow for Bird-Worthy Weeds

The plants that we humans regard as weeds are often great seed sources for wild birds. Although goldenrods are highly valued as garden plants in many parts of the world, here in North America most of us think of them as weeds and pull them out if they voluntarily show up in our cultivated beds. But we shouldn't, because they produce amazing amounts of seeds. That's why you'll always find birds on them in winter. Jewelweed, a

> *"In my suburban Philadelphia yard, pokeweed attracts all kinds of birds to its berries. I've seen American robin, wood thrush, gray catbird, cedar waxwings, northern mockingbird, European starlings, great-crested flycatcher, hermit and Swainson's thrush, ruby-crowned kinglet, Nashville warbler, yellow warbler, black-throated blue warbler, common yellowthroat, ovenbird [eating the berries], and ruby-throated hummingbirds taking nectar from the white flowers."*
>
> **CINDY AHERN,** Huntingdon Valley, PA

member of the impatiens family that grows wild in wet ditches and along creeks and streams, is another plant considered to be a weed, even though its yellow or orange flowers are very pretty. But it's a major seed producer, and it spreads them by exploding its seedpods when they're ripe. Grosbeaks are birds of the woods known for sometimes cleaning out a feeder's supply of sunflower seeds, but they can often be found feeding near the ground in jewelweed patches, because they know that when they close

their bills around ripe seedpods, the contents will explode into their mouths. That way they don't have to do any work at all.

Some familiar weeds that produce abundant seeds and shelter for birds, but whose proper identities aren't commonly known, are Virginia knotweed (*Tovara virginiana*) and phragmites (*Phragmites* spp.). Virginia knotweed is a tall member of the Polygonum family, the same one that the common smartweeds belong to. You probably know what smartweed is, even if you think you don't: Look at the edges of fields, ditches, or untended places of your garden from early summer on, and you'll be almost certain to find plants with thin stems topped by oval or club-shaped seedheads with hundreds of tiny pink, red, or white seeds on them. Sometimes in early fall, untended fields or recently harvested fields will turn pink from blooming smartweeds. Wild turkeys will often take a blooming or seed-covered stalk of Virginia knotweed in their bills and eat everything on it from bottom to top in zipperlike fashion. Phragmites are reeds that resemble those you see growing along ocean shorelines. They'll grow in disturbed sites and even in spots where you'd never expect to find them, sometimes looking totally out of place—but they offer a lot of shelter to birds.

Thistles can be the bane of gardens and wild areas, but they're great seed producers. You'll always find goldfinches on them once their flowers have turned into puffy seedheads that get carried freely on the wind.

Other unwanted weeds that produce lots of seeds are the many members of the amaranth family and also curly dock (*Rumex crispus*). Some amaranths are grown for grain production, but there are many more that grow wild in fields and waste places. They get tall and their fat seedheads are literally covered with seeds, just like those of curly dock are. One dock seedhead can have as many as 40,000 seeds on it. Ragweed (*Ambrosia* spp.) is another prolific seed pro-ducer and often is visited by migrating Connecticut warblers, as well as many other seed-eating birds, but it's extremely disliked and unwanted by gardeners because its pollen is a major allergen.

Mullein (*Verbascum thapsus*) is easily recognized by its tall stalks of bright yellow flowers and soft velvety leaves. It's a pioneer plant, meaning it's one of the first to germinate in disturbed ground, probably because one seedhead alone can produce more than 100,000 seeds.

If you are able to allow a small area of your property to "go wild" and give weeds free rein there, you'll undoubtedly enjoy seeing birds in it that never appear at your

This young mockingbird represents just one species of the many fruit-loving birds that relish dark purple pokeberries. Pokeweeds will attract lots of birds to your landscape, but they also spread vigorously via seedlings (planted by birds) and sprouts from the wide-ranging fleshy roots.

feeders or in more cultivated parts of your landscape. But be responsible and don't let your weed patch become a source of problems for your neighbors' gardens. Keep an eye on what pops up and do all you can to limit their weedy presence to their designated space. To keep things from looking unkempt, mow a border around the weed patch (this will also limit the spread of some

of its occupants) and consider a simple fence—not for containment, but to give an aura of civilization to your wild-'n'-weedy corner.

Weeds for Seeds

To a hungry bird, food is food, and the seeds and fruits borne by weeds are just as tempting as the plants you've cultivated

The View from Deb's Window

Convinced by my bird-wise friend, Sally Roth, that pokeberries were a surefire way to attract bluebirds to my yard, I allowed a few pokeweeds to bloom and produce fruit in the garden below my deck. After all, I'd heard dedicated plant enthusiasts talking about *Phytolacca americana* as a promising "new" perennial, and the plants are quite attractive with bright green leaves and reddish stalks producing clusters of small white flowers that become deep purple berries with bright red stems.

A few different birds enjoyed those berries that first fall, as evidenced by purplish droppings spattered here and there. And Sally was right—in the dark, gray days of late February, I was delighted to see bluebirds feeding on the remaining pokeberries as the birds made their forays in search of suitable housing for the breeding season ahead.

What I didn't count on was the vigorous nature of pokeweed. Not only did a crop of seedlings sprout the following spring, courtesy of the purple bird "deposits" from the previous fall, but plenty of pokeweed popped up from the roots of the original plants, turning what had been a mixed garden of perennials and annuals into a pokeweed thicket. When I tried to thin things out a bit, I found out about the sturdy nature of pokeweed roots: Mature plants had crowns as thick as my arm and fleshy roots that extended both deep into the ground and widely into the surrounding soil. My few plants for the bluebirds became a forest of pokeweed that took a lot of hard labor to tame. In addition, every broken piece of root that I left behind became the source of new plants, so that pokeweed removal remains a regular item on my gardening to-do list.

Still, I treasure the moments when I see a flash of blue in the otherwise dull landscape and can watch bluebirds dining on the pokeberries. What the pokeweed costs me in labor is more than repaid by the sight of bluebirds on a late winter's day.

specifically for their bird-worthy features. If you have unkempt areas where weedy plants grow unchecked near your property, you may notice birds enjoying this free-range abundance, as well as the more civilized offerings at your feeders. It's worth noting that weeds that are attractive to birds often are adapted to distribution by the wildlife that visits them. Seed- and fruit-bearing weeds growing near your property are likely to pop up in your lawn and gardens, as your feathered guests deliver their seeds wherever they pause to rest. As long as you are quick to remove unwanted weed seedlings while they're young, they are unlikely to become a problem in your landscape. Whether you welcome these weedy plants or not, these prolific seed-bearers are some of the most attractive to hungry birds.

Weeds That Attract Birds

Pigweed (*Amaranthus* spp.)

Chicory (*Cichorium intybus*)

Thistles (*Cirsium* spp.)

Jewelweed (*Impatiens capensis*)

Mulberries (*Morus* spp.)

Phragmites (*Phragmites* spp.)

Pokeweed (*Phytolacca americana*)

Knotweeds and smartweeds
(*Polygonum* spp.)

Chokecherry (*Prunus virginiana*)

Curly dock (*Rumex crispus*)

Greenbriers (*Smilax* spp.)

Climbing nightshade (*Solanum dulcamara*)

Goldenrods (*Solidago* spp.)

Chickweed (Stellaria media)

Dandelion (*Taraxacum officinale*)

Poison ivy (*Toxicodendron radicans*)

Common mullein (*Verbascum thapsus*)

ten

Birds at the Buffet

Birds don't observe political boundaries, and because they can fly, they're not particularly limited by geographical ones, either. Because they instinctively follow patterns of migration and breeding behavior established over hundreds of generations, we can narrow down an individual bird's identity based solely on its location at a particular time of the year. But opportunity and necessity also may guide birds in their search for food and suitable nesting sites, and the occasional odd bird—or flock—may find its way to your feeders along with more familiar guests.

A cardinal, goldfinches, and a house finch find the seeds in this tube feeder to their liking.

The birds described in this chapter include the most common/widespread species seen across North America, as well as significant regional and/or related species. The profiles are arranged alphabetically by a bird's main common name (blackbird, cardinal, dove, etc.) and focus on the birds most likely to visit feeders for seeds, suet, nectar, fruit, or other goodies.

Because place and season are the first, best keys to use in matching names to the feathered faces at your feeders, the lists that follow are a quick guide to the birds most likely to be where you live at a particular time of year. Exceptions will occur, of course, along with birds that will visit your yard but have no interest in your feeders. For those "mystery guests" and for non-feeder birds, you'll want a field guide that's specific to the birds common to your region and maybe one that covers all of North America also. Your local chapter of the Audubon Society may have recommendations for field guides that are particularly useful where you live; you'll also find a few of the best-known guides listed in Resources in the back of this book.

Who's Who at Your Feeders

To identify the birds at your feeder, start with those listed under the "Widespread" heading on page 187 and then move on to the heading that best describes the region where you live, bearing in mind that these designations are for our purposes, not those of the birds. There are no hard and fast lines keeping the birds of one region from venturing into a neighboring area, particularly when climate, mating opportunities, and/or abundant food drive their movements. And while a bird that's common in the Arizona desert is unlikely to appear at a feeder in New Hampshire, it's not unusual to see some of the same species at feeders in the Midwest, the Southeast, and the Northeast.

Make Your Observations Count

As you become more adept at recognizing your feeder visitors, try to note when different species begin showing up in your landscape, as well as which foods they seem to prefer and how long they stay around. Jot your observations in a journal or notebook, and you'll gradually create a record of the seasonal movements and habits of the wild birds outside your windows.

Consider participating in a bird count, such as Project Feederwatch. By reporting the numbers and species of birds at your feeders, you can contribute to important scientific studies of wild bird populations. Since 1987, more than 40,000 people have contributed checklists to Project Feederwatch, supplying scientists with valuable assistance in monitoring fluctuations in the distribution and populations of bird species throughout North America.

Tufted titmouse

Northeast

These birds appear in the area that extends roughly from Maine south along the Atlantic coastline to Virginia, and west along the Great Lakes to eastern Ohio.

Year-Round

Northern cardinal, page 198

Black-capped chickadee, page 202

Red crossbill, page 206

White-winged crossbill, page 207

Purple finch, page 214

Common grackle, page 218

Blue jay, page 229

Dark-eyed junco, page 233

Golden-crowned kinglet, page 236

Chipping sparrow, page 258

Song sparrow, page 258

White-crowned sparrow, page 259

White-throated sparrow, page 256

Tufted titmouse, page 270

Cedar waxwing, page 277

Pileated woodpecker, page 280

Red-bellied woodpecker, page 281

Red-headed woodpecker, page 282

Carolina wren, page 284

Spring into Fall

Eastern bluebird, page 190

Indigo bunting, page 196

Gray catbird, page 200

Rose-breasted grosbeak, page 222

Ruby-throated hummingbird, page 224

Baltimore oriole, page 244

Yellow-bellied sapsucker, page 254

Field sparrow, page 259

Scarlet tanager, page 264

Brown thrasher, page 265

Hermit thrush, page 268

Wood thrush, page 267

Eastern towhee, page 273

Winter

Evening grosbeak, page 220

Pine siskin, page 255

American tree sparrow, page 260

Northern cardinal

Far North

The following birds inhabit Canada and Alaska, northern New England, the northern Great Lakes states, and the Upper Midwest.

Year-Round

Northern cardinal, page 198

Black-capped chickadee, page 202

Boreal chickadee, page 204

Red crossbill, page 206

White-winged crossbill, page 207

Evening grosbeak, page 220

Pine grosbeak, page 221

Blue jay, page 229

Gray jay, page 231

Dark-eyed junco, page 233

Pine siskin, page 255

Cedar waxwing, page 277

Red-headed woodpecker, page 282

Common grackle, page 218

Rose-breasted grosbeak, page 222

Ruby-throated hummingbird, page 224

Ruby-crowned kinglet, page 235

Baltimore oriole, page 244

American robin, page 252

Fox sparrow, page 261

Song sparrow, page 258

White-throated sparrow, page 256

Scarlet tanager, page 264

Brown thrasher, page 265

Hermit thrush, page 268

Wood thrush, page 267

Eastern towhee, page 273

Spring into Fall

Yellow-headed blackbird, page 189

Eastern bluebird, page 190

Indigo bunting, page 196

Purple finch, page 214

Winter

Common redpoll, page 250

American tree sparrow, page 260

Painted bunting

Southeast and South

Birds in the following lists appear in southern Virginia; west to southern Missouri, Arkansas and Texas, and south to the Gulf Coast and Florida.

Year-Round

Eastern bluebird, page 190
Northern bobwhite, page 194
Northern cardinal, page 198
Carolina chickadee, page 203
Boat-tailed grackle, page 219
Common grackle, page 218
Brown-headed nuthatch, page 242
Field sparrow, page 259
Brown thrasher, page 265
Tufted titmouse, page 270
Eastern towhee, page 273
Pileated woodpecker, page 280
Red-bellied woodpecker, page 281
Red-headed woodpecker, page 282
Carolina wren, page 284

Spring into Fall

Indigo bunting, page 196
Painted bunting, page 197
Blue grosbeak, page 223

Ruby-throated hummingbird, page 224
Baltimore oriole, page 244
Summer tanager, page 262
Wood thrush, page 267

Winter

Brewer's blackbird, page 189
Gray catbird, page 200
Purple finch, page 214
Evening grosbeak, page 220
Rose-breasted grosbeak, page 222
Rufous hummingbird, page 227
Dark-eyed junco, page 233
Ruby-crowned kinglet, page 235
Pine siskin, page 255
Fox sparrow, page 261
Song sparrow, page 258
White-throated sparrow, page 256
Scarlet tanager, page 264
Hermit thrush, page 268
Cedar waxwing, page 277

Ruby-throated hummingbird

Midwest

These birds show up in Indiana westward through the Plains to the Rockies, including southern Minnesota and South Dakota, and south to northern Texas, New Mexico, and Arkansas.

Year-Round

Northern bobwhite, page 194

Northern cardinal, page 198

Black-capped chickadee, page 202

Common grackle, page 218

Field sparrow, page 259

Song sparrow, page 258

Tufted titmouse, page 270

Eastern towhee, page 273

Red-bellied woodpecker, page 281

Red-headed woodpecker, page 282

Carolina wren, page 284

Spring into Fall

Yellow-headed blackbird, page 189

Eastern bluebird, page 190

Indigo bunting, page 196

Painted bunting, page 197

Gray catbird, page 200

Blue grosbeak, page 223

Rose-breasted grosbeak, page 222

Ruby-throated hummingbird, page 224

Baltimore oriole, page 244

Orchard oriole, page 246

Scarlet tanager, page 264

Summer tanager, page 262

Brown thrasher, page 265

Wood thrush, page 267

Winter

Purple finch, page 214

Evening grosbeak, page 220

Dark-eyed junco, page 233

Pine siskin, page 255

American tree sparrow, page 260

White-throated sparrow, page 256

Steller's jay

West

These birds frequent the Rocky Mountains from Montana south to New Mexico and Arizona, and west through eastern Oregon and the Sierra Nevada Mountains.

Year-Round

Black-capped chickadee, page 202

Mountain chickadee, page 203

Red crossbill, page 206

Evening grosbeak, page 220

*Pine grosbeak, page 221

*Gray jay, page 231

Steller's jay, page 230

Western scrub-jay, page 232

Golden-crowned kinglet, page 236

Black-billed magpie, page 238

*Clark's nutcracker, page 240

Pine siskin, page 255

Spotted towhee, page 274

Carolina wren, page 284

Spring into Fall

Yellow-headed blackbird, page 189

Mountain bluebird, page 193

Western bluebird, page 192

Lazuli bunting, page 197

Black-headed grosbeak, page 223

Broad-tailed hummingbird, page 226

Ruby-crowned kinglet, page 235

Fox sparrow, page 261

Western tanager, page 263

Hermit thrush, page 268

Winter

Dark-eyed junco, page 233

American tree sparrow, page 260

* At high elevations

Female (left) and male purple finches

Southwest and California

The following birds appear in coastal and desert California and east into Nevada, Arizona, New Mexico, and western Texas.

Year-Round

Mountain bluebird, page 193
Western bluebird, page 192
Chestnut-backed chickadee, page 204
Mountain chickadee, page 203
Purple finch, page 214
Evening grosbeak, page 220
Anna's hummingbird, page 228
Pygmy nuthatch, page 242
California quail, page 247
Pine siskin, page 255
California towhee, page 274
Carolina wren, page 284

Spring into Fall

Black-headed grosbeak, page 223
*Allen's hummingbird, page 227
*Broad-tailed hummingbird, page 226
*Calliope hummingbird, page 226
*Costa's hummingbird, page 228
*Rufous hummingbird, page 227

* Hummingbirds may be year-round in some areas; migration visitors in others.

Winter

Dark-eyed junco, page 233
Oregon junco, page 234
Ruby-crowned kinglet, page 235
Fox sparrow, page 261
Eastern towhee, page 273
Cedar waxwing, page 277

Anna's hummingbird

Northwest

These are the birds of Washington and Oregon, western Idaho, and northern California.

Year-Round

Black-capped chickadee, page 202

Chestnut-backed chickadee, page 204

Red crossbill, page 206

Evening grosbeak, page 220

Anna's hummingbird, page 228

Steller's jay, page 230

Western scrub-jay, page 232

Oregon junco, page 234

Pine siskin, page 255

Varied thrush, page 268

Cedar waxwing, page 277

Pileated woodpecker, page 280

Carolina wren, page 284

Spring into Fall

Lazuli bunting, page 197

Black-headed grosbeak, page 223

Calliope hummingbird, page 226

Rufous hummingbird, page 227

Ruby-crowned kinglet, page 235

Fox sparrow, page 261

Western tanager, page 263

Winter

Purple finch, page 214

Dark-eyed junco, page 233

Oregon junco, page 234

Golden-crowned sparrow, page 260

Widespread

These birds are seen year-round—in most cases—throughout the lower 48 states and across southern Canada.

Red-winged blackbird, page 188

American crow, page 208

Mourning dove, page 211

House finch, page 212

American goldfinch, page 216

Horned lark, page 237

Northern mockingbird, page 239

White-breasted nuthatch, page 243

American robin, page 252

Wild turkey, page 275

Yellow-rumped warbler, page 276

Downy woodpecker, page 278

Hairy woodpecker, page 278

White-breasted nuthatch

Red-Winged Blackbird *(Agelaius phoeniceus)*

- 7 to 9½ inches
- Straight, sharp bill
- Male: Glossy black; red shoulders lined with yellow (epaulettes) mostly visible when displaying
- Female: Striped brown
- Resident year-round: Throughout United States
- Spring into fall: Canada

These birds may swoop in *as a noisy flock, or you may notice a male perched alone singing and displaying his red shoulders to impress a female. If you encourage red-winged blackbirds to dine at your feeders, you may find yourself feeding dozens of them, so be ready. Offer cracked corn and mixed seed on a low tray at the edge of your yard to draw this crowd away from your sunflower-seed feeders, so other birds can have a chance.*

Natural Foods
- Insects
- Seeds
- Grains

Feeder Fill-Ups
- Mixed seed
- Sunflower seed
- Cracked corn
- Millet
- Milo
- Chicken scratch
- Raisins
- Apples
- Oranges
- Nuts
- Peanuts
- Suet
- Crushed cornflakes
- Cheerios
- Dog food

Favored Feeders
- Ground feeders

Attracting Red-Winged Blackbirds
- Gardens with plenty of insects (including pests such as Japanese beetles, beetle grubs, gypsy moths, and tent caterpillars)
- Harvested fields with corn and seed remaining
- Blackberries
- Raspberries
- Wineberries

Special Treats for Red-Winged Blackbirds
Serve up a breakfast bar for blackbirds. String Cheerios and apple chunks and drape them over the edge of low tray feeders. Add a small dish of dog food or chopped suet to complete the balanced meal.

Similar Species

Yellow-Headed Blackbird *(Xanthocephalus xanthocephalus)*

- 8 to 11 inches
- Black body
- Yellow head and chest
- White wing patch
- Spring into fall: Southern Canada, western United States, upper Mississippi Valley to northwest Mexico
- Winter: Southwestern United States and Mexico

This blackbird with the vibrant yellow head may be seen at feeders in the West.

Brewer's Blackbird *(Euphagus cyanocephalus)*

- 9 inches
- Straight, sharp bill
- Male: Black with purplish highlights on head and greenish highlights on body; distinctive pale yellow eye
- Female: Brownish gray body; dark eye
- Spring into fall: Canada and Northwest
- Winter: Midwestern United States and southwest into Mexico

Looking truly like a blackbird, this bird has purple and green highlights that glisten in the sun.

Eastern Bluebird *(Sialia sialis)*

Though not attracted *by a feeder full of seeds, these beautiful birds can become diners at your table. Tempt them with protein treats and fruits, and they will be return visitors.*

- 7 inches
- Orange throat and chest
- White belly
- Male: Bright blue head, back, tail
- Female: Duller, more brown than blue on back and head

- Resident year-round: Southeastern United States
- Spring into fall: Eastern North America, from southern Canada through Gulf States, southeast Arizona to Nicaragua
- Migrates: Southeastern United States

Natural Foods
- Insects: Beetles, crickets, grasshoppers, katydids
- Berries and fruit

Feeder Fill-Ups
- Mealworms
- Suet
- Raisins
- Peanut butter/cornmeal mix
- Baked goods
- Pine nuts
- Blueberries
- Bayberries
- Blackberries
- Raspberries

Favored Feeders
- Table feeders
- Roofed feeders (once the birds have become regulars)

Attracting Eastern Bluebirds
- Date palms
- Mountain ash
- Black gum
- Camphor trees
- Winterberry
- Virginia creeper
- Hollies
- Cedars
- Junipers
- Spicebush
- Mulberries
- Chokecherries
- Sumacs
- Dogwoods
- Elderberries
- Wax myrtles
- Flowering fuchsia
- Gooseberries
- Blackberries
- Raspberries
- Wineberries
- American bittersweet

Special Treats for Eastern Bluebirds
Got a fence post? Make it a No. 1 stop for hungry bluebirds. Rest a piece of plywood on top of the fence post and attach with screws or nail. Place a few shallow plastic containers or tuna-fish cans spaced apart on the board and nail securely. Then, serve up a buffet for bluebirds—mealworms in one container, raisins in another, a mix of peanut butter and cornmeal in a third. You can add berries or crumbled baked goods to change things up!

Western Bluebird *(Sialia mexicana)*

This western beauty *will also come to feeders for mealworms and berries, so keep them well filled and enjoy the view!*

- 7 inches
- Male: Deep blue head, throat, back, tail; chestnut breast; some chestnut across back; blue underneath
- Female: Duller, more gray/brown than blue on back and head; blue tail

- Spring into fall: Pacific Northwest, California coast, southwest down into Mexico
- Winter: In southern parts of range

Natural Foods
- Insects
- Fruits and berries

Feeder Fill-Ups
- Mealworms
- Raisins
- Peanut butter/cornmeal mix
- Baked goods
- Pine nuts
- Suet
- Blueberries
- Bayberries
- Blackberries
- Raspberries

Favored Feeders
- Tray and table feeders

Attracting Western Bluebirds

- Elderberries
- Chokecherries
- Grapes
- Redberry buckthorn
- Toyon
- Coffeeberry
- Mistletoe
- Hackberries

Special Treats for Western Bluebirds

Offer a bouquet of delights to your western bluebirds: Gather a few berry branches from your outlying bushes and tie them together with twine in a bouquet. Lay the berry bough bouquet on a tray feeder or hang it from a pole feeder to bring a bit of your berry hedge—and berry-loving bluebirds—to your feeding station.

Similar Species

Mountain Bluebird (Sialia currucoides)

- 7 inches
- Male: Bright blue on body, head, wings, and tail; slightly lighter below
- Female: Brown/blue; blue on rump, wings, tail; bluish-gray back
- Spring into fall: Western mountains from Mexico to Alaska
- Migrates: To southern areas of range

This is the bluebird that truly is blue, although it's lighter blue underneath. If you live in the western mountains, offer protein and fruit goodies to make this visitor happy.

Northern Bobwhite *(Colinus virginianus)*

Keep a lookout *at dawn and dusk for these quietly friendly birds, as they prefer to remain hidden during the day when predators may be about. These birds spend most of their time at ground level, so tempt them by scattering grain beneath your brush pile or bushes.*

- 9¾ to 10½ inches
- Round and plump
- Black-and-white breast
- Black-and-white connected by red-brown on sides, wings, and back
- Short gray tail
- Male: White throat and white brow stripes
- Female: Buff throat and buff brow stripes

- Resident year-round: Eastern United States from southwestern Maine west to South Dakota; eastern Washington, Wyoming, eastern Colorado, eastern New Mexico, eastern Mexico

Natural Foods
- Seeds
- Insects, including beetles and crickets
- Spiders

Feeder Fill-Ups
- Cracked corn
- Whole corn
- Chicken scratch
- Mixed seed
- Millet

- Black-oil sunflower seeds
- Milo
- Crumbled baked goods

Favored Feeders
- Tray feeders at ground level
- Ground, under bushes

Attracting Northern Bobwhites
- Brush pile
- White ash
- American beech
- Sandcherry
- Redbud

- Bittersweet
- Blackberries
- Mulberries
- American beautyberry
- Clover

- Alfalfa
- Lespedeza
- Amaranth
- Buckwheat
- Sorghum

Special Treats for Northern Bobwhites

Pass along the stale odds and ends of bran flakes and shredded wheat from your cereal cupboard to neighborhood bobwhites. Crush the cereal with a rolling pin and serve in a ground feeder. If the cereal attracts too many of the less desirable birds such as pigeons, house sparrows, and starlings, try spreading some cereal beneath a shrub or under an evergreen tree with low hanging branches to diminish its appeal to the pests.

Like other game birds, bobwhites are shy birds that prefer to take their meals in sheltered spots where they can feed out of the sight of creatures that might eat them. This means they are happiest dining low to the ground beneath tall groundcovers or bushes that give them cover while allowing room to move about. Also, like most game birds, foodwise bobwhites are easy to please: Scatter cracked corn or scratch grains (sold for feeding poultry) on the ground in a secluded area, and they will feast to their hearts' content.

Indigo Bunting *(Passerina cyanea)*

- 4½ to 5½ inches
- Conical bill
- Male: Deep blue, becomes more brown in winter
- Female: Plain brown with no obvious markings
- Spring into fall: Eastern United States
- Migrates: West Indies, Mexico, and Panama

These brilliant blue birds *(at least the males of the species) add color and song to your backyard. If you have shrubs and brush where they can hide from danger, and plants that produce abundant small seeds, indigo buntings will feel at home in your yard and may easily adopt your feeders.*

Natural Foods
- Insects
- Seeds

Feeder Fill-Ups
- Canary seed
- Mixed seeds
- Millet
- Chopped peanuts
- Nuts
- Rape seed
- Untreated grass seed
- Crushed cornflakes

Favored Feeders
- Low or ground tray feeders

Attracting Indigo Buntings
- Hedges, brush piles
- Blackberries
- Raspberries
- Wineberries
- Zinnias
- Marigolds
- Cosmos

- Mexican sunflower
- Purple coneflower
- Gloriosa daisy
- Pigweeds
- Ragweeds
- Lamb's quarters
- Chicory
- Filarees
- Chickweed
- Dandelions

Special Treats for Indigo Buntings
Plant a brilliant garden full of annuals that will produce small seeds for indigo buntings to devour. Include marigolds, zinnias, cosmos, and/or coreopsis. Let any stray dandelions grow undisturbed in the mix, as well. You will love the bright colors and your bunting friends will feast!

Similar Species

Lazuli Bunting *(Passerina amoena)*

- 4½ inches
- Conical bill
- Male: Blue head, back, wings, tail; white wing bars; chestnut breast
- Female: Brown; pale wing bars
- Spring into fall: Great Plains and southern Canada west and south to Baja California
- Migrates: Southeastern Arizona, Mexico

The western counterpart to the indigo bunting, the lazuli bunting can be tempted by similar feeder foods.

Painted Bunting *(Passerina ciris)*

- 5¼ inches
- Conical bill
- Male: Dark blue head and nape, green back, red rump and underparts, dark gray wings and tail
- Female: Plain greenish head, back, and tail; lighter green underparts
- Spring into fall: Southern central and eastern United States to northeastern Mexico
- Migrates: Into Panama

These stunning birds feast on seeds and insects in the wild and can be tempted to the feeder with bread crumbs, mixed seeds, peanut hearts, and cracked corn.

Northern Cardinal (Cardinalis cardinalis)

The dashing red plumage *of the male cardinal is a delight to any backyard birder. Cardinals are frequent feeder visitors, and you can easily tempt these lovely birds to brighten the scenery in your yard.*

- 7½ to 9 inches
- Heavy, conical orange bill
- Crest
- Male: Bright red with a distinctive black mask
- Female: Light grayish brown; red touches in wings, tail, and head
- Resident year-round: Eastern United States and southern Canada, Mexico

Natural Foods
- Weed seeds
- Leaf buds
- Almonds
- Fruits and berries
- Insects: Ants and beetles

Feeder Fill-Ups
- Safflower seeds
- Black-oil sunflower seeds
- Cracked corn
- White proso millet
- Nuts
- Peanut butter goodies
- Watermelon, cantaloupe seeds

Favored Feeders

- Ground feeders
- Tray feeders
- Hopper feeders with room to perch
- Hanging feeders with a bottom tray

Attracting Northern Cardinals

- White ash
- American elm
- Dogwoods
- Blackberries
- Wild grapes
- Hackberries
- Elderberries
- Grapes
- Mulberries
- Sumac
- Thicket of honeysuckle and brambles
- Evergreens for winter protection

Special Treats for Northern Cardinals

Plant sunflower seeds in your garden for cardinals to eat naturally as the seeds ripen. Try 'Russian Giant' for towering 12-foot stalks bearing flower heads up to 20 inches across, or the more demure 'Italian White', a 4-foot cultivar with multiple creamy white flowers on each plant.

Similar Species

Pyrrhuloxia *(Cardinalis sinuatus)*

- 7½ to 9 inches
- Curved, yellowish bill
- Both sexes have red crest
- Male: Gray wings, back, and sides with red mask, belly, and wingtips
- Female: Grayish brown with less red marking overall and no red mask
- Resident year-round: southern Arizona and New Mexico, southwestern Texas, northern Mexico

Looking like a gray cardinal, *the closely related pyrrhuloxia sports a red crest and mask. In the southwestern states and northern Mexico where they live, pyrrhuloxias feed mainly on seeds from weeds and grasses but will also take a meal at a feeder or on the ground below one, just as their cardinal relatives often do.*

Gray Catbird *(Dumetella carolinensis)*

You may hear *a resident catbird in the thickets or brambles before you see it or tempt it to your feeders. The catbird mimics many other birdcalls and regularly alerts you to its identity with its characteristic catlike mewing sound.*

- 9 inches
- Rich slate gray
- Black on head
- Black bill
- Russet under tail

- Spring into fall: Eastern United States and southern Canada, west to Utah and Texas, south to Gulf States, except for Florida
- Migrates: Eastern United States coast from Long Island south and into Mexico

Natural Foods
- Insects, including crickets, grasshoppers, beetles (especially Japanese beetles!)
- Some fruit

Feeder Fill-Ups
- Mealworms
- Suet
- Grapes
- Oranges
- Raisins
- Raspberries
- Blackberries
- Elderberries
- Currants
- Apples

Favored Feeders
- Ground feeders

Attracting Gray Catbirds

- Shrubs near deciduous trees
- Hedgerows, brambles, or brushy areas
- Water features
- Serviceberries
- Persimmons
- Black cherries
- Hawthorn
- Black gum
- Dogwoods
- Spicebush
- Sandcherries
- Winterberries
- Blackberries
- Mulberries
- Elderberries
- Huckleberries
- Bayberries
- Wax myrtle
- Virginia creeper
- Buckthorns
- Pokeberries
- Hollies
- Boston ivy
- Blueberries
- Honeysuckle
- Sumacs
- Cedars
- Junipers

Special Treats for Gray Catbirds

Unlike their feline namesakes, catbirds love water. Use an old frying pan or a plastic plant saucer with a stone in the middle to provide a perfect bathtub for this bird. Place it on or low to the ground near a thicket or brambles where catbirds hang out for the best chance of catching sight of a catbird happily splashing as it bathes.

Catbirds will show little interest in seed feeders but may be attracted to visit offerings of fruity treats of the sort that also draw the attention of orioles and mockingbirds. A cup of jelly or an orange half on a skewer may bring these rather secretive birds to a feeder. A tray feeder with chopped apples, berries, grapes, raisins, and/or crumbled suet will also tempt catbirds, as long as the feeder hasn't already been claimed by noisy jays or a territorial mockingbird.

Black-Capped Chickadee *(Poecile atricapillus)*

- 4¾ to 5¾ inches
- Plump
- Small-billed
- Black cap and bib
- White cheeks
- Buff sides
- Gray wings
- White patches in wings
- Resident year-round: Parts of Alaska, southern Canada, northern United States

Perky, jaunty, cute, cheery . . . *all words that describe chickadees to a T! These common feeder birds are friendly residents and stay busy at backyard feeders in their locales.*

Natural Foods

- Winter
  - Seeds and berries
  - Insects
  - Spiders
  - Suet
- Spring, summer, and fall
  - 80 to 90 percent insects and spiders

Feeder Fill-Ups

- Suet
- Mealworms
- Sunflower seeds

- Peanut hearts
- Shelled peanuts
- Peanut butter mixed with seeds
- Safflower seeds
- Pine nuts
- Acorns
- Almonds
- Doughnuts
- Raw hamburger

Favored Feeders

- Globe feeders
- Tube feeders
- Window feeders
- Suet feeders

Attracting Black-Capped Chickadees

- Pines
- Virginia creeper
- Blackberries
- Raspberries
- Wineberries
- Tickseed sunflower
- Annual sunflowers
- Zinnias

Special Treats for Black-Capped Chickadees

With a bit of patience and stillness, you may tempt a chickadee to eat out of your hand. Try sitting comfortably outdoors in the same place at the same time every day for several days in a row, your hands resting palm up on your knees and full of black-oil sunflower seeds.

Similar Species

Depending on your location, you may see other chickadee species in your backyard. They can be tempted by the same kinds of foods as those enjoyed by black-capped chickadees.

Carolina Chickadee (Poecile carolinensis)

- 4½ inches
- Almost identical to black-capped chickadee, except for size and absence of white wing patches
- Resident year-round: Southeastern United States through northern Florida, west to parts of Texas, north to southern Illinois, Indiana, Ohio, and Pennsylvania
- Range overlaps with black-capped chickadee

Chickadees are great birds for window feeders. Purchase a small lightweight plastic feeder, a lightweight bracket, and suction cups at your local hardware store or bird-feeder supply store, and hang a small feeder at your window. You will be amazed by how close you will be to these busy birds.

Mountain Chickadee (Poecile gambeli)

- 5¼ inches
- Similar to black-capped chickadee except white eyebrow through its black cap makes it appear masked; gray underside
- Western mountains from Canada through western United States

Water can be a great attraction for chickadees and other birds. Chickadees will happily use a hanging water source. The swaying doesn't deter them at all.

Boreal Chickadee *(Poecile hudsonica)*

- 5 to 5½ inches
- Similar to other chickadees but with brownish cap, black bib, brown back, ruddy flanks
- Resident year-round: Throughout northern boreal forests, Canada, and a few areas in northernmost United States

In their northern forest homelands, *these birds feast upon tree seeds, but if you are lucky enough to live near them, you can bring them to your feeders with suet, seeds, and baked goodies.*

Chestnut-Backed Chickadee *(Poecile rufescens)*

- 4½ to 5 inches
- Similar to other chickadees but with rich chestnut back, flanks either brown or gray
- Resident year-round: United States West Coast, Pacific Northwest into Canada

These friendly chickadees *will often figure out your feeder schedule and wait for you, following you encouragingly as you restock their feeders.*

Brown Creeper *(Certhia americana)*

- 5 inches
- Slim
- Brown above
- White below
- Slightly downward curved, slender bill
- Stiff tail, braced when climbing
- Resident year-round: Southern Canada, New England, around Great Lakes; Alaska down through most western states into Mexico
- Migrates: Throughout United States

You'll need sharp eyes *to spot this well-camouflaged bird. The brown creeper's dark brown back blends in with the bark of the trees it frequents. It feeds by spiraling up the trunk of a tree, searching for insects in the bark.*

Natural Foods
- Insects (from bark crevices)
- Insect and spider eggs and larvae

Feeder Fill-Ups
- Suet
- Chopped peanuts
- Peanut butter

Favored Feeders
- Hanging feeders
- Suet feeders

Attracting Brown Creepers
- Pines
- Rough-barked trees

Special Treats for Brown Creepers
Bring brown creepers to your backyard trees for easy viewing. Mix equal parts peanut butter and cornmeal. Spread the mixture in gaps in the bark on your trees and watch these birds feast. Or attach a suet feeder to the side of a tree to make it easy for these birds to stay camouflaged against the bark but still get a fatty treat.

Red Crossbill *(Loxia curvirostra)*

The tips of this bird's bill *cross each other, giving the species its name. A crossbill will voraciously attack pinecones for the seeds, sticking its bill into the cone, opening it, and extracting the seeds with its tongue. Crossbills may dangle like parrots when feeding.*

- 5¼ to 6½ inches
- Upper and lower bill crossed at tip
- Notched, short tail
- Long pointed wings
- Male: Dull red; brighter red rump, with blackish wings and tail
- Female: Olive with dark wings and tail
- Newfoundland to northeastern Pennsylvania, west to Alaska, south through western mountains into South America
- Migrates: Unevenly through much of United States, particularly if northern tree seeds are scarce

Natural Foods
- Tree seeds
- Weed seeds
- Insects
- Buds

Feeder Fill-Ups
- Pine nuts
- Sunflower seeds
- Conifer cones

Favored Feeders
- Tray feeders

Attracting Red Crossbills

- Hemlock
- Spruces
- Pines
- Birches
- Balsam

- Larch
- Willows
- Poplars
- Maples
- Beech

- Elms
- Huckleberries
- Ragweeds

Similar Species

White-Winged Crossbill (*Loxia leucoptera*)

- 6 to 6¾ inches
- Two white wing bars
- Male: Dull rose with black wings and tail
- Female: Olive-gray
- Resident year-round: Canada, northern New England, and Great Lakes
- Winter: Northern United States and as far south as West Virginia, Kansas. and northern New Mexico

These northern birds *can be regulars in your backyard if you live in their environs. Offer them water in winter when natural water sources may freeze over.*

Special Treats for Red Crossbills

Provide much-needed minerals for crossbills and other birds: Place a salt block and a dish of crushed oyster or clam shells (for calcium) on a stump or rock near your feeding areas.

American Crow *(Corvus brachyrhynchos)*

- 17 to 21 inches
- Long, strong bill
- All-over black, including bill and feet
- Breeds: Canada to southern United States
- Northern populations may migrate
- Resident year-round: Across nearly all of the United States
- Short tail, broad wings with feather "fingertips," and steady flapping flight distinguish crows from other large birds in the air

These intelligent birds *often flock together, and a group of them can create quite a ruckus in a home landscape. People may find crows' loud and persistent cawing annoying, but the uproar often serves as an early warning system for other birds in the area. Sharp-eyed crows are quick to sound the alarm whenever they spot a potential threat such as a prowling cat. Crows also will harass birds of prey that soar too close to where crows are nesting and roosting.*

Natural Foods
- Grains
- Insects
- Carrion
- Small reptiles
- Garbage

Feeder Fill-Ups
- Bones with marrow and meat
- Baked goods

- Dog food
- Eggs, raw or cooked
- Leftovers
- Meat scraps
- Cooked pasta
- Suet
- Corn

Favored Feeders
- On the ground
- Low tray feeders

Attracting American Crows
- Strawberries
- Sumacs
- Blackberries
- Raspberries
- Wineberries
- Bayberries
- Wax myrtles

Special Treats for American Crows

Set up a smorgasbord from your leftovers for these hungry birds. They will eat practically anything from your kitchen (or Fido's bowl), so be creative. Someone didn't finish his eggs and bacon? Set them out on a low tray feeder for a brunch treat. Leftover spaghetti? Toss it with vegetable oil, add a bit of hamburger if you have some, and you can have a great time watching the crows slurp up the long strands.

Though they will feed side by side with songbirds, crows are big eaters—and opportunistic nest raiders—and their presence may discourage smaller birds from visiting your feeders. You may want to set up a ground feeding area off to the side for crows, and keep it stocked with leftovers and meaty treats to entice them.

Similar Species

Fish Crow *(Corvus ossifragus)*

- 16 to 20 inches
- Black, including feet and bill
- Long, strong bill
- Coastal: Southern New England to Florida, eastern Texas
- Resident year-round: Coastal areas from southern New England to Florida and Gulf Coast to eastern Texas; moving inland along rivers especially in urban areas

The sometimes smaller fish crow *is almost identical to the American crow in appearance, although its wings and tail may appear a bit longer. Identify this species by its different voice—a nasal-sounding "car" instead of a true "caw."*

Common Raven *(Corvus corax)*

- 22 to 27 inches
- Black
- Large head
- Heavy bill
- Shaggy feathers at throat
- Wedge-shaped tail
- Resident year-round: Alaska and throughout Canada and western United States; visits eastern United States irregularly
- Voice is a harsh, almost guttural croak

Though often maligned *as dangerous to young or otherwise weak farm animals, these large black birds also help out by dining voraciously on pesky rodents.*

The View from Deb's Window

It's a pretty safe bet that the only ravens I ever encountered near my home in southeastern Pennsylvania were a resident pair at the small zoo housed in our local game preserve. Crows are plentiful here, but ravens rarely turn up this far to the east and south of their normal range. But I did have a memorable encounter with ravens while on a trip "across the pond." Touring the Tower of London, one gets to see the Tower Ravens, a cadre of these large black birds that live on the Tower grounds and are tended by the Ravenmaster, a specially appointed Beefeater. At least six common ravens, the same species as ravens found in North America, are kept at the Tower at all times. Legend has it that if the ravens leave, the Great White Tower will crumble and disaster will befall England. Whether that's true or not, it is both fascinating and a little scary to be close to these imposing and powerful birds.

Mourning Dove *(Zenaida macroura)*

- 9 to 13 inches
- Gray/brown
- Slim with small head
- Pointed tail edged in white
- Resident year-round: Entire United States and into Mexico
- Summer breeding into central Canada
- Some birds do migrate and may winter as far south as Central America.

You won't find it difficult to attract mourning doves to your backyard. These mild-mannered birds are veritable chowhounds that may eat the equivalent of up to 20 percent of their body weight each day! A mourning dove fills its crop (an enlargement of its esophagus) with thousands of seeds and then flies to a more protected spot to digest its meal away from neighborhood pets and other predators.

Natural Foods
- Weed seeds
- Grains from cultivated fields
- Beechnuts
- Small acorns

Feeder Fill-Ups
- Nyjer seed
- Millet
- Cracked corn

- Hulled sunflower seeds
- Buckwheat kernels
- Breadcrumbs
- Crushed cereal—bran flakes, cornflakes, shredded wheat

Favored Feeders
- Tray feeders on the ground
- Low table feeders

- Open feeders with perches

Attracting Mourning Doves
- Allow some areas of weeds and grass to go to seed
- Violets
- Mexican sunflowers

Special Treats for Mourning Doves

Provide water and grit alongside seeds, and your backyard can be a mourning dove paradise. Fill a pie plate with coarse sand, crushed eggshells, small washed gravel, or crushed oyster shells to provide the grit the birds need to digest seed. If you provide a protected, low birdbath with a few inches of water, you can enjoy watching these birds drink. They don't fill their bills with water and tip their heads back to drink like most other birds do. Instead, a dove will simply lower its head into the water and suck up the good stuff!

House Finch *(Carpodacus mexicanus)*

- 5 to 5¾ inches
- Short wings
- Slightly flat head
- Male: Bright red on chest, head, rump; brown streaks on sides and lower chest; brown back, wings, tail
- Female: Lightly striped brown; no markings on face
- Resident year-round: Western United States to southern Mexico, eastern United States, Hawaii
- Once-discreet house finch populations in the western and eastern United States are gradually expanding their ranges into the middle states.

Originally from the West, these birds are now friendly feeder birds all over the United States. House finches were illegally introduced in New York City in the 1940s as cage birds but were released into the wild. They have been quite successful in the East, feeding side by side with purple finches, goldfinches, sparrows, and other backyard birds. They can be considered pests, cleaning out gardens and orchards and competing for nesting spots. However, they also consume many weed seeds, are colorful, and have a lovely song.

Natural Foods
- Seeds
- Fruits
- Insects

Feeder Fill-Ups
- Sunflower seeds, especially black-oil
- Millet
- Cracked corn
- Milo
- Fruits
- Bread
- Peanuts
- Suet
- Crushed eggshells
- Salt
- Nectar
- Nyjer

Favored Feeders
- Hopper feeders
- Tray feeders
- Hanging feeders
- Ground feeders
- Tube feeders

Attracting House Finches

- Cherries
- Peaches
- Pears
- Plums
- Strawberries
- Blackberries

- Figs
- Thistle
- Mulberry
- Cactus
- Dandelions
- Tickseed sunflowers

- Cosmos
- Zinnias
- Purple coneflowers
- Gloriosa daisy

Pay Special Attention

If your feeders are being visited by large flocks of house finches, you may notice some birds with swollen, crusty, or reddened eyes. Once widespread in Eastern house finch populations, mycoplasmal conjunctivitis still affects as much as 10 percent of all Eastern house finches. Ten years after house finch eye disease reached epidemic levels among eastern birds, an outbreak occurred in Western house finches in the Pacific Northwest.

An infected bird's eyes may swell or crust over to the point that the bird can't see, interfering with its ability to find food and shelter and to escape predators. These factors, more than the disease itself, contribute to most bird deaths from the eye infection. While mycoplasmal conjunctivitis mainly affects house finches, infections have been reported in other members of the finch family, including purple finches, goldfinches, and grosbeaks.

Although house finch eye disease is far less prevalent than the epidemic levels it reached in years past, it remains a threat to the health of birds at feeders throughout North America. Because house finches travel together in large, mobile flocks, infected birds may come in contact with many other birds and visit multiple feeding stations. In the eastern states, particularly, house finches lack genetic diversity and thus may be more susceptible to this bacterial infection than their western counterparts.

Keeping feeders clean is a key element of limiting the spread of house finch eye disease. Even when no infected birds are present, regularly cleaning feeders with a mild bleach solution is a recommended preventive measure. You can also contribute to scientists' understanding of the spread of this disease by reporting sightings of birds with symptoms to the House Finch Disease Survey at the Cornell University Laboratory of Ornithology. To learn more about the survey and to sign up to participate, visit www.birds.cornell.edu/hofi/ or call 800-843-BIRD.

Purple Finch *(Carpodacus purpureus)*

The male of this species *is a lovely raspberry wine color. Its lower belly is pale, but any streaks on its breast are reddish, not brown as in the similar house finch. You'll also note that the male house finch has more brown coloring overall, with its bright cherry red coloring mainly on its head, back, and breast.*

- 5½ to 6 inches
- Male: Rose red, bright on rump and head
- Female: Brown, heavily striped; dark jaw and ear stripes; light eye stripe
- Resident year-round: Northeastern United States and Great Lakes, Pacific Northwest, and California
- Spring into fall: Canada through the Pacific Northwest, California; mountains of West Virginia
- Winter: Eastern United States

Natural Foods

- Seeds
- Buds
- Fruits
- Insects

Feeder Fill-Ups

- Sunflower seeds
- Bread crumbs

- Crushed eggshells
- Nyjer
- Salt
- Millet

Favored Feeders

- Platform feeder on a tall pole
- Tube feeders

- Hopper feeders
- Tray feeders
- Hanging feeders
- Ground feeders

Attracting Purple Finches

- Ash
- Elms
- Birch
- Beeches
- Box elders
- Balsam
- Spruce

- Honeysuckle
- Butternut
- Cotoneaster
- Snowberries
- Wild grapes
- Junipers
- Pines

- Tickseed sunflower
- Cosmos
- Zinnias
- Purple coneflowers
- Gloriosa daisy

Special Treats for Purple Finches

Serve a mix made just for finches in tube feeders with small perches to keep the larger birds at bay. Finch mixes may include black-oil sunflower, millet, and nyjer seeds. Add some canary seed and flaxseed for extra finch appeal!

In addition to purple finches, American goldfinches and house finches will enjoy a feeder that holds a customized finch mix. In the West, rosy Cassin's finches will join the throng seeking nyjer and black-oil sunflower seeds.

Sorting out the rosy finches—house, purple, and Cassin's—at your feeders can be quite a challenge, particularly where these species overlap. While eastern bird feeders are likely to host both house finches and purple finches, all three species may share space at feeders in parts of the western United States. While the males are more useful in distinguishing one species from another, it's still not easy. The females of all three are brown, streaky birds of about the same size. Male purple finches are the most extensively rosy-purple; house finches tend toward orange-red hues and have the least rosy coloring overall. The western Cassin's finch has a noticeable bright red crown and a pinkish tint overall.

American Goldfinch (Spinus tristis)

Goldfinches are one of *the most colorful reasons to fill your feeders all summer. Although they are rather drab in their yellow-olive plumage in winter months, the male goldfinch seems to spontaneously burst into glorious yellow garb in summer. Besides being easy to tempt to feeders, goldfinches are easy to identify, even at a distance. Their characteristic undulating flight gives them away, even when they're not dressed in their bright yellow breeding plumage.*

- 5 inches
- Black wings and tail
- Conical, heavy bills
- Male: Breeding/summer plumage is brilliant yellow with black forehead; winter plumage is dull yellow/olive

- Female: Dull yellow/olive
- Year-round resident: Central United States, Mid-Atlantic, and much of Northeast and Pacific Northwest
- Spring into fall: Northern United States and southern Canada
- Winter: Southern United States and Mexico

Natural Foods

- Deciduous tree seeds
- Grass seeds
- Flower seeds
- Berries

Feeder Fill-Ups

- Nyjer
- Black-oil sunflower seeds

- Chopped peanuts
- Millet
- Flax seed
- Canary seed
- Salt
- Rapeseed

Favored Feeders

- Tube feeders
- Upside-down-feeding tube feeders (discourage house finches)
- Hopper feeders
- Tray feeders

Attracting American Goldfinches

- Pines
- Dandelion
- Pigweed
- Star thistles
- Lamb's quarters
- Filarees

- Chickweed
- Asters
- Bachelor's buttons
- Coreopsis
- Coneflowers
- Cosmos

- Zinnia
- Milkweed
- Joe-pye weed
- Black-eyed Susan

Special Treats for American Goldfinches

Grow a garden filled with late summer- and fall-blooming perennials, and you will enjoy the company of goldfinches even when your feeders are empty. Goldfinches are seed-eaters supreme—they are one of the very few songbird species that feeds seeds to their young—and they naturally seek out a varied diet of seeds from trees, grasses, weeds, and flowers. While they appreciate a feeder filled with nyjer or black-oil sunflower, they will be among the birds that glean seeds from the many perennials that bloom in summer and fall.

Place a finch-friendly tube feeder in the midst of perennials such as purple coneflowers (*Echinacea* spp.), black-eyed Susans (*Rudbeckia* spp.), joe-pye weeds (*Eupatorium* spp.), asters (*Symphytotrichum* spp.), butterflyweed (*Asclepias tuberosa*), and goldenrods (*Solidago* spp.). You'll enjoy colorful flowers into the fall while providing an ongoing treat for these lovely birds. As the flowers go to seed, the goldfinches will perch on the flower heads and pick off the seeds with great enthusiasm. Inevitably, a few seeds will escape the birds' beaks and become the source for next year's crop—more flowers for you and more seeds for the goldfinches, without any extra effort or expense on your part.

In addition to feasting on the seeds of many perennials and grasses, goldfinches use seed fibers from milkweeds, dandelions, and bluestars (*Amsonia* spp.) in building their nests. A diverse planting of perennials will offer them plenty to eat and help with housing, too.

Common Grackle *(Quiscalus quiscula)*

- 11 to 13½ inches
- Iridescent black
- Purplish highlights on head
- Bronze or purple highlights on back
- Yellow eyes
- Long, wedge-shaped tail (keel shaped like the V at the bottom of a boat)
- Year-round resident: Canada, United States east of the Rockies

Grackles walk along *the ground and can stroll right into your feeding area and disrupt your other diners. If grackles become too aggressive at your feeders, squirt them with a water pistol to discourage them. These strutting birds can be fun to watch, but their croaking, squeaky vocalizations are decidedly nonmusical.*

Natural Foods

- Insects
- Fruits
- Field grains
- Weed seeds
- House sparrows
- Mice

Feeder Fill-Ups

- Corn
- Suet
- Acorns
- Beechnuts
- Sunflower seeds
- Bread crumbs
- Apples
- Bayberries
- Grapes
- Leftovers
- Vegetable scraps
- Meat scraps
- Chopped suet
- Millet
- Cooked pasta

Favored Feeders

- Ground
- Low tray feeders

Attracting Common Grackles

- Oak trees
- American beech
- Cabbage palmetto
- Grain
- Mulberries
- Blackberries
- Raspberries
- Wineberries
- Grapes
- Bayberries

Special Treats for Common Grackles

It may seem a bit unusual, but grackles love cat food. Put out a dish of dry cat food on the ground near your feeders for them. Or, if you're trying to minimize their pushy behavior at your feeders, place the cat food at the far reaches of your yard, so you can enjoy the bossy grackles without encouraging them to overtake your entire buffet

Grackles are among the birds that take advantage of suburban lawns, hunting in the grass for grubs, beetles, caterpillars, and other live prey. Grackles are big enough to dine on vertebrates as well; and their diets may include mice, salamanders, frogs, and even other birds.

Similar Species

Boat-Tailed Grackle *(Quiscalus major)*

- Male: 16½ inches
- Female: 13 inches
- Yellow eyes
- Very long, keeled tail
- Male: Iridescent black
- Female: Soft brown to gray brown
- Resident year-round: Atlantic and Gulf Coasts from New Jersey to central Texas

This bird is larger than the common grackle, and its tail is much longer. It can often be seen along the coasts acting like a shorebird in the surf. Boat-tailed grackles on the Gulf Coast have dark eyes rather than yellow. This helps birders distinguish them from the similar but larger yellow-eyed great-tailed grackle, which shares its range with boat-tailed grackles along the Gulf of Mexico.

Evening Grosbeak (Coccothraustes vespertinus)

- 8 inches
- Stocky
- Large, conical, pale bill
- Black wings with large, white wing patches
- Male: Dull yellow, dark head, yellow eyebrow stripe
- Female: Silvery gray with some yellow, white, and black
- Resident year-round: Southern Canada, New England, portions of western United States
- Winter resident: United States except southern Gulf States and Florida; Mexico

A member of the finch family, this large yellow, black, and white bird looks like a larger version of the American goldfinch. The evening grosbeak is mostly a bird of the North, but irruptions bring it to many areas of the United States, albeit somewhat randomly.

Natural Foods
- Buds
- Fruits
- Seeds
- Insects

Feeder Fill-Ups
- Sunflower seeds, especially black oil
- Safflower seeds
- Cracked corn
- Peanut hearts or pieces

Favored Feeders
- High tray feeders
- Hanging feeders with large perches

Attracting Evening Grosbeaks
- Box elders
- Cottonwoods
- Catalpas
- White and green ash
- Elm
- Beech
- Maple
- Sweetgum
- Spruce
- Dogwood
- Sumac
- Honeysuckle
- Elderberries
- Serviceberry

Special Treats for Evening Grosbeaks
Never throw away a cherry pit again. As you devour cherries in season, wash and dry the pits and store them in the freezer. Throughout your bird-feeding season, offer these treats to the evening grosbeaks, who love them! These birds will also partake of rock salt offered on a tray feeder or in a dish.

Similar Species

Pine Grosbeak (*Pinicola enucleator*)

- 9¾ inches
- Heavy bill
- Reddish
- Dark wings
- White wing bars
- Spring into fall: Alaska, northwestern Canada, and parts of northern United States
- Winter: Northern United States to Kansas and Kentucky

The pine grosbeak looks like a large purple finch—and is one. Unlike its smaller finch relatives, the pine grosbeak is not a regular at feeders but can be tempted to a yard planted with such favorites as conifers, crabapples, sumac, mountain ashes, maples, willows, ashes, elms, blackberries, and grapes. Within its normal range, it may occasionally visit feeders for sunflower seeds; water is also attractive to these birds.

Rose-Breasted Grosbeak *(Pheucticus ludovicianus)*

- 7 to 8½ inches
- Heavy bill
- Male: Black head, back, tail, and wings; white tail patch and wing bars
- Female: Brown, heavily streaked; white wing bars; striped crown; white eyebrow stripe; yellow under wings
- Spring into fall: Central Canada south to Plains States, northeast south to Georgia and Appalachia
- Winter: Mexico, Central America, South America

The name says it all—a bird with a brilliant red breast and a big bill perfectly designed for cracking open its food. The male is easily identified when he visits, but the females may be deceptively dull and not easily spotted amid similarly colored finches and sparrows.

Natural Foods
- Insects
- Seeds
- Fruits

Feeder Fill-Ups
- Sunflower seeds
- Acorns
- Cherries
- Corn
- Crackers
- Figs

Favored Feeders
- Tray feeders
- Hopper feeders
- Tube feeders with perches
- Ground feeders
- High feeders

Attracting Rose-Breasted Grosbeaks
- Beeches
- Redbud
- Cedars
- Junipers
- Dogwood
- Sumac
- Virginia creeper
- Wheat
- Strawberries
- Cherries
- Mulberries
- Bramble fruits
- Elderberries
- Grapes

Special Treats for Rose-Breasted Grosbeaks

When grosbeaks swoop down on your feeder, you'll need all the sunflower seeds you can provide. Raid your recycling bin and thoroughly wash out large plastic soda bottles or milk cartons. A few inches up from the bottom of each, cut out a large opening with a utility knife. Fill the bottom of your impromptu feeder with sunflower seeds and hang it from a branch or feeder pole to feed the masses!

Similar Species

Black-Headed Grosbeak (*Pheucticus melanocephalus*)

- 6½ to 7¾ inches
- Heavy bill
- Male: Black head; black and white wings; orange-brown chest, sides, and tail patch
- Female: Brown, heavily streaked; yellow-brown, unstreaked chest
- Spring into fall: Southwest Canada, western United States, and Mexico
- Winter: Mexico

The black-headed grosbeak is built very much like the rose-breasted, but it is more orange-brown than rose colored on its breast. It is mostly a western bird but occasionally will find its way to eastern feeders. Add some bread to your tray feeders in addition to sunflower seeds to make this lovely bird feel at home.

Blue Grosbeak (*Passerina caerulea*)

- Silvery, heavy bill
- Male: Deep blue; broad rusty wing bars
- Female: Light brown, lighter below; light blue in rump; buff wing bars
- Spring into fall: Southern United States, from California to New Jersey and down to Florida; Mexico
- Winter: Arizona, Mexico, Panama

The blue grosbeak may visit feeders in the southern states. Sunflower seeds and berries are a welcoming treat for this rather stocky songbird.

Ruby-Throated Hummingbird (*Archilochus colubris*)

- 3 to 3¾ inches
- Needlelike bill
- Iridescent green back and head
- Dull white breast
- Greenish gray underneath
- Males: Ruby red throat feathers (gorget), dark green and black tail, black patch below each eye
- Female: Light-colored throat, green tail with black tips
- Spring into fall: Eastern United States
- Migrates: Mexico and Central America

Fast and furious feeders, these tiny birds are a treat to watch. Their wings move so quickly that they appear blurred. They visit nectar feeders and flowers of trees, shrubs, vines, annuals, and perennials.

Natural Foods

- Nectar
- Sap
- Tiny insects or spiders

Feeder Fill-Ups

- Sugar water: Mix 4 parts water to 1 part sugar. Boil mixture and let cool. Fill clean nectar feeders.

Favored Feeders

- Nectar feeders with some red parts to attract the birds (add a bit of red ribbon if you like!)
- Consider these things when choosing feeders:
    - Easy to clean—simply shaped, easy to take apart and reassemble
    - Made of thick plastic (glass is breakable)
    - Flat feeder ports (easier to clean than cute flower-shaped ports)
    - Ant guards (though tolerant of many things, hummers don't like ants!)
- Mount securely, but so they're easy to take down for cleaning
- Hang several feeders, as male birds are quite territorial

Attracting Ruby-Throated Hummingbirds

FLOWERS
- Asters
- Bee balms
- Cardinal flowers
- Columbines
- Delphiniums
- Fuchsias
- Gladiolas
- Goldenrods
- Larkspurs
- Lupines
- Mexican sunflowers
- Petunias
- Phlox
- Salvias
- Snapdragons
- Zinnias

VINES
- Trumpet honeysuckle
- Trumpet vine
- Cypress vine

SHRUBS
- Azaleas
- Chinaberry
- Flowering quince
- Honeysuckles
- Viburnums
- Flowering currant
- Butterfly bush
- Fire bush
- Hibiscus

TREES
- Red buckeye
- Tulip poplar
- Desert willow
- Mimosa

A Note from Arlene

HUMMINGBIRDS NEAR AND FAR

More than practically any other kind of wild bird, hummingbirds are responsible for inspiring even the most sofa-bound couch potatoes to get up and take a look at what nature has to offer. Even people who are uninterested in other wild birds are captivated by hummingbirds, drawn by their small size, their quickness, and the fact that they're not very wary of being around humans. There are more than 325 hummingbird species in the world, all in the Americas. While there are hummingbird species that may be seen as far north as Alaska and as far south as Chile, the greatest number of species are found in the middle, close to the equator.

I became fascinated with hummingbirds early in my birding career. I love to garden, so it just seemed logical to plant new and different kinds of flowers full of nectar to attract them to my property. The only hummingbird that breeds in the eastern part of North America is the ruby-throated, so eventually I traveled west and south and saw another 15 species. Then my quest to see more of them took me to Central and South America, where many are brilliantly colored and have tufted head feathers or extremely long tails. But no matter if you just watch the antics of a ruby-throated hummingbird in your backyard or travel great distances to walk through rain forests to see these tiny birds, they truly are amazing little creatures.

Similar Species

Though there is only one hummingbird species that regularly is seen in the eastern United States, the western states play host to many more lovely hummingbirds. Here are a few of the more common birds that may zip around your hummingbird-friendly yard in the West. Compared to male hummingbirds, the females of the various species are nondescript and are best identified by range, rather than by markings.

Allen's Hummingbird *(Selasphorus sasin)*

- 3½ inches
- Male: Green head and back; scarlet-orange gorget; rufous on tail and along sides of front; dark bill
- Female: Very similar to female rufous; nondescript, with faint rufous color on tops of tail feathers and above eyes; rufous sides and under tail; pale, speckled gorget with faint reddish central spot
- Spring into fall: Pacific coastline from Oregon through southern California
- Migrates: South-central Mexico

Although the Allen's hummingbird looks very similar to the rufous hummingbird, it is not nearly so wide-ranging, nesting only along the coast of California and southernmost Oregon.

Anna's Hummingbird *(Calypte anna)*

- 3½ to 4 inches
- A bit stocky-looking
- Male: Coppery red gorget, forehead, around eyes; blue to bluish green back; deeply notched tail; black bill; gray front
- Female: Similar appearance to female ruby-throated; light-colored throat, very lightly speckled with small red spot; green tail with black tips
- Resident year-round: California coast
- Winter: Coastal British Columbia to northern Mexico

Anna's hummingbirds are a familiar sight at feeders and flowers all along the Pacific Coast, from Canada to the Baja Peninsula and northern Mexico.

Broad-Tailed Hummingbird *(Selasphorus platycercus)*

- 3¾ to 4¼ inches
- Male: Green back and head, white breast, rufous coloring at base of long tail, gorget dark pink to rose red
- Female: Similar to male, except rusty sides and under tail, gorget pale with rusty brown speckles
- Central Idaho through Central America
- Summer: Rocky Mountains and high elevations from central Idaho to Southern California, Arizona, and New Mexico
- Resident year-round: mountains and high elevations in Mexico and Central America

By slowing their metabolic rate and entering a state of torpor, broad-tailed hummingbirds can withstand the cold nighttime temperatures that are common in the mountainous areas where they nest.

Calliope Hummingbird *(Stellula calliope)*

- 3½ inches
- Male: Gorget is long, skinny, with wine-red to reddish purple stripes on white background; green back; white front with green along sides; rufous feathers at base of tail; short, dark bill
- Female: Similar coloring to broad-tailed female; green back and head; pale, buffy breast and sides; pale, lightly speckled gorget
- Spring into fall: Pacific Northwest
- Migrates: Southwestern Mexico

The Calliope hummingbird is the world's smallest long-distance migratory bird and the smallest bird in the United States.

Costa's Hummingbird *(Calypte costae)*

- 3 to 3½ inches
- Slightly down-curved, dark bill
- Male: Purple violet gorget, long colored feathers down sides, white feathers under eyes, white breast, gray belly, deep-green back
- Female: Similar appearance to female ruby-throated; pale, unmarked chest and belly; green tail with black tips
- Resident year-round: Southern California, New Mexico, Arizona
- Breeds: Desert areas of California and Arizona

The handsome Costa's hummingbird *ranges over the arid Southwest, nesting in the Mojave and Sonoran Deserts.*

Rufous Hummingbird *(Selasphorus rufus)*

- 3½ to 4 inches
- Male: Orange head, back, tail, and sides; white belly; top of head green
- Female: Nondescript, with faint rufous color on tops of tail feathers and above eyes; rufous sides and under tail; pale, speckled gorget with faint reddish central spot
- Spring into fall: Pacific Northwest into southern Alaska
- Migrates through western mountains to southern Mexico

Starting in late winter, *rufous hummingbirds begin their long journey to the northernmost breeding grounds of any hummingbird species. Increasingly, during their migrations in early spring and late summer, these feisty hummers are being spotted at nectar feeders in the eastern United States.*

Blue Jay *(Cyanocitta cristata)*

- 11 to 12½ inches
- Blue crest
- White face
- Large bill
- Blue back and tail
- Blue wings with white
- White and gray underneath
- Black "necklace" marking
- Resident year-round: Eastern United States south to Gulf of Mexico
- Some short migration

Strikingly marked and brightly colored, the blue jay is a beautiful addition to your yard. However, the blue jay can be a noisy, pesky diner. Jays will swoop into a feeding area, push other birds out of the way, and clean fare out quickly, eating on the spot and hoarding food for later dining.

Natural Foods
- Acorns
- Other nuts
- Fruits
- Insects—Beetles, tent caterpillars, gypsy moth caterpillars, grasshoppers
- Spiders
- Birds' eggs or nestlings

Feeder Fill-Ups
- Sunflower seeds
- Peanuts
- Acorns
- Hazelnuts
- Fruits and berries
- Cracked corn
- Peanut butter
- Suet
- Crumbled bread
- Meat scraps
- Hard-boiled or scrambled eggs
- Mealworms
- Cheerios
- Cornflakes; crisped rice mixed in peanut butter or in suet
- Fruit/nut cereals
- Cooked pasta

Favored Feeders
- Ground feeders
- Tray feeders

Attracting Blue Jays

- Oaks
- Hazel
- Manzanitas
- Hackberries
- Pines

- Wild grapes
- Hollies
- Elderberries
- Blackberries
- Raspberries

- Wineberries
- Sumacs
- Viburnums

Special Treats for Blue Jays

As the fall harvest offers up lovely orange pumpkins for pies and Halloween jack o' lanterns, prepare a special treat for the blue jays in your yard. Simply separate the pumpkin seeds from the pumpkin pulp, rinse and dry them, and offer them on a tray feeder. The large seeds are just right for these birds—big in size and personality.

If you have a lot of pumpkin or winter squash seeds all at once, clean them and then dry them thoroughly in your oven or in a food dehydrator. Store the dried seeds in an airtight container for serving to jays and other large seed lovers over the winter months.

Similar Species

Steller's Jay (Cyanocitta stelleri)

- 13 inches
- Dark blue body
- Blackish crest, head, and front
- Resident year-round: Western United States and Canada, pine forests from the Pacific to New Mexico and into Alaska

This darkly beautiful blue-and-black jay is a striking sight in western conifer and oak woodlands. Crested like its eastern counterpart—and unlike other western jays—the Steller's jay will come to your feeder for a variety of foods, including seeds, nuts, berries, suet, and leftovers.

Gray Jay *(Perisoreus canadensis)*

A crestless jay, this species is a well-known thief in the North and West, as it will steal food from camps and game from traps. It's also known as an Oregon jay or a Canada jay.

- 11 to 13 inches
- Gray with black patch on back of head
- White forehead
- No crest
- Short, dark bill
- Resident year-round: Much of Canada; northern New England and Michigan; Rockies into New Mexico

Natural Foods
- Insects
- Fruit
- Carrion

Feeder Fill-Ups
- Meat
- Baked beans
- Leftovers
- Dry dog food

Favored Feeders
- Tray feeders

Attracting Gray Jays
- Conifers

Special Treats for Gray Jays

Invite a gray jay to your backyard barbecue. Take a metal skewer with a ring on the end (meant to act as a handle for the chef). Cut a couple of cooked hamburgers into fourths and slide the quarters onto the skewer. Hang the skewer by the ring from a branch or a nail on the edge of one of your wooden feeders, and see if these thieves will come steal a meal from you.

Be careful about encouraging gray jays to get used to grabbing food from outdoor areas where you and your family spend time. These bold birds have little fear of humans and will even take food from your hand. What starts as a fun way to see wild birds up close can become a problem when gray jays lay claim to any food in sight, whether it's meant for them or not.

Similar Species

Western Scrub-Jay *(Aphelocoma californica)*

- Solid blue wings and tail
- Gray back
- White underneath
- No crest
- Resident year-round: Western United States to southern Mexico, also central Florida (subspecies: Florida scrub-jay)

Western scrub-jays are dynamic birds that move boldly, turning their heads sharply to keep an eye on everything around them. They steal shamelessly from other birds' caches and are quite mischievous.

Dark-Eyed Junco *(Junco hyemalis)*

These ground feeders are often the first migrating birds you'll notice at your winter feeder, busily vacuuming up the seeds that fall to the ground.

- 5½ to 6¾ inches
- Male: Slate-gray back and head; no streaks; brown, pink, or gray flanks; white outer tail feathers, striking in flight; white belly; pinkish bill
- Female: Similar but slightly duller
- Spring into fall: Across much of Canada, Alaska, New England
- Migrate: South across United States

Natural Foods
- Insects
- Fruits
- Seeds

Feeder Fill-Ups
- Cracked corn
- Millet
- Peanuts
- Sunflower seeds
- Wheat
- Cracker and bread crumbs
- Peanut butter

Favored Feeders
- Ground feeders
- Peanut butter on feeders placed low to ground

Attracting Dark-Eyed Juncos

- Bunchberry
- Junipers
- Trumpet vine
- Bachelor's buttons
- Cosmos
- Coneflowers
- Zinnias
- Weeds

Special Treats for Dark-Eyed Juncos

Take good care of these birds when the snow falls and covers their usual sustenance at ground level. When the white stuff blankets the landscape, fill two or three trays with cracked corn, millet, and sunflower seeds and put them under your feeders for your juncos. Add a bit of chopped suet or peanut butter mixed with cornmeal to provide extra fat and protein.

Similar Species

Oregon Junco *(Junco hyemalis, Oregon subspecies)*

- 5½ to 6¾ inches
- Showy black hood
- Chestnut sides and back
- White outer tail feathers, striking in flight
- White belly
- Spring into fall: Across much of Canada, Alaska, New England
- Migrate: Western half of United States

There are several variants *of the dark-eyed, slate-colored junco described above that differ in appearance and location. They are all simply subspecies, including the Oregon junco.*

Ruby-Crowned Kinglet *(Regulus calendula)*

- 4 inches
- Short tail
- Olive gray above
- Light underparts
- White broken eye ring
- Wing bars
- Male: Red crown patch, visible when agitated
- Spring into fall: Canada, Alaska into California, and east to New Mexico
- Winter: Southern United States and Mexico

These tiny birds *are so full of energy and jerky in their movement that you may have trouble keeping an eye on them as they flit through the treetops in search of insects. Ruby-crowned kinglets spend their summers in North America's northernmost forests and high up in tall trees, where they hunt for insects on bark and leaves. They may build their nests as much as 100 feet off the ground. They will enjoy some of your feeder offerings, particularly in winter when insects are absent.*

Natural Foods
- Insects
- Some seeds and berries

Feeder Fill-Ups
- Nuts
- Peanuts
- Suet, block or chopped
- Suet or peanut butter and cornmeal mixtures
- Nectar
- Raw hamburger bits

- Elderberries
- Persimmons

Favored Feeders
- Hanging nut feeders
- Fruit feeders with perches
- Nectar feeders

Attracting Ruby-Crowned Kinglets
- Sumac
- Elderberry

- Pine
- Spruce
- Hemlock
- Fir
- Oak
- Aspen
- Dogwood

Special Treats for Ruby-Crowned Kinglets
Hang a few extra hummingbird feeders for these busy birds. Though tiny compared to other songbirds, kinglets will look rather gigantic next to the petite hummers. But they will welcome the extra nectar feeders, as male hummingbirds can be quite territorial and unwilling to share.

To provide kinglets with protein when insects are scarce in winter months, place small bits of raw hamburger on a high tray feeder. To make sure you have plenty of the small offerings, divide a package of hamburger into morsels and freeze on a tray. When frozen, place in a plastic bag and pull out a few to serve each day.

Similar Species

Golden-Crowned Kinglet (*Regulus satrapa*)

- 3½ inches
- Short tail
- Olive gray above
- Light underparts
- Whitish eyebrow stripe over short black eye stripe
- Wing bars
- Male: Orange crown patch with black border
- Female: Yellow crown patch with black border
- Spring into fall: Southeastern Canada and New England, west to British Columbia and Alaska
- Year-round: Atlantic and Pacific coasts of Canada; Pacific Northwest and coastal California; Rockies and Appalachians
- Winter: Throughout United States and into Mexico

The two species of kinglets in North America are both tiny and similar in markings and behavior. They often inhabit the same areas, so look for the eyebrow stripe of the golden-crowned to distinguish the two.

Horned Lark *(Eremophila alpestris)*

- 7 to 8 inches
- Male: Brown above, white below, black "sideburns" and "necklace" markings, yellow face, black feather tufts
- Female: Similar markings, slightly duller
- Resident year-round: Most of United States
- Spring into fall: Northern and southern Canada and Alaska
- Migrates: Middle of Canada
- Winter: Gulf Coast and through Florida

These birds turn up occasionally to snack on the ground beneath feeders. When you get a good look at a horned lark with its "horns" that make it look both quizzical and devilish, you can't help but smile at this bird.

Natural Foods
- Weed seeds
- Grain

Feeder Fill-Ups
- Corn
- Grain
- Bayberries
- Canary seed
- Grass seeds
- Millet
- Milo
- Oats
- Suet (chopped, at ground level)
- Black-oil sunflower seed

Favored Feeders
- Ground
- Low tray feeders

Attracting Horned Larks
- Open lawn, preferably a bit rough
- Pigweed
- Ragweed
- Lamb's quarters
- Amaranth

Special Treats for Horned Larks
Gather a few bouquets of pigweed and ragweed as they go to seed. Tie them upside down at the base of your feeder poles to give the horned larks easy access to some of their favorite weeds.

Black-Billed Magpie *(Pica hudsonia)*

- 17½ to 22 inches
- Slender
- Black and white
- Large white wing patches
- Long, wedge-shaped tail (9½ to 12 inches)
- Wings and tail iridescent green, purple, blue, and black
- Resident year-round: South-central Alaska, western Canada and United States

These birds are beautiful bullies, *and they love meat—even in the form of pretty songbirds. Magpies also devour grasshoppers and mice, so they do provide a valuable pest-control service. If you don't want them around to interfere with other feeder birds, serve food in weight-baffled feeders that don't allow heavier creatures to get to the seed.*

Natural Foods
- Insects
- Plants
- Carrion
- Reptiles
- Crustaceans
- Scorpions
- Rodents

Feeder Fill-Ups
- Suet
- Meat scraps
- Bones
- Peanuts
- Dry dog food
- Corn
- Apples
- Blueberries
- Grapes
- Cereal

Favored Feeders
- Ground feeders
- Tray feeders

Attracting Black-Billed Magpies
- Tall grass (preferably full of grasshoppers!)

Special Treats for Black-Billed Magpies

It isn't all that difficult to entice these birds to your feeders, as they are feisty and forceful. They may keep other birds away, so set up a separate magpie feeding area and fill it first with treats they love—it may give your other guests a head start. Keep a magpie busy by stuffing the inside of a resilient rubber dog toy with suet and making the big bird work to get the good stuff out!

Northern Mockingbird *(Mimus polyglottos)*

- 9 to 11 inches
- Large, slim
- Gray
- Long tail
- Large white patches on wings and tail, particularly noticeable in flight
- Resident year-round: Southeastern Maine west to northern California, Mexico to the Gulf States and Florida

These birds are more than a pleasure to watch—they create their own symphony. As their name suggests, mockingbirds are able to mimic a wide variety of birdcalls and can sound like dogs, frogs, crickets, and rusty gates. So prepare a spread for them and sit back to enjoy the concert.

Natural Foods
- Insects
- Fruits
- Berries
- Seeds

Feeder Fill-Ups
- Raisins
- Berries
- Currants
- Apples
- Nutmeats
- Peanut butter
- Suet
- Small grains
- Stale donuts

Favored Feeders
- Open feeders.
- Hanging suet feeders

Attracting Northern Mockingbirds
- Mulberry
- Blueberries
- Cherries
- Barberry
- American beautyberry
- Cabbage palmetto
- Date palms
- Euonymus
- Cotoneaster
- Camphor tree
- Sour gum
- Sumac
- Yucca
- Cactus
- Persimmons

Special Treats for Northern Mockingbirds

Dish up a perfectly balanced mockingbird meal by setting out a small dish of raisins and crumbled stale doughnuts on a corner of your table feeder or on a large stone or tree stump near your feeding station. Don't put out too much at a time, as dew and rain may cause leftover doughnuts to mold.

If you find these birds have laid claim to your suet feeder and are chasing other birds away, just give in and hang up another one. Mockingbirds can be very territorial when it comes to suet!

Clark's Nutcracker *(Nucifraga columbiana)*

- 11 inches
- Gray with black wings
- Long, sharp black bill
- Tail white underneath and along outer tail feathers
- White wing patches
- Resident year-round: Mountain forests of the West, from central British Columbia to Baja California
- May move from higher to lower elevations in range to find reliable sources of food

These bold, inquisitive birds often can be seen in western states, robbing campsites and feasting on scraps left by visitors at roadside rest stops and ski areas. In the wild, a Clark's nutcracker can carry dozens of seeds at a time in a pouch under its tongue to stash away for later meals.

Natural Foods
- Pine nuts
- Seeds
- Nuts
- Berries
- Insects
- Eggs and nestlings of other birds
- Carrion
- Seeds (cached in soil on hillsides)

Feeder Fill-Ups
- Meat
- Peanuts and acorns
- Baked goods
- Chicken scratch
- Crackers
- Suet
- Sunflower seeds
- Cracked and whole corn

Favored Feeders
- Open feeders
- Hanging suet feeders

Attracting Clark's Nutcrackers
- White fir
- Pinyon pines
- Juniper

Special Treats for Clark's Nutcrackers

Soup bones can be a great treat for a Clark's nutcracker. Either purchase one at the meat counter or serve up the bone from your Sunday roast. Tie a string around the bone and tie the other end to a tree branch near your feeding station to supply a protein treat for these friendly birds.

Red-Breasted Nuthatch *(Sitta canadensis)*

- 4½ inches
- Male: Broad black line through eye area, black cap, slate gray back, rusty underparts
- Female: Cap and line not as dark
- Resident year-round: Northeastern United States, into Canada and southeastern Alaska; most of western United States
- Winter: Throughout many states, including Central Plains and Southeast

This tiny, perky bird *is friendly and a great addition to your backyard. It is often a willing participant in hand-feeding, if you are so inclined.*

Natural Foods
- Insects, spiders
- Insect eggs
- Seeds
- Acorns
- Beechnuts

Feeder Fill-Ups
- Suet
- Sunflower seeds

- Peanut hearts and pieces
- Peanut-butter mixtures

Favored Feeders
- Hanging feeders
- Wire suet feeders
- Hopper feeders
- Tray feeders

Attracting Red-Breasted Nuthatches
- Nut trees
- Mountain ash
- Juniper
- Spruce
- Pine
- Elderberries
- Virginia creeper

Special Treats for Red-Breasted Nuthatches
Get a perfect view of these beautiful birds by making a hanging window feeder. Purchase a small lightweight plastic feeder, a lightweight bracket, and suction cups. Attach the suction cups to your window, add the bracket, and hang a feeder full of sunflower hearts or peanuts.

Similar Species

Two other small nuthatches are residents in the United States. Like their nuthatch relatives, they share a love of suet, nuts, and seeds.

Brown-Headed Nuthatch *(Sitta pusilla)*

- 4 to 4½ inches
- Brown head
- White underneath
- Blue-gray back, nape, wings, rump
- Resident year-round: Southeastern United States, Atlantic Coast

The tidy brown-headed nuthatch climbs up and down tree trunks with ease. This bird makes its home in pine forests throughout the Southeast.

Pygmy Nuthatch *(Sitta pygmaea)*

- 3½ inches
- Gray cap
- Gray back
- Light underneath
- Resident year-round: Southwestern South Dakota westward and down into Mexico

In western pine forests, the smallest of the nuthatches roosts in groups to stay warm on cold nights. Multiple pygmy nuthatches may crowd together in a cavity to conserve body heat.

White-Breasted Nuthatch *(Sitta carolinensis)*

- 6 inches
- Strong, thick bill
- Short, square tail
- Black cap
- Black eyes in white face
- Chestnut under tail
- Year-round resident: United States, from southern Canada to Mexico

These birds are great fun to watch at your feeder and in your backyard trees. They travel headfirst down tree trunks in search of food. They eat many insects in the wild and enjoy suet and seeds at the feeder. The white-breasted nuthatch stores food for later indulgence, so it will be busy flying to and from your feeder.

Natural Foods
- Insects, spiders
- Insect eggs
- Seeds
- Acorns
- Beechnuts

Feeder Fill-Ups
- Suet
- Sunflower seeds

- Peanut hearts and pieces
- Peanut-butter mixtures
- Carrots
- Pumpkin and squash seeds

Favored Feeders
- Hanging feeders
- Wire suet feeders
- Hopper feeders
- Tray feeders

Attracting White-Breasted Nuthatches
- Nut trees
- Mountain ash
- Juniper
- Spruce
- Pine
- Elderberries
- Virginia creeper

Special Treats for White-Breasted Nuthatches
Crush dry cereal (cornflakes, crisped rice, fruit and nut cereals, oatmeal, grits) with a rolling pin. Melt peanut butter, bacon drippings, or suet (or a mixture) and mix equal parts cereal and melted fats. Pour or pack mixture into a small, low can, such as the kind that holds tuna or cat food. Poke a hole in the side of the can, thread a 12-inch piece of twine or wire through the hole, and tie on a branch or hook to provide a treat for clinging nuthatches.

Baltimore Oriole *(Icterus galbula)*

- 7 to 8 inches
- Two white wing bars
- Male: Bright orange and black body, black head
- Female: Olive-brown above, burnt orange-yellow below
- Spring into fall: South-central Canada through most of eastern United States
- Migrates: Into Florida and southern Texas
- Winter: Southernmost Florida and Texas, Gulf Coast of Mexico, Central America, northernmost parts of South America

These brightly colored members of the Blackbird family are a great addition to your backyard. They love fruit and suet and often can be lured in from neighboring trees to sample these delights.

Natural Foods
- Insects
- Caterpillars
- Fruits

Feeder Fill-Ups
- Oranges
- Peaches
- Pears
- Green peas
- Berries
- Nuts

- Suet
- Nectar
- Grape jelly

Favored Feeders
- Tray feeders
- Hanging feeders
- Nectar feeders

Attracting Baltimore Orioles
- Black locusts
- Trumpet vines

- Mulberries
- Blackberries
- Raspberries
- Wineberries
- Blueberries
- Green peas
- Mountain ash
- Hollyhocks
- Sunflowers

Special Treats for Baltimore Orioles

A skewer of oranges is a great treat for these fruit-loving birds. Cut two oranges in half and skewer them parallel to the cut onto a long metal skewer with a hook at one end. Tie a string to the hooked end and hang the fruit kebab from a branch or a feeder pole.

You can also offer fruit in wire suet feeders. Cut oranges, peaches, apples, or pears in half, put them into suet feeders, and hang in a shady spot.

Water is a key attraction for these birds. Include a birdbath near your nectar feeders to make your yard the ultimate oriole rest stop.

Similar Species

Bullock's Oriole *(Icterus bullockii)*

- 7 to 8 inches
- Long tail
- Long, straight bill
- White wing patch
- Male: Bright orange with black back, throat, top of head, nape; orange cheeks
- Female: Grayish olive-brown above, pale yellowish-gray below
- Summer: Throughout western United States
- Migrates: Into Mexico
- Winter: Mexico and Central America

In the western states, *Bullock's oriole takes the place of the Baltimore oriole as the resident showy orange-and-black nest weaver. In the center of the country where their ranges overlap, hybrids of the two species occur.*

Hooded Oriole *(Icterus cucullatus)*

- 7 inches
- White wing bars (one narrow, one wide)
- Slightly curved bill
- Male: Orange-yellow body; black bib, mask, back, wings
- Female: Olive-yellow body, back grayer, underparts brighter
- Spring into fall: Southwestern United States
- Migrates: Into Mexico

In the Southwest, you may spot this orange-hooded bird sipping nectar. Nectar will often tempt orioles, but they can be a bit big for the hummingbird feeders you may already fill. Consider purchasing a nectar feeder designed for orioles—it's larger with bigger ports and perches and probably orange instead of red. Hang near your trees for birds to easily access.

Orchard Oriole *(Icterus spurius)*

- 6 to 7 inches
- Two white wing bars
- Male: Very dark bird, black with deep chestnut color underneath
- Female: Olive green above, yellowish below
- Spring into fall: South-central Canada, eastern United States to Florida, northern Mexico
- Winters: Mexico to northern South America

Though most likely to inhabit neighborhood orchards, as its name implies, mulberries or bread and jam may bring this dark bird to your feeder.

California Quail *(Callipepla californica)*

One of several *small game birds that inhabits forests or chaparral across the United States, the California quail is a quaint, cute, chubby bird that travels in small groups called coveys. They are ground feeders whose diet is mainly vegetarian, and they will happily clean up any spilled seed below your feeders.*

- 9½ to 10½ inches
- Small head and bill
- Short necked
- Plump
- Short, broad wings
- Long, square tail
- Curled feathers bobbing over forehead
- Males: Gray and brown body, black face with bold white stripes
- Females: Plainer brown body, no facial markings
- Resident year-round: Pacific Northwest, California, Baja California

Natural Foods
- Seeds
- Leaves
- Flowers
- Grain
- Berries
- Acorns
- Insects

Feeder Fill-Ups
- Acorns
- Persimmons
- Apples
- Berries
- Dried peas and beans
- Cracked corn
- Sunflower seed
- Mixed seed
- Safflower seed
- Millet
- Milo

- Peanuts
- Pine nuts
- Nuts

Favored Feeders
- Ground
- Low tray feeders

Attracting California Quail
- Dandelions
- Goldenrod
- Ragweed

- Smartweed
- Brushy areas and hedgerows
- Bayberry
- Blackberries
- Bearberries
- Blueberries
- Grapes
- Dogwood
- Greenbrier
- Raspberries
- Sumac

Special Treats for California Quail

Plant a crop just for quail and other game birds in your yard: Sow some buckwheat, and just let it grow for these birds to enjoy as it ripens. Other crops that will welcome California quail include millet, milo (also known as sorghum), amaranths, wheat, and other grains. Choose ornamental types of these seedy plants, and create a birdseed garden that pleases your eyes as well as birds' palates.

If you live outside the range of California quail, don't let that deter you from sowing the seeds of grains and other plants favored by game birds. Species local to your area—wild turkeys, pheasants, bobwhites, ruffed grouse, partridges, or other quails—will all find a homegrown buffet of seeds to their liking, as will many songbird species.

While they scratch on the ground for seeds, quail and other game birds often add a side order of protein to their meals. California quail eat their share of beetles, caterpillars, and other invertebrates, although seeds, fruits, flowers, and other vegetation typically make up more than two-thirds of their diet.

Also popular with quail are berries, berries, and more berries. Put out saucers or trays of berries for these birds, and they will keep coming back for more. During the fall and winter months, California quail—and other game bird species—form flocks that feed and roost together. Such a group of birds, known as a covey in the case of quail, can quickly clean up the seeds from your birdseed garden, any fruit you put out, and all the dropped seeds beneath your bird feeders. If you're in the habit of hosting game birds, lay in a supply of inexpensive cracked corn or poultry scratch to keep the flock satisfied without breaking your birdseed budget.

Similar Species

Ring-Necked Pheasant (*Phasianus colchicus*)

- 20 to 28 inches
- Wingspan 22 to 34 inches
- Long tail, angled up
- Male: Gold and black back, copper and black underside, maroon breast, white ring at base of throat, iridescent green head and neck, featherless bright red face
- Female: Amazingly dull by comparison! Mottled brown with some black
- Resident year-round: Western and northern states

These visually showy birds (at least the males) look like they are from another world—and they are. Imported from Asia into Oregon in 1881, they now run wild across much of the northern United States and nearly all of California.

Ruffed Grouse (*Bonasa umbellus*)

- 14 inches
- Red-brown or gray-brown
- Chickenlike
- Fan-shaped tail with black band near tip
- Resident year-round: Throughout Canada and into Alaska, New England and northern Great Lakes, southward along the Appalachians and northern Rockies

This bird, like most game birds, explodes into flight when it is startled and needs to get to cover quickly. Ruffed grouse eat goldenrod, clover, cottonwood, birch, hazelnuts, apples, and dandelions.

Common Redpoll *(Acanthis flammea [or Carduelis flammea])*

The redpoll *is an exciting sight at the feeder, because it is not common, even in the northern United States. A small, streaked finch, it may at first be mistaken for a small sparrow—but it is distinguished from other little brown birds by its bright red cap. Male purple and house finches are larger, redder, and more common, so take some time to carefully identify your guests!*

- 5 inches
- Streaked
- Gray-brown
- Black chin
- Dark streaks on flanks
- Male: Bright red cap; reddish or pink rump, cheeks, breast

- Female: Red only on crown; darker and more streaked than male
- Spring into fall: The Arctic, Newfoundland west to northern Alaska
- Winters: Occasionally in northern United States
- Resident year-round: Alaska and Yukon, Northwest Territories, and Nunavut

Natural Foods

- Seeds
- Buds
- Insects

Feeder Fill-Ups

- Nyjer
- Black-oil sunflower seeds
- Sunflower hearts and pieces
- Oats
- Millet
- Grass seeds
- Finch mix

Favored Feeders

- Hanging feeders
- Tube feeders
- Hopper feeders
- Tray feeders

Attracting Common Redpolls

- River birch
- Alder
- Willows
- Dandelion
- Ragweed
- Lamb's-quarters
- Smartweeds
- Catalpa
- Tickseed sunflower
- Cosmos
- Zinnias
- Buttercups
- Black-eyed Susans

Special Treats for Common Redpolls

Hang out an invitation for redpolls with a quick and easy nyjer feeder. Cut off the leg of an old pair of pantyhose. Pour in enough nyjer seed to fill it about 10 inches deep, and knot the open end of the stocking a couple of inches above the seed. Tie that end to a post or tree branch and trim the excess. As birds eat and the "feeder" gets holey, you can just toss it in the trash and make a new one from the other hose leg.

To survive the harsh conditions and low temperatures in their subarctic range, redpolls may take their meals to go. A special throat pouch, known as an esophageal diverticulum, lets a redpoll gather a quantity of seeds from a feeder or a natural source (birch seeds are favorites) and fly with the food to a sheltered location to eat it. Redpolls may use this survival strategy during severe weather or when nighttime temperatures are extremely low.

Like other small finches, redpolls also puff up their feathers during cold weather to better retain their body heat. This makes them look deceptively chunky, but it helps them stay warm.

American Robin *(Turdus migratorius)*

The American robin *is a year-round resident in much of the United States. When robins appear on our lawns in early spring, giving us hope that cold winter months are ending, they may be migrating from the South, or they may simply be emerging from protective hedges and shrubs where they spent the winter. Though many of us envision the robin as a worm-gobbling machine, it actually eats many kinds of insects and grubs and will happily dine at your fruit bushes and trees.*

- 10 inches
- Dark head
- Gray-brown back and wings
- Orange breast and belly
- White eye ring

- Females duller than males
- Resident year-round: Throughout United States
- Spring into fall: Most of Canada and into Alaska
- Migrates: Southern states and Mexico in winter

Natural Foods

- Insects
- Worms
- Grubs
- Fruits

Feeder Fill-Ups

- Sunflower seeds
- Fruits
- Bread crumbs
- Dried blueberries and cherries
- Raisins
- Grapes
- Baked goods
- Crackers
- Mealworms
- Suet
- Berries
- Cracked corn

Favored Feeders

- Tray feeders
- Low feeders

Attracting American Robins

- Lawn
- Shadbush
- Creeping juniper
- Common spicebush
- Cabbage palmetto
- Saw palmetto
- Buffalo berry
- Dogwoods
- Sumac
- Toyon
- Blueberries
- Blackberries
- Strawberries

- Mulberries
- Serviceberry
- Elderberries
- Barberries
- Hollies
- Honeysuckle
- Sumac
- Crabapples
- Hawthorn
- Cherries
- American bittersweet
- Virginia creeper
- Viburnum

Special Treats for American Robins

Bake a fruit treat for robins and have it handy to share in winter after storms make native foods hard to find and in early spring when the migrants are passing through. Using your favorite recipe or a packaged mix, make a batch of cornbread and stir 2 cups of mixed berries, raisins, and/or other dried fruits into the batter. Bake in a shallow pan. When cool, crumble into low tray feeders.

Yellow-Bellied Sapsucker *(Sphyrapicus varius)*

- 8 to 9 inches
- Black and white
- Long white wing patch
- Red forehead patch
- Slight flush of yellow on underside
- Male: Red throat patch
- Female: White throat patch
- Spring into fall: Canada to southern Rockies and southern Appalachians
- Winter: Southern United States into Central America and West Indies

Though not as common *as some of its woodpecker cousins, the yellow-bellied sapsucker can be lured to your feeders from sap-providing trees nearby. It's a great addition to any neighborhood, as it drills rows of neat sap holes in tree trunks that attract hummingbirds and butterflies.*

Natural Foods
- Mostly sap
- Insects
- Fruits
- Berries

Feeder Fill-Ups
- Apple bits
- Cherries
- Strawberries
- Occasionally nuts or suet

Favored Feeders
- Open tray (place food in the shade to delay rotting)

Attracting Yellow-Bellied Sapsuckers
- Large trees
- Hollies
- Cedars
- Junipers
- Elderberries
- Magnolias
- Wild grapes
- Virginia creeper

Special Treats for Yellow-Bellied Sapsuckers

Serve bits of fruit in a real fruit cup: After eating your morning grapefruit, scoop out the remaining pulp. Fill the rind with some chopped fruit and set it out to tempt a nearby sapsucker. You can either set it on a large rock or fence post near your feeders, or use string or wire to secure it to a tree branch.

Pine Siskin *(Spinus pinus [or Carduelis pinus])*

- 4½ to 5 inches
- Darkly streaked finch
- Yellow in wings and base of tail (sometimes hidden)
- Notched tail
- Pointed bill
- Spring into fall: Southern Canada across to southern Alaska and down to northern rim of United States, West Coast and into coastal Mexico
- Winter: Throughout most of United States, except southern Florida; Mexico

A bird of the Far North in summer breeding season, the pine siskin acts a bit like a goldfinch, is heavily streaked like a sparrow, and flashes yellow in its wings in flight.

Natural Foods
- Insects
- Buds
- Seeds
- Sap

Feeder Fill-Ups
- Nyjer
- Millet
- Nuts
- Sunflower hearts and pieces
- Ground oyster shells

Favored Feeders
- Tube feeders
- Hanging feeders
- Hopper feeders
- Tray feeders

Attracting Pine Siskins
- Spruces
- Birch
- Sweetgum
- Hemlock
- Alder
- Scotch thistle
- Star thistle
- Filarees
- Pines
- Bachelor's button
- Cosmos
- Zinnia
- Ragweed
- Tickseed sunflower
- Marigolds
- Purple coneflower
- Gloriosa daisy

Special Treats for Pine Siskins
Hang coconut halves and offer hulled sunflowers, small servings of nyjer, or flower seeds you've harvested from your annual bed to attract pine siskins.

White-Throated Sparrow *(Zonotrichia albicollis)*

One of many sparrows *that you may host at your feeder, the white-throated sparrow is easily identi-fied and easy to please. A little brown bird (as are most of the sparrows you'll see), it has a pure white throat. When you provide plenty of seeds for them to munch on, you will be buying time so you can sort out the many sparrow species in your backyard.*

- 6 to 7 inches
- Small, conical beak
- Brown above
- Gray breast
- Black eye stripes at crown and at eyes
- Yellow marks just above beak lead into white or buff eyebrow

- Spring into fall: Canada
- Migrates: Upper Midwest and Central Plains states
- Winter: Eastern United States, New York to Florida, and west into Texas; coastal California

Natural Foods

- Seeds
- Insects
- Fruits
- Berries
- Tree buds and blossoms

Feeder Fill-Ups

- Sunflower seed
- Millet
- Cracked corn
- Peanut hearts
- Baked goods
- Birdseed mix
- Berries
- Cereal
- Cherries
- Chicken scratch
- Bread and cracker crumbs
- Grapes
- Grass seed
- Millet
- Milo
- Suet, chopped

Favored Feeders

- Ground
- Low tray feeders
- Hopper feeders

Attracting White-Throated Sparrows

- Hollies
- Strawberries
- Blackberries
- Blueberries
- Elderberries
- Wineberries
- Bachelor's buttons
- Marigolds
- Sweet alyssum
- Mexican sunflower
- Zinnias
- Buttercups
- Violets
- Cockscomb
- Weeds
- Pigweeds
- Ragweed
- Lamb's-quarters
- Tarweed
- Crabgrass
- Filarees
- Yellow wood sorrel
- Smartweed
- Knotweeds
- Common purslane
- Sheep sorrel
- Docks
- Foxtail grasses
- Nightshades
- Chickweed
- Cosmos
- Amaranths
- Millet
- Buckwheat
- Sumac
- Dogwoods
- Mountain ash
- Oaks
- Maples
- Beeches
- Elms

Similar Species

Chipping Sparrow (*Spizella passerina*)

- 4¾ inches
- Gray breast
- Reddish cap
- Forked tail
- White eye stripe
- Resident year-round: Eastern seaboard and Gulf States
- Spring into fall: Canada and northern United States, Alaska, Central America
- Winter: Florida, Texas, California, into Mexico

Small, friendly sparrows, *"chippies" will almost certainly visit your feeder in the East and you may see them at times in the western United States, as well.*

Song Sparrow (*Melospiza melodia*)

- 5 to 6½ inches
- Small, conical bill
- Brown head and back
- Heavy breast streaks
- Brown dot on center of breast
- Resident year-round: Northeastern United States, western states, Pacific Northwest
- Spring into fall: Alaska, Canada
- Winter: Southern United States, Central Plains, and Mexico

You may stop and listen *in delight when you first hear these birds. The melody lilts and dances and is reminiscent of human songs. Take the time to listen to the entire repertoire—a song sparrow may sing about two dozen different songs.*

White-Crowned Sparrow *(Zonotrichia leucophrys)*

- 6½ to 7½ inches
- Unmarked gray breast and throat
- Black and white striped crown
- Small, pinkish, conical bill
- Spring into fall: Northern and western Canada and Alaska, south through British Columbia to Cascades
- Migrates: Throughout Canada, Upper Midwest, Great Lakes, and New England states
- Winter: Throughout most of United States, Mexico, Cuba

If you see one *white-crowned sparrow, you'll probably see more. These birds tend to travel in flocks.*

Golden-Crowned Sparrow *(Zonotrichia atricapilla)*

- Gray face and chest
- Yellow crown with black border
- Back brown with black stripes
- Long tail
- White wing bars
- Spring into fall: Western Canada, Alaska
- Winter: Pacific Coast of United States

Watch for this visitor *if you stock winter feeders in the West. After breeding in cold Canada, the golden-crowned enjoys the slightly milder winter weather of the United States' Pacific Coast states.*

American Tree Sparrow (*Spizella arborea*)

- 5¼ inches
- Reddish cap
- Gray breast with black spot
- Brown wings and tail
- Spring into fall: Edge of tundra and throughout Alaska
- Winter: Western Canada, all but southernmost United States

With its rusty cap *and white wing bars, the tree sparrow resembles the field sparrow in both size and coloring. Two features are useful in determining which species is which: The American tree sparrow's beak is dark on top and yellow on the bottom, compared with the field sparrow's pink bill; and the tree sparrow has a dark spot in the center of its gray breast, where the field sparrow's gray breast is unmarked. While tree sparrows nest in the Far North and turn up at feeders in the lower 48 states during winter months, field sparrows are year-round residents over much of the eastern two-thirds of the United States.*

Field Sparrow (*Spizella pusilla*)

- 5¼ inches
- Unmarked gray breast
- Brown back, tail, wings
- Rusty cap
- Light eye ring and light stripe over eye
- Pink bill
- Resident year-round: Central and eastern United States to Florida
- Spring into fall: Across much of northeastern United States
- Winter: Florida, Texas, Gulf Coast

These birds are often seen *in the eastern United States. They may flock with chipping sparrows and will feed on the ground, as most sparrows do.*

Fox Sparrow (*Passerella iliaca*)

- 6¾ to 7½ inches
- Reddish, rusty looking
- Heavily streaked breast
- Gray around side of neck
- Spring into fall: Western Canada, Alaska, through mountains of California, Nevada, Utah, Colorado
- Winter: Across much of eastern United States, Texas Gulf Coast, coastal California

The color of a red fox, *the fox sparrow is easy to recognize with its rusty back and head and rusty streaks on its breast. These sparrows are apt to visit your feeder when snow has blanketed the area, making natural food sources a challenge to find. Similar to a towhee, the fox sparrow hunts with both feet, hopping/ kicking backward to uncover insects hidden under leaf litter.*

Special Treats for Sparrows

Keep little seeds safe for your small sparrow visitors. They like to feed on the ground, but so do some of the big eaters like crows, starlings, and grackles. So, place a hopper feeder on the ground full of the small seeds sparrows adore, and place a wire mesh cage around it. The wire mesh should have holes big enough for the sparrows to go through easily, but it will dissuade squirrels, grackles, crows, and other potential pests that might be tempted by the promise of easy food!

Summer Tanager *(Piranga rubra)*

- 7 to 7¾ inches
- Thick yellowish, notched bill
- Male: All-over red
- Female: Olive above, yellow below
- Spring into fall: Central through southern United States to northern Mexico
- Migrates: Mexico to Brazil

This glorious red bird *is a wonderful addition to your backyard and is relatively easy to attract to the feeder with fruits, suet, and baked goods.*

Natural Foods
- Insects, particularly bees
- Weevils
- Spiders
- Berries

Feeder Fill-Ups
- Fruit
- Suet
- Millet
- Mealworms

- Baked goods
- Peanut butter

Favored Feeders
- Hopper feeders
- Tray feeders

Attracting Summer Tanagers
- Blackberries
- Mulberries
- Raspberries
- Wineberries
- Elderberries
- Huckleberries
- Figs
- Sumacs

Special Treats for Summer Tanagers

Make a nearby fence or branch into a smorgasbord for tanagers. String berries and small cubes of bread spread with peanut butter onto strong thread using a large needle. Fill up a nice long strand (18 to 24 inches), tie it in a circle for easy hanging, and drape it over a fence or branch.

Similar Species

Western Tanager *(Piranga ludoviciana)*

- 7 inches
- Thick, notched bill
- Male: Yellow with black back, wings, and tail; red head; two distinct wing bars
- Female: Olive above, yellowish below; white and yellow wing bars
- Spring into fall: Western North America
- Migrates: Plains states and Mexico
- Winter: Mexico and Central America

The colorful Western tanager is a willing participant at backyard feeders, particularly when fruit of any kind is on the menu.

Hepatic Tanager *(Piranga flava)*

- 8 inches
- Dark-colored bill
- Male: Bright red overall with grayish back, tail, and cheek patch
- Female: Gray back with yellow below
- Resident year-round: Western Mexico mountains, parts of Central and South America
- Spring into fall: Mountain forests of southwestern United States, primarily New Mexico, Arizona, southern Nevada, and California

In the forested mountains of the southwestern United States, the flash of bright red you spot in the treetops may be the male hepatic tanager.

Scarlet Tanager *(Piranga olivacea)*

- 7 inches
- Light, thick, notched bill
- Male: Brilliant scarlet with black wings
- Female: Dull green back and tail; yellowish below; brown/black wings
- Spring into fall: Southeastern Canada and eastern United States
- Migrates: Southeastern United States, Cuba, Central America
- Winter: Colombia to western Amazon rainforest

The scarlet tanager *is less likely than its kin to appear at feeders in your backyard, but you may spot it nearby. It makes a brilliant flash of color high in surrounding trees.*

The View from Deb's Window

A person could get a serious kink in her neck while trying to get a good look at the showy scarlet tanager. In spite of its eye-catching red-and-black color scheme, the scarlet tanager is somewhat secretive and spends nearly all of its time high in the treetops, where it gleans insects from bark and foliage and takes flying insects in midair.

Attracting scarlet tanagers is not as simple as offering its favorite foods at your feeders. What these birds want most of all is unbroken tracts of mature forestland with the tall trees they favor for feeding and nesting in. I'm fortunate to have mature oaks and ashes around my home, in a neighborhood that still has wooded areas around it, and I've caught the occasional glimpse of a male scarlet tanager flitting about the canopy. With binoculars, patience, and maybe a chaise lounge to recline on, I might someday enjoy the sight of a tanager snatching an insect midflight and carrying it to a branch to beat it to death. Until then, I'll have to be satisfied knowing that scarlet tanagers are finding food and shelter in our neighborhood and enjoy the chance to spot one now and then.

Brown Thrasher *(Toxostoma rufum)*

- 11½ inches
- Reddish brown
- Wing bars
- Yellow eye
- Streaked breast
- Long, slightly curved bill
- Long tail
- Spring into fall: East of the Rocky Mountains, including southern Canada, New England and Mid-Atlantic States, south to Virginia and west to the Plains.
- Resident year-round: Atlantic coastal states from the Carolinas to Florida and throughout the Gulf Coast states
- Winter: Southern tip of Florida and Texas Gulf Coast

At first glance you might think the bird rustling in the undergrowth is a thrush, given its rusty brown back and streaky brown-and-white breast. The brown thrasher's size, its long curved bill, and its long tail set it apart from the smaller thrushes and make it look more like a mockingbird dressed in thrush's plumage! You may see these birds of the low brush scratching among leaves and mulch to uncover insects. Slim and brown, they often run rather than fly between patches of cover as they approach your feeder.

Natural Foods
- Insects
- Grubs
- Worms
- Caterpillars
- Berries
- Fruits
- Seeds

Feeder Fill-Ups
- Suet
- Shelled peanuts
- Hulled sunflower seeds
- Cornbread
- Dried berries
- Cheese
- Apples
- Raisins
- Grapes
- Cracked corn
- Walnut meats
- Baked goods
- Cooked pasta
- Leftovers
- Meat scraps

Favored Feeders
- Ground feeders

Attracting Brown Thrashers

- Shrubs with mulched areas beneath
- Thickets
- Holly
- Dogwood
- American beauty bush
- Black gum
- Virginia creeper
- Sumac
- Cedars
- Junipers
- Currants
- Blackberries
- Blueberries
- Raspberries
- Elderberries
- Mulberries
- Cherries
- Strawberries

Special Treats for Brown Thrashers

When fruits are abundant, slice and dry them in the sun on old window screens, then bag them up and save for winter. When the cold weather comes, put a few pieces of dried apple or a handful of cherries on a low tray feeder near a hedge, and see if you can tempt the skulking brown thrasher to venture out for a sweet treat.

Similar Species

California Thrasher (*Toxostoma redivivum*)

- 10 inches
- Brown
- Unstreaked breast
- Long, sicklelike bill
- Resident year-round: Sacramento to Baja California

The California thrasher is an energetic, aggressive bird that will eat a variety of fruits, suet, seeds, and grains at your feeder.

Wood Thrush *(Hylocichla mustelina)*

- 7 to 8 inches
- Rusty brown head
- Brown back and wings
- Buff-colored chest with round brown spots
- Pinkish long legs
- Brown-tipped stout bill
- Spring into fall: Eastern United States and Canada; southern Ontario to Gulf Coast and northern Florida
- Migrates: Central America

Thrushes feed on the ground, *whether scratching through leaves for insects or nibbling at feeders. Most species are well camouflaged with their brown backs and spotted breasts, so you will often hear them scuffling in the underbrush before you spot them.*

Natural Foods
- Insects
- Fruits

Feeder Fill-Ups
- Crumbled suet
- Raisins
- Mixed peanut butter and cornmeal

Favored Feeders
- Ground
- Low tray feeders

Attracting Wood Thrushes
- Spicebush
- Leaf litter left on ground
- Open compost pile

Special Treats for Wood Thrushes
Create a self-perpetuating feast for wood thrushes with shredded leaves. Pick a spot or two in your yard under shrubs or trees where it's shaded and moist. Load the areas up with several inches of chopped leaves and allow them to decompose. Thrushes will scratch in the leafy litter and eat the creepy-crawly creatures they uncover.

Similar Species

Hermit Thrush (*Catharus guttatus*)

- 7 inches
- Brown
- Spotted breast
- Reddish tail
- Spring into fall: Far north Canada and Alaska; western United States
- Migrates: Central United States
- Winter: Southwestern and southeastern United States and Mexico

The hermit thrush may grace your feeder in winter when all other true thrushes leave North America for warmer climes. Be sure to keep some fruit low to the ground for these visitors.

Varied Thrush (*Ixoreus naevius*)

- 9½ inches
- Male: Burnt-orange throat, chest; black to dark gray V on chest; dark face mask and back; orange wing bars and stripe above eye
- Female: Brown-gray; burnt-orange throat and chest; lighter orange eye stripe and wing bars
- Year-round resident: Pacific Northwest
- Spring into fall: Through Alaska and western Canada
- Winter: Pacific Coast of California and Baja Peninsula

These colorful, robin-size birds nest along the Pacific Coast of Canada and throughout nearly all of Alaska, residing year-round in coastal Washington and Oregon and spending winter on the coast of California as far south as Baja, Mexico.

Veery *(Catharus fuscescens)*

- 7 inches
- Light, rusty brown back
- Buff to white underside with indistinct spots on breast
- Spring into fall: Southern Canada, New England and Northeast south along Appalachians, upper Great Lakes and Northern Plains south along Rockies
- Migrates: Southeast, Midwest, south-central states
- Winter: Brazil

This inhabitant of wet woodlands is a paler, slightly larger version of the related hermit thrush. Colored for maximum camouflage in the leafy underbrush where it nests and feeds, the veery is an infrequent feeder guest but may drop in to dine when mealworms are on the menu. The sound of trickling water may draw these birds out of the woods and into your yard.

Special Treats for Thrushes

The veery and its spotted thrush relatives are rather shy birds that spend most of their time hunting for insects in leaf litter and brushy areas. Few common feeder foods will tempt them to leave the shelter of the shady undergrowth they prefer. A low tray feeder with grapes, berries, or chopped apples may give thrushes reason to emerge for a bite, and a low feeder with mealworms is also a potential attraction for these insect-eaters.

A moist, uncovered compost pile that offers opportunities to rummage for worms and other invertebrates may be the most appealing "feeder" you can provide. Thrushes also find water attractive and will visit a low basin, especially if it has a dripper to let the birds know it's there.

Tufted Titmouse *(Baeolophus bicolor)*

- 6 to 6½ inches
- Soft gray
- Small crest
- White underneath
- Rusty sides
- Black eyes
- Black forehead patch just above beak
- Resident year-round: Eastern United States

The titmouse is a lovely soft-gray bird with a strikingly dark eye and a jaunty crest. It is easily tempted to your feeders and will be a friendly and constant diner.

Natural Foods
- Insects (70 percent of diet)
- Seeds
- Berries

Feeder Fill-Ups
- Suet
- Shelled peanuts and peanut hearts
- Peanut butter with crushed cereal, hulled seeds
- Sunflower seed
- Corn

- Acorns
- Beechnuts
- Fruit: Apples, cherries
- Cheerios
- Doughnuts, crackers, other baked goods

Favored Feeders
- Tube feeders
- Tray feeders
- Hopper feeders
- Globe feeders

Attracting Tufted Titmice
- Virginia creeper
- Mulberries
- Blackberries
- Raspberries
- Wineberries
- Elderberries
- Tickseed
- Annual sunflowers
- Mexican sunflowers
- Zinnias

Special Treats for Tufted Titmice
Make a simple suet feeder for your titmouse guests. Tie a string around a pinecone so it is easy to hang. Melt suet (carefully over low heat) and dip the pinecone in it several times, letting the suet cool between dips. Hang the pinecone from a tree branch or a feeder hook to watch the local titmice perch and devour.

Similar Species

There are several more *localized species of titmice that you may see in your backyard depending on your location.*

Juniper Titmouse (Baeolophus ridgwayi [or Baeolophus griseus])

- 5¾ inches
- Slightly larger than oak titmouse
- Plain gray
- Resident year-round: Southwest United States, east of California

These titmice, *like other small birds, will welcome shallow dishes of water where they can enjoy a quick drink. In some guides, you'll find the juniper titmouse combined with the oak titmouse as the catch-all species "plain titmouse," because these two birds are virtually indistinguishable, apart from where you might see them. They don't even stick to the trees for which they were named!*

Oak Titmouse (Baeolophus inornatus)

- 5½ to 5¾ inches
- Slightly smaller than juniper titmouse
- Plain gray underside
- Gray-brown back
- Resident year-round: California

Titmice love suet *and can hang at almost any angle to eat it. If larger birds are crowding out these little gray beauties, provide a hanging mesh bag full of suet for the smaller birds. The larger birds won't be able to get a good grasp on the bag without perches, and they will soon spend their time at feeders better suited to their size.*

Bridled Titmouse (*Baeolophus wollweberi*)

- 5½ inches
- Black throat
- Black-edged crest
- Black C on cheeks
- Resident year-round: Mexico into the mountains of southern New Mexico and Arizona

These distinctive titmice *are only found in the Southwest and Mexico. They are friendly and busy at a feeder.*

Black-Crested Titmouse (*Baeolophus atricristatus*)

- 6 to 6½ inches
- Similar to tufted titmouse
- White forehead
- Black crest
- Resident year-round: Texas and Mexico

If you live in the neighborhood *of the black-crested titmouse, you can tempt it to feeders with seeds and suet. Sometimes called "Mexican" titmouse and counted as a regional variation of the tufted titmouse, the black-crested is great fun to watch with its perky black crest making it appear at times quite surprised. The dark crest sometimes looks like the wild hair of a punk rocker!*

Eastern Towhee *(Pipilo erythrophthalmus)*

- 7 to 8 inches
- Rufous sides
- White belly
- Male: Black head, chest, back, tail
- Female: Brown head, chest, back, tail
- Year-round resident: Midwest and Southeast
- Spring into fall: Canada and New England
- Winters: Texas and some of Southwest

Towhees are distinctive *as they scratch for food among the leaves. They jump forward with tail and head high, then kick back with both feet at the same time. The leaves fly, and seeds and yummy invertebrates are exposed to snack upon.*

Natural Foods
- Insects
- Spiders
- Berries
- Seeds

Feeder Fill-Ups
- Mixed seed
- Mealworms
- Cracked corn
- Sunflower seeds
- Cracker and bread crumbs
- Peanut pieces
- Acorns
- Berries

Favored Feeders
- Ground feeders

Attracting Eastern Towhees
- Thicket or hedge
- Magnolia
- Wax myrtle
- Trumpet vine
- Pines
- Oaks

- Blackberries
- Cherries
- Blueberries
- Elderberries
- Hollies
- Hackberries

- Pigweeds
- Ragweeds
- Star thistles
- Filarees
- Chickweed
- Dandelions

Special Treats for Eastern Towhees
Provide a birdbath with several inches of water in it, placed low to the ground to allow these birds to splash with abandon. A garbage can lid sunk into the ground works well. Provide protection from cats and other predators, so towhees can enjoy their ground-level bath in peace.

Similar Species

Spotted Towhee *(Pipilo maculatus)*

- 7 to 8 inches
- Rufous sides
- White belly
- White wing bars
- White spots on back
- Male: Black head, chest, back, tail
- Female: Brown head, chest, back, tail
- Resident year-round: Western United States
- Some migration from Montana to Mexico

A very close relative of the Eastern towhee, this bird is the Western version, though the two species may hybridize where their ranges overlap. The two species were once grouped under the name "rufous-sided towhee."

California Towhee *(Pipilo crissalis)*

- 8½ to 9 inches
- Brown, stocky
- Faint streaks around throat
- Rusty under tail
- Resident year-round: Pacific Coast from Oregon to southern Baja California peninsula

If you live in the California towhee's range, plant mesquite, wolfberry, and flowering currant to attract this dark brown bird.

Wild Turkey (Meleagris gallopavo)

- 43 to 55 inches
- Chestnut feathers with dark bars, bronze tips
- Male: Featherless bluish head, pink wattle, red throat, feathers hanging like a beard
- Female: Duller
- Resident year-round: Across continental United States; more common in eastern states

Tempted to tempt our not-quite-national bird to your backyard? It can be done if you live near wooded areas where turkeys are already in residence. If they come in large numbers, be ready to replenish your food stock often—these big birds are big eaters.

Natural Foods
- Nuts
- Berries
- Plants
- Grains
- Insects

Feeder Fill-Ups
- Corn: Whole or cracked
- Acorns and other nuts

- Scratch grain (chicken feed)
- Fruit pieces

Favored Feeders
- Tray feeders
- Ground feeders

Attracting Wild Turkeys
- Oak trees
- Cranberries
- Inkberries
- Madrone
- American bittersweet

Special Treats for Wild Turkeys

Draw turkeys from the woods by scattering corn along the edge of any wooded areas near your feeding stations. If there are turkeys near, they may wander out at dusk and dawn to feed. Also, if you appreciate the irony of serving them *to* turkeys instead of *with* turkey, place a saucer of dried cranberries on the ground for these big birds.

Yellow-Rumped Warbler (Dendroica coronata)

- 4¾ to 6 inches
- White throat
- Yellow rump
- Yellow patches on the side of its breast
- Male, spring: Blue-gray above, heavy black breast patch like an inverted U, yellow patch on head
- Female: Similar but browner
- Spring into fall: Throughout North America into Alaska
- Winter: Southern New England, southwest to central California, south to Central America, Pacific Coast

Most warblers are not feeder birds, but the yellow-rumped species may snack on your suet, peanut-butter treats, and fruits if you provide them in areas these birds frequent.

Natural Foods
- Insects

Feeder Fill-Ups
- Suet
- Peanut-butter mixes
- Figs
- Bayberries
- Persimmon
- Red cedar berries
- Sumac
- Bread
- Nutmeats
- Sunflower seeds

Favored Feeders
- Open feeders

Attracting Yellow-Rumped Warblers
- Persimmon
- Juniper
- Wax myrtle

Special Treats for Yellow-Rumped Warblers
Mix peanut butter and cornmeal and press into crevices in tree bark and where side branches arise from tree trunks.

Cedar Waxwing *(Bombycilla cedrorum)*

- 7 inches
- Sleek
- Brown
- Crest
- Black mask through eye
- Waxy red tips on secondary wing feathers
- Yellow band at tail
- Resident year-round: Much of northern United States
- Spring into fall: Into southern third of Canada
- Migrates: Irregularly into southern United States and parts of Mexico in winter

Often swooping into your yard *as a mob, these handsome masked marauders can make short work of your berry bushes and your fruit feeders. Entice them by planting a variety of fruit and berry bushes to provide them with plenty to nibble on all year.*

Natural Foods
- Fruit
- Insects

Feeder Fill-Ups
- Raisins
- Apples
- Oranges
- Sunflower seeds

Favored Feeders
- Tray feeders

Attracting Cedar Waxwings
- Junipers

- Mountain ash
- Dates
- Cotoneaster
- Cranberries
- Currants
- Blue gum eucalyptus blossoms
- Elm buds
- Pyracantha berries
- Sandcherries
- Japanese barberry
- Asparagus
- Birch

- Crabapples
- Honeysuckle
- Hollies
- Mulberries
- Blackberries
- Raspberries
- Wineberries
- Viburnum
- Filarees
- Serviceberry
- Hawthorn
- Red cedar

Special Treats for Cedar Waxwings
Tempt cedar waxwings with a simple water feature: Suspend a capped soda bottle filled with water over your birdbath. Poke a tiny hole in the bottom and one near the top to let the water slowly drip into the bath. The dripping will invite waxwings and others to stop and sip.

Downy Woodpecker *(Picoides pubescens)*

- 6 to 7 inches
- Wing spots create a black-and-white "checkered" effect
- White back
- Male: Small red patch on back of head
- Resident year-round: Most of United States, Canada, and Alaska

Hairy Woodpecker *(Picoides villosus)*

- 7 to 10 inches
- Coloring identical to downy
- Larger, heavier bill than downy
- Mostly resident year-round: Across United States; Alaska and Canada, along western mountains in Mexico and Central America

These two small feeder-friendly birds are great fun to watch. Be sure to include suet and nut feeders to bring them in. Downy woodpeckers are by far the most prevalent out our back windows, but the somewhat larger hairy woodpecker will also make an occasional appearance. Because their markings are so similar, these two species are difficult to tell apart.

Natural Foods

- Insects (75 to 85 percent of their diet)
- Sap
- Seeds
- Fruit

Feeder Fill-Ups

- Suet
- Peanut-butter mixtures
- Sunflower seeds
- Peanut hearts
- Millet
- Nuts

Favored Feeders

- Hanging or mounted suet feeders
- Hanging or mounted nut feeders
- Hanging or mounted hopper feeders
- Nectar feeders

Attracting Downy and Hairy Woodpeckers

- Mature trees
- Dead trees (20 feet tall is ideal)
- Viburnums (arrowwood, possumhaw)

- Elderberry
- Sumac
- Hollies
- Mulberries
- Virginia creeper
- Buckthorn (for pileated woodpeckers)
- Blackberries
- Raspberries
- Annual sunflowers
- Goldenrods
- Oaks
- Corn

Special Treats for Downy and Hairy Woodpeckers

Make your own rustic feeder to offer customized treats for these agile, small woodpeckers. Start with a section of a log or tree limb, about a foot long and at least 3 inches in diameter. Install a screw eye into one end of the log for easy hanging. Drill several holes, 1 inch in diameter by 1 inch deep, scattered over the surface of the log. Pack the holes with a mixture made of $1/4$ cup peanut butter and 1 cup crushed cereal (such as cornflakes or crisped rice) to tempt these friendly woodpeckers. Use a cable or chain to hang the log from a branch or hook that's sturdy enough to support the feeder's weight.

Experiment with different concoctions to see what your local woodpecker population finds most appealing. Softened suet, suet and peanut butter combinations, or mixes of suet and/or peanut butter and cornmeal are just a few other options for serving on your log feeder.

Although downy and hairy woodpeckers may be the main customers at this feeder, other birds will visit as well. Any of the larger woodpeckers that live in your area may give it a try, as will local nuthatches, chickadees, and titmice. Depending upon the mixture you're serving, mockingbirds, jays, starlings, and crows may attempt to grab a bite, although most of these large birds will have difficulty clinging to the log to feed.

Similar Species

More than a dozen species *of woodpeckers can be found in North America, but not all are normally seen at feeders. Some, such as the northern flicker, may not even immediately register to viewers as woodpeckers, a group that also includes nuthatches (pages 241, 242, and 243), brown creeper (page 205), and sapsuckers (page 254).*

Pileated Woodpecker (Dryocopus pileatus)

- 16 to 19 inches (crow size)
- Large red crest
- Mostly black with a few white markings
- Much of Canada; eastern half of United States, including Florida and eastern Texas; upper Midwest and Pacific Northwest; largely absent in western mountains, Plains, and desert Southwest

At the opposite end *of the woodpecker size spectrum from the relatively petite downy woodpecker is the pileated, a large black and white bird with a bold red crest.*

The View from Deb's Window

As a youthful fan of Woody Woodpecker cartoons, I was delighted when, many years later, I heard—and then saw—my first pileated woodpecker. Its loud, stuttering call startled me while I was working in my yard, and I looked up to catch a glimpse of an impressively large bird high in the trees. When I finally got a better look at them—a pair of pileated woodpeckers—I felt like I was finally seeing the model my childhood entertainment was based upon. I was thrilled that our neighborhood had enough mature trees to provide food and housing for these dramatic, large woodpeckers.

Red-Bellied Woodpecker *(Melanerpes carolinus)*

- 9 to 10½ inches
- Black and white, ladder-backed (or zebra-backed) feather pattern
- White, red-blushed belly
- White rump
- Male: Red cap and nape
- Female: Red nape
- Resident year-round: Eastern United States into New York and southern Great Lakes, south to Florida and Texas Gulf Coast

Your first instinct upon spotting the more common red-bellied woodpecker is likely to assume that the large black-and-white bird with the bright red nape, crown, and forehead must be the red-headed woodpecker. Think again: It takes a fully red head to claim the title "red-headed," and the red-bellied woodpecker must rely on the blush of red on its otherwise pale underside for its name.

Natural Foods
- Insects (one-third of its diet)
- Nuts
- Seeds
- Fruit

Feeder Fill-Ups
- Oranges
- Suet
- Peanut butter
- Peanuts
- Cracked corn
- Sunflower seed

Favored Feeders
- Hanging or mounted suet feeders
- Hanging or mounted nut feeders
- Hanging or mounted hopper feeders
- Tray feeders
- Nectar feeders

Attracting Red-Bellied Woodpeckers
- Pines
- Bayberries
- Wax myrtle

Special Treats for Red-Bellied Woodpeckers
Old pieces of wood and a few nails can make a feeder fit for a king—or a hungry red-bellied woodpecker. Hammer several large nails through a small board from the back, spaced evenly around the board. Attach two screw eyes and string or wire to one end for easy hanging on a nearby tree or hook. Then fill 'er up! Skewer whole ears of dried corn, orange halves, and bunches of grapes on the nails to treat red-bellied woodpeckers.

Similar Species

Red-Headed Woodpecker (*Melanerpes erythrocephalus*)

- 8½ to 9½ inches
- Red head
- White-barred black wings
- White chest
- Resident year-round: South and eastern United States; Canada, New England
- Migrates: Some migration from northern to southern parts of range
- Breeds: Northern Great Lakes, upper Midwest, and northern to Central Plains states

Acorn Woodpecker (*Melanerpes formicivorus*)

- 9 inches
- Black back and chest
- White at forehead and between bill and eyes
- Male: Red cap from nape to forehead
- Female: Smaller cap, just at nape
- Resident year-round: Southwestern United States forests, coastal California, Mexico

This striking bird makes holes in trees to stash acorns for winter feeding. Its white rump and wing patches are only visible when it takes flight.

Gila Woodpecker *(Melanerpes uropygialis)*

- 9 inches
- Medium to large
- Black-and-white barred back
- Brown face and neck
- Male: Red cap
- Resident year-round: Deserts in US Southwest and Mexico

The Gila woodpecker *stands in for the red-bellied in a limited portion of the desert Southwest where it frequents cactus deserts and city parks.*

Special Treats for Woodpeckers

Many species of woodpeckers will visit feeders offering suet or sunflower seeds, but habitat and natural food sources are what keep these strikingly marked birds in the neighborhood. For woodpeckers, one of the biggest attractions is a dead tree or at least a sizeable dead branch or two. While a snag—a standing dead tree—can be a difficult feature to include in a suburban landscape, leaving such a tree where you can is a great benefit to woodpeckers. Your local birds will glean the trunk and branches for insects and may create nest cavities. Species such as red-headed and acorn woodpeckers may use it as a place to cache seeds and other treats. If it's not possible to give woodpeckers their own dead tree, even a section of log will offer them a place to hunt for bark insects, borers, carpenter ants, and other woodpecker favorites. Prop or rest it in a corner of your landscape, perhaps near a suet feeder, which woodpeckers will also appreciate.

Carolina Wren *(Thryothorus ludovicianus)*

- 5¾ inches
- Warm, reddish brown above
- White stripe
- Warm buff breast
- Bill turns down slightly
- Resident year-round: Eastern United States and eastern Mexico

These reddish brown birds *are perky and fun to watch. Their habit of cocking their tails is an identifying characteristic.*

Natural Foods
- Insects: Beetles, cotton boll weevils, stink bugs, leafhoppers, scale insects, crickets, grasshoppers

Feeder Fill-Ups
- Suet
- Hulled peanuts
- Peanut-butter mixes
- Chopped or sliced apples
- Baked goods

- Elderberries
- Mealworms
- Meat scraps

Favored Feeders
- Table feeders
- Hanging feeders

Attracting Carolina Wrens
- Pines
- Bayberries

- Wax myrtles
- Sweetgum
- Sumacs
- Blackberries
- Raspberries
- Wineberries
- Brush pile

Special Treats for Carolina Wrens
Whip up a peanut butter and jelly sandwich for the Carolina wren. Spread peanut butter and jelly on a slice of bread, sprinkle it with cornmeal, and top it with another slice of bread. Cut into small pieces and serve on a low tray feeder.

Similar Species

Cactus Wren (*Campylorhynchus brunneicapillus*)

- 7 to 9 inches
- Brownish with scattered white streaks above
- White eye stripe
- Barred wings
- Brown, black-barred tail
- Resident year-round: Southwest United States, Baja Peninsula, and Mexico

While many wrens visit backyards across the country, only the Carolina wren and its western counterpart, the cactus wren, are readily tempted to feeders.

Special Treats for Cactus Wrens

If you live in the southwestern desert areas where this large wren makes its home, you may tempt it to visit your landscape with offerings of fruit, suet, or peanut butter–based treats. Fruits and seeds make up as much as 20 percent of the cactus wren's diet—more than most other wren species. Don't bother with a birdbath—these desert dwellers get the moisture they need from their food and get along fine without open water. Thorny native plants, such as mature cacti and tree yuccas, provide cactus wrens with places to hunt for insects and suitably protected nest sites. These birds will also appreciate a sheltered corner of your yard where they can hunt in leaf litter for insects and spiders.

resources

Conservation and Education Organizations

American Bird Conservancy
PO Box 249
4249 Loudoun Avenue
The Plains, VA 20198-2237
540-253-5780
888-247-3624
www.abcbirds.org

American Birding Association
4945 North 30th Street, Suite 200
Colorado Springs, CO 80919
800-850-2473
www.aba.org

Birding.com
Hillclimb Media
710 Second Avenue, Suite 1130
Seattle, WA 98104
www.birding.com

Birdingonthe.Net
www.birdingonthe.net

Cornell Lab of Ornithology
159 Sapsucker Woods Road
Ithaca, NY 14850
800-843-2473
www.birds.cornell.edu

eNature.com
1811 36th Street NW
Washington, DC 20007
www.enature.com

The Hummingbird Society
6560 Highway 179, Suite 204
Sedona, AZ 86351
928-284-2251
800-529-3699
www.hummingbirdsociety.org

International Migratory Bird Day
Environment for the Americas
2129 13th Street, Suite I
Boulder, CO 80302
866-334-3330
303-499-1950
www.birdday.org

National Audubon Society
225 Varick Street
New York, NY 10014
212-979-3000
www.audubon.org

National Wildlife Federation
11100 Wildlife Center Drive
Reston, VA 20190-5362
800-822-9919
www.nwf.org

North American Bluebird Society (NABS)
PO Box 43
Miamiville, OH 45147
812-988-1876
www.nabluebirdsociety.org

Operation RubyThroat: The Humming-bird Project
Hilton Pond Center for Piedmont
    Natural History
York, SC
803-684-5852
www.rubythroat.org

Smithsonian Migratory Bird Center
National Zoological Park
PO Box 37012-MRC 5503
Washington, DC 20013
nationalzoo.si.edu/scbi/migratorybirds

U.S. Fish & Wildlife Service
1849 C Street NW
MailStop MIB
Washington, DC 20240
800-344-WILD (9453)
www.fws.gov

Bird-Feeding Supplies

Audubon Workshop
5200 Schenley Place
Lawrenceburg, IN 47025-2182
513-354-1485
www.audubonworkshop.com

Droll Yankees, Inc.
55 Lathrop Road Extension
Plainfield, CT 06374
800-352-9164
860-779-8980
www.drollyankees.com

Duncraft, Inc.
102 Fisherville Road
Concord, NH 03303
888-879-5095
www.duncraft.com

eBirdseed.com
PO Box 162
Hawley, MN 56549
866-324-7373
218-486-5607
www.ebirdseed.com

Enterprises of Garden Gate
6473 Ruch Road
Bethlehem, PA 18017
610-837-1114
www.gardengatebirdhouses.com

Kester's Wild Game Food Nurseries Inc.
PO Box 516
Omro, WI 54963
800-558-8815
www.kestersnursery.com

Wild Bird Centers of America, Inc.
7370 MacArthur Boulevard
Glen Echo, MD 20812
800-WILDBIRD (945-3247)
301-229-9585
www.wildbirdcenter.com

Wild Bird Place
c/o Shop By Night LLC
137 Torrey Pines Court
Mankato, MN 55601
866-277-2972
www.wildbirdplace.com

Wild Birds Unlimited, Inc.
11711 North College Avenue, Suite 146
Carmel, IN 46032
888-302-2473
317-571-7100
www.wbu.com

Field Guides and Further Reading

Burton, Robert and Stephen W. Kress. 2005. *Audubon North American Birdfeeder Guide.* DK Publishing. New York, New York.

Dolezal, Robert J. 2009. *Birds in Your Backyard.* Reader's Digest Association. Pleasantville, New York.

Dunn, Jon L. and Jonathan Alderfer. 2006. *National Geographic Field Guide to the Birds of North America,* Fifth Edition. National Geographic. Washington, DC.

Dunn, Jon L. and Jonathan Alderfer. 2008. *National Geographic Field Guide to the Birds of Eastern North America.* National Geographic. Washington, DC.

Dunn, Jon L. and Jonathan Alderfer. 2008. *National Geographic Field Guide to the Birds of Western North America.* National Geographic. Washington, DC.

Griggs, Jack. 1997. *American Bird Conservancy's Field Guide to All the Birds of North America.* Harper Collins Publishers, Inc. New York, New York.

Heintzelman, Donald S. 2000. *The Complete Backyard Birdwatcher's Home Companion.* McGraw-Hill. Blacklick, Ohio.

Kaufman, Kenn. 2005. *Kaufman Field Guide to Birds of North America.* Houghton Mifflin Harcourt. New York, New York.

Kress, Stephen W. 2006. *The Audubon Society Guide to Attracting Birds.* Cornell University Press. Ithaca, New York.

Louv, Richard. 2008. *Last Child in the Woods.* Algonquin Books of Chapel Hill. Chapel Hill, North Carolina.

Martin, Deborah L. 2008. *Best-Ever Backyard Birding Tips.* Rodale Inc. Emmaus, Pennsylvania.

Mizejewski, David. 2004. National Wildlife Federation's *Attracting Birds, Butterflies, and Other Backyard Wildlife.* Creative Homeowner. Upper Saddle River, New Jersey.

Peterson, Roger Tory. 2008. *Peterson Field Guide to Birds of North America.* Houghton Mifflin Company. New York, New York.

Peterson, Roger Tory. 2010. *Peterson Field Guide to Birds of Eastern and Central North America,* Sixth Edition. Houghton Mifflin Harcourt. New York, New York.

Peterson, Roger Tory. 2010. *Peterson Field Guide to Birds of Western North America,* Fourth Edition. Houghton Mifflin Harcourt. New York, New York.

Robbins, Chandler S., Bertel Bruun, Herbert S. Zim. 2001. *Birds of North America, Revised and Updated: A Guide to Field Identification* (Golden Field Guide Series). St. Martin's Press. New York, New York.

Roth, Sally. 1998. *Attracting Birds to Your Backyard.* Rodale Inc. Emmaus, Pennsylvania.

Roth, Sally. 2001. *Attracting Hummingbirds and Butterflies to Your Backyard.* Rodale Inc. Emmaus, Pennsylvania.

Roth, Sally. 2007. *The Backyard Bird Lover's Field Guide.* Rodale Inc. Emmaus, Pennsylvania.

Sargent, Robert R. 1999. *Wild Bird Guides, Ruby-throated Hummingbird.* Stackpole Books. Mechanicsburg, Pennsylvania.

Schneck, Marcus H. 2005. *The All-Season Backyard Birdwatcher.* Quarry Books. Gloucester, Massachusetts.

Sibley, David A. 2003. *The Sibley Field Guide to Birds of Eastern North America.* Alfred A. Knopf, Inc. New York, New York.

Sibley, David A. 2003. *The Sibley Field Guide to Birds of Western North America.* Alfred A. Knopf, Inc. New York, New York.

Sibley, David A. 2000. *The Sibley Guide to Birds.* Alfred A. Knopf, Inc. New York, New York.

Sibley, David A. 2009. *The Sibley Guide to Trees.* Alfred A. Knopf, Inc. New York, New York.

Tallamy, Douglas W. 2007. *Bringing Nature Home.* Timber Press. Portland, Oregon.

photo credits

about the writers

Deborah L. Martin enjoys the sights and sounds of birds outside the windows of her home near Allentown, Pennsylvania. Although a pair of peacocks once visited her yard (having escaped from their pen on a nearby farm), a more typical day finds her watching chickadees, titmice, nuthatches, and cardinals at her feeders. Eastern towhees, indigo buntings, rose-breasted grosbeaks, and northern magpies are among the occasional visitors to her feeders, and once in a while, she spots a hawk or kestrel that is also watching the songbirds. For fun, Deb likes to mix up "kitchen-cupboard concoctions" for the birds, to see which tidbits they like best. Deb has edited, written, and/or contributed to several birding books and gardening books and magazines; she appreciates a thriving earthworm-compost bin every bit as much as she does a pileated woodpecker.

Arlene Koch has been birding for more than 35 years and is owner, with her husband, David, of 27 acres in a farm valley in eastern Pennsylvania. After their barn was struck by lightning and burned in 1993, they converted their fields from conventional farm crops to grains and wildlife food crops that they leave standing for birds and other wildlife. To date, 238 species of birds have been documented on or from their property, including Pennsylvania's first ash-throated flycatcher, in 1997. Other rarities documented there include the western kingbird, rufous hummingbird, clay-colored sparrow, northern shrike, and dickcissel.

Arlene is past president of both the Lehigh Valley Audubon Society and the Pennsylvania Society for Ornithology, and is a long-time official hawk counter for Hawk Mountain Sanctuary in Kempton, Pennsylvania. She has written a weekly nature-watch column for Easton, Pennsylvania's *Express-Times* for more than 15 years and has been published in many other birding publications, including *Birding, Pennsylvania Birds, Birder's World,* and *WildBird* magazines. An avid hummingbird enthusiast who has seen many tropical hummingbird species, Arlene gives tours through her gardens that she plants exclusively for hummingbirds. She also lectures on nature topics and teaches about the advantages of using native plants in the landscape.

Sue Burton owes the bird facts bouncing around in her head to her father, who peruses Peterson and Sibley bird guides for fun and still urges her to join him on dark, cold mornings to be out "by first light" to watch the birds. Since she grew up watching birds at the feeder, from the car, in the woods, and along the shore, Sue was embarrassingly old before she realized that most people did not mean they had spotted a vulture when they said they had watched "TV"—birders' abbreviation for turkey vulture. Sue lives in Pennsylvania with her two daughters, who patiently endure her enthusiasm for bird feeders, birdhouses, bird books, and bird-friendly plants.

bird-feeding friends
who shared their thoughts

Cindy Ahern has planted all kinds of native and nectar-rich plants in her bird- and wildlife-rich backyard in Montgomery County, Pennsylvania. She participated in the recent Pennsylvania Five-Year Breeding Bird Atlas.

Photographer Donna Chiarelli relaxes in her bird-friendly gardens around her home in Kutztown, Pennsylvania, and occasionally points her camera in the direction of her colorful guests.

Dave DeReamus began learning to identify raptors as a teen at Hawk Mountain Sanctuary. Dave compiles the Eastern Pennsylvania Birdline (a list of regional bird sightings), is active in the Lehigh Valley Audubon Society, works with the Pennsylvania Ornithological Records Committee, and has participated in both the recent Breeding Bird Atlas and the first one 25 years ago.

Mike Fialkovitch is an extremely knowledgeable and longtime birder from the Pittsburgh area who has done atlas work and contributed much data to bird census projects across Pennsylvania.

Ron French is a past president of Bucks County (Pennsylvania) Bird Club and has been birding for more than 50 years. He is one of the most knowledgeable birders in the Southeast. He has worked with many organizations, leading walks and teaching his skills to others while contributing to and/or taking part in all kinds of conservation projects.

Al Guarente, former wild-bird store owner and current member of the Pennsylvania Ornithological Records Committee, is a longtime birder who's extremely knowledgeable and always willing to learn and to teach.

Jen H. is a transplanted Massachusetts native who is getting to know the flora and fauna of the Pacific Northwest and enjoys sharing her discoveries and observations with her son.

Naturalist Thomas Leckey is a longtime birder and advocate for the preservation and creation of natural habitats for wild birds.

Geoff Malosh, editor of *Pennsylvania Birds* magazine, is a very skilled birder and photographer.

Terry Master, professor of biology at East Stroudsburg University and contributor to numerous articles and books on bird habitat and conservation issues, makes frequent birding/conservation trips to Costa Rica with his students.

Elaine Mease has been a backyard bird feeder for more than 40 years and is a longtime member (along with husband, Don) of the Eastern Bird Banders Association. Elaine is responsible for making many people aware of birds and is someone to whom Arlene Koch is very indebted.

Betsy Mescavage entered the birding world after her children were grown. She has established a backyard habitat in a small suburban area that attracts many bird species, she counts hawks at Lehigh Gap in Danielsville, Pennsylvania, has volunteered for Hawk Mountain Sanctuary, and was very active in the recent Pennsylvania Breeding Bird Atlas.

acknowledgments

It's hard to imagine writing a book about bird feeding without being able to look out my window and see birds going about their lives conveniently close to where I go about mine. For the wonder and beauty birds bring to my daily existence, I owe them a debt of thanks that I try to settle—at least in part—with seeds, suet, and other tidbits. They are as unaware of my gratitude as the squirrels are of my frustration with their destructive, feeder-raiding ways, but all the wild creatures that visit my yard have contributed in some way to the creation of this book.

Many people are owed thanks as well. Birder extraordinaire Arlene Koch contributed a wealth of useful information based on her years of bird-feeding experiences and those of her network of fellow bird lovers. My friend Sue Burton brought her lifelong love of birds to the task of writing the feeder-bird profiles found in Chapter 10 and also made sure I was well supplied with chocolate. Many friends generously shared accounts of their own relationships with the birds; others shared a laugh with me on days when it was most needed.

My editor, Karen Bolesta, kept me going with grace and good humor every step of the way; without her patient encouragement, this book would not have been possible. Senior project editor Hope Clarke made sure all the pieces came together and reunited me with sharp-eyed copy editor Claire McCrea, whose deft touch with the manuscript was deeply appreciated. Chris Rhoads's design produced the attractive package you see here, and Faith Hague put it on the pages with style. My thanks also go to photographers Mitch Mandel and Troy Schneider for making the mealworms look good, to Sean Sabo for his editorial assistance, and to Sarah Hadley for tracking down beautiful bird photos to go with the words.

My family has endured months of my laptop on the dining room table, birdseed on the kitchen floor, lard and suet in the refrigerator, countless crazy projects, and coming home to find a treat for the birds in the oven instead of dinner. I am grateful for their unfailing patience and support, and for the fact that they still come to the window when I spot a bird they just have to see.

index

Bold page references indicate photographs. <u>Underscored</u> references indicate boxed text.

Abies spp. *See* Firs (*Abies* spp.)
Acacia greggii. See Catclaw-acacia
  (*Acacia greggii*)
Acanthis flammea. See Common
  redpoll (*Acanthis flammea*)
Acer spp. *See* Maples (*Acer* spp.)
  A. negundo (*see* Box elder)
Achillea spp. *See* Yarrows (*Achillea*
  spp.)
Acorns, birds attracted to, <u>36</u>
Acorn woodpecker (*Melanerpes
  formicivorus*), 282, **282**
Adiantum pedatum. See Maidenhair
  fern (*Adiantum pedatum*)
Aesculus spp.
  A. californica (*see* California
    buckeye)
  A. pavia (*see* Red buckeye; Red
    buckeye [*Aesculus pavia*])
Agapanthus (*Agapanthus* spp.), <u>165</u>
Agastache
  Agastache foeniculum (*see* Anise
    hyssop)
  Agastache rupestris (*see* Sunset
    hyssop)
  for hummingbird attraction, 77,
    77
Agaves (*Agave* spp.), <u>165</u>
Agelaius phoeniceus. See Red-winged
  blackbird (*Agelaius
  phoeniceus*)
Albizia julibrissin. See Mimosa tree
  (*Albizia julibrissin*)
Alders (*Alnus* spp.), <u>173</u>
Allegheny spurge (*Pachysandra
  procumbens*), <u>168</u>
Allelopathy, <u>24</u>
Allen's hummingbird (*Selasphorus
  sasin*), 226, **226**
Almonds, birds attracted to, <u>36</u>
Alnus spp. *See* Alders (*Alnus* spp.)
Altricial, 12
Amaranthus spp. *See* Pigweed
  (*Amaranthus* spp.)
  A.caudatus (*see* Love-lies-bleeding)
Ambrosia spp. *See* Ragweed
  (*Ambrosia* spp.)
Amelanchier spp. *See* Juneberries
  (*Amelanchier* spp.);
  Serviceberries (*Amelanchier*
  spp.)
American beautyberry (*Callicarpa
  americana*), **90**, 95

American beech (*Fagus grandifolia*),
  <u>173</u>
American bittersweet (*Celastrus
  scandens*), <u>96</u>, 97, <u>166</u>
American cranberry bush (*Viburnum
  trilobum*), <u>171</u>
American crow (*Corvus
  brachyrhynchos*)
  diverting away from feeders, <u>120</u>,
    146–47
  food choices
    bread, 113
    cooked pasta and rice, 115
    corn, 34–35
    pet food, 116, 117
    suet, 53, 62
  profile of, **208**, 208–9
  seed-hoarding, <u>23</u>
  special treats for, <u>209</u>
American goldfinch (*Spinus tristis*),
  14, **178**
  author's experiences with, 15
  food choices
    nyjer/niger seed, <u>26</u>
    sunflowers, **161**
    thistles, 175
  profile of, **216**, 216–17
  special treats for, <u>217</u>
  summer feeding, 15
  tube feeder use, 40–41
American holly (*Ilex opaca*), <u>91</u>, 95
American robin (*Turdus migratorius*)
  earthworms and grubs, **107**, 107–8
  nesting, **12**, <u>151</u>, 152
  profile of, **252**, 252–53
  roosting in Boston ivy, 167
  special treats for, <u>253</u>
American tree sparrow (*Spizella
  arborea*), 260, **260**
Ampelopsis brevipedunculata. See
  Porcelain berry (*Ampelopsis
  brevipedunculata*)
Andropogon gerardii. See Big bluestem
  (*Andropogon gerardii*)
Anemone clematis (*Clematis
  montana*), <u>166</u>, 168
Anise hyssop (*Agastache foeniculum*),
  77, <u>79</u>, <u>165</u>
Anna's hummingbird (*Calypte anna*),
  77, **187**, 226, **226**
Annual sunflowers (*Helianthus* spp.),
  <u>163</u>
Ant eaters, <u>7</u>

Ants, 73–74, <u>108</u>, 108–9
Aphelocoma californica. See Western
  scrub-jay (*Aphelocoma
  californica*)
Aphids, birds attracted by, <u>108</u>
Apples, birds attracted by, <u>86</u>, 117, <u>127</u>
Aquilegia spp. *See* Columbines
  (*Aquilegia* spp.)
Archilochus colubris. See Ruby-
  throated hummingbird
  (*Archilochus colubris*)
Arctostaphylos spp.
  A. columbiana (*see* Hairy
    manzanita)
  A. uva-ursi (*see* Bearberry)
Aronia arbutifolia. See Red
  chokecherry (*Aronia
  arbutifolia*)
Arrowwood (*Viburnum dentatum*), <u>171</u>
Asclepias spp. *See* Milkweed
  (*Asclepias* spp.)
  A. tuberosa (*see* Butterfly weed)
Ash-throated flycatcher, <u>159</u>
Asters (*Eucephalus, Eurybia,* and
  Symphotrichum spp.), 164, <u>165</u>
Autumn clematis (*Clematis
  terniflora*), <u>167</u>, 168
Autumn olive (*Elaeagnus umbellata*),
  <u>159</u>
Avian pox, 152

*B*achelor's buttons (*Centaurea
  cyanus*), <u>162</u>
Bacillus thuringiensis var. *kurstaki*
  (BTK), 104
Bacon, birds attracted by, <u>127</u>
Bacon grease, 48
Baeolophus spp.
  B. atricristatus (*see* Black-crested
    titmouse)
  B. bicolor (*see* Tufted titmouse)
  B. griseus (*see* Juniper titmouse)
  B. inornatus (*see* Oak titmouse)
  B. ridgwayi (*see* Juniper titmouse)
  B. wollweberi (*see* Bridled titmouse)
Bagels, <u>113</u>
Baked goods, feeding, 112, <u>113</u>, 113–14
Baltimore oriole (*Iterus galbula*), 244,
  244, <u>245</u>
Bark bug eaters, <u>7</u>
Basswood (*Tilia americana*), <u>78</u>
Bayberry (*Myrica pensylvanica*), <u>91</u>,
  95, <u>171</u>

Bearberry (*Arctostaphylos uva-ursi*), 96, 168
Bears, 148–49
Bee balm (*Monarda* spp.), 79, 165
Bees, nectar feeders and, 73
Beetles, birds attracted by, 108
Berchemia scandens. See Rattan vine (*Berchemia scandens*)
Berries. *See also* Fruit; *specific berry types*
  bramble patches, 89, 93
  color, 97
  digestibility of, 82
  fermented, 94
  marking calendar for availability times, 95
  of native plants, 5
  protecting from birds, 93–94
  species attracted by particular berry types, 82, 88
Berry eaters, 82, 88
Betula spp. *See* Birches (*Betula* spp.)
Bidens aristosa. See Tickseed sunflower (*Bidens aristosa*)
Big bluestem (*Andropogon gerardii*), 169
Birches (*Betula* spp.), 173
Birdbath
  choosing, 143
  heated, 142, 143
  maintenance of, 143–44
Bird counts, 180
Birdhouses, 152
Bird Screen Company, 134
Bird's-foot trefoil (*Lotus corniculatus*), 163
Birds of prey, 3–4, 4, 149, 150–51
Blackberries, birds attracted by, 86, 88
Black-billed magpie (*Pica hudsonia*), 238, 238, 238
Blackbirds
  at feeders, 146, 147
  flocks of, 146, 147, 147
  safflower seeds and, 28
  species
    Brewer's blackbird, 189, 189
    red-winged blackbird, 178, 178, 178
    yellow-headed blackbird, 189, 189
  suet and, 53
Black-capped chickadee (*Poecile atricapillus*)
  hand-feeding, 153
  profile of, 202, 202
  special treats for, 202
Black-crested titmouse (*Baeolophus atricristatus*), 272, 272
Black current (*Ribes nigrum*), 171
Black-eyed Susan (*Rudbeckia hirta*), 163
Black gum (*Nyssa sylvatica*), 173

Black hawthorn (*Crataegus douglasii*), 90
Black-headed grosbeak (*Pheucticus melanocephalus*), 223, 223
Bleeding heart (*Dicentra* spp.), 79
Blueberries (*Vaccinium* spp.), 86, 92, 168
Bluebirds
  mealworms for, 105, 105–7, 106
  pokeweed for, 176
  species
    Eastern bluebird, 98, 190, 190–91, 191
    mountain bluebird, 193, 193
    Western bluebird, 192, 192–93, 193
Blueblossom (*Ceanothus thyrsiflorus*), 90
Blue elderberry (*Sambucus mexicana*), 92
Blue flax (*Linum perenne*), 165
Blue grama grass (*Bouteloua gracilis*), 169
Blue grosbeak (*Passerina caerulea*), 223, 223
Blue jay (*Cyanocitta cristata*)
  food choices
    cat food and, 116
    peanuts and, 29
    safflower seeds and, 28
    special treats for, 230
  profile of, 229, 229–30
Boat-tailed grackle (*Quiscalus major*), 219, 219
Bobwhite. *See* Northern bobwhite (*Colinus virginianus*)
Body temperature of birds, 5
Bohemian waxwing, 154, 169
Bombycilla cedrorum. See Cedar waxwing (*Bombycilla cedrorum*)
Bonasa umbellus. See Ruffed grouse (*Bonasa umbellus*)
Boreal chickadee (*Poecile hudsonica*), 204, 204
Boston ivy (*Parthenocissus tricuspidata*), 167, 167
Bouteloua gracilis. See Blue grama grass (*Bouteloua gracilis*)
Bouvardia ternifolia. See Firecrackerbush (*Bouvardia ternifolia*)
Box elder (*Acer negundo*), 173
Box huckleberry (*Gaylussacia brachycera*), 171
Brambles (*Rubus* spp.), 92
Brazil nuts, 119
Breads, feeding, 113, 113–14, 126, 127
Brewer's blackbird (*Euphagus cyanocephalus*), 189, 189
Bridled titmouse (*Baeolophus wollweberi*), 272, 272

Broad-billed hummingbird, 74
Broad-tailed hummingbird (*Selasphorus platycercus*), 227, 227
Brown creeper (*Certhia americana*), 205, 205, 205
Brown-headed nuthatch (*Sitta pusilla*), 242, 242
Brown thrasher (*Toxostoma rufum*), 265, 265–66, 266
BTK, 104
Buckthorns (*Rhamnus* spp.), 88
Buddleia davidii. See Butterfly bush (*Buddleia davidii*)
Bug eaters, 7, 100, 100–101, 108–9
Bullock's oriole (*Iterus bullockii*), 72, 84, 245, 245
Bunchberry (*Cornus canadensis*), 168
Bunting
  indigo, 196, 196, 196
  lazuli, 197, 197
Bush clover (*Lespedeza* spp.), 163
Buttercups (*Ranunculus* spp.), 165
Butterfly bush (*Buddleia davidii*), 75
Butterfly weed (*Asclepias tuberosa*), 79

Cactus wren (*Campylorhynchus brunneicapillus*), 285, 285, 285
Cake, birds attracted by, 127
California, birds of, 186
California buckeye (*Aesculus californica*), 78
California quail (*Callipepla californica*), 247, 247–48, 248
California thrasher (*Toxostoma redivivum*), 266, 266
California towhee (*Pipilo crissalis*), 274, 274
Callicarpa americana. See American beautyberry (*Callicarpa americana*)
Calliope hummingbird (*Stellula calliope*), 227, 227
Calliopsis (*Coreopsis tinctoria*), 162
Callipepla californica. See California quail (*Callipepla californica*)
Callistephus chinensis. See China aster (*Callistephus chinensis*)
Calypte spp.
  C. anna (see Anna's hummingbird)
  C. costae (see Costa's hummingbird)
Campsis radicans. See Trumpet creeper (*Campsis radicans*)
Campylorhynchus brunneicapillus. See Cactus wren (*Campylorhynchus brunneicapillus*)
Canary seed
  birds attracted by, 18, 33
  in seed mixes, 31, 33
Cankerworms, birds attracted by, 108
Canola. *See* Rapeseed (canola)

Cantaloupe, 117
Cardinal. *See* Northern cardinal
    (*Cardinalis cardinalis*)
Cardinal creeper (*Ipomoea x
    multifida*), **76**, 167
Cardinal flower (*Lobelia cardinalis*),
    79, 165
Cardinalis spp.
    C. cardinalis (*see* Northern
        cardinal)
    C. sinuatus (*see* Pyrrhuloxia)
Carduelis spp.
    C. flammea (*see* Common redpoll)
    C. pinus (*see* Pine siskin)
Carolina buckthorn (*Rhamnus
    caroliniana*), 92
Carolina cherry laurel (*Prunus
    caroliniana*), 91
Carolina chickadee (*Poecile
    carolinensis*), 203, **203**
Carolina wren (*Thryothorus
    ludovicianus*), 284, 284, **284**
Carpodacus spp.
    C. mexicanus (*see* House finch)
    C. purpureus (*see* Purple finch)
Catbird. *See* Gray catbird (*Dumetella
    carolinensis*)
Catclaw-acacia (*Acacia greggii*), 90
Caterpillars, 100–101, 104, 108, 158
Catharus spp.
    C. fuscescens (*see* Veery)
    C. guttatus (*see* Hermit thrush)
Cats, 147–48
Cattail (*Typha latifolia*), 169
Ceanothus thyrsiflorus. See
    Blueblossom (*Ceanothus
    thyrsiflorus*)
Cedars, birds attracted by, **88**, 171
Cedar waxwing (*Bombycilla
    cedrorum*)
    intoxication from fermented fruit,
        94
    profile of, 277, **277**
    special treats for, 277
Celastrus scandens. See American
    bittersweet (*Celastrus
    scandens*)
Celtis spp. *See* Hackberries (*Celtis*
    spp.)
    C. ehrenbergiana (*see* Spiny
        hackberry)
Centaurea cyanus. See Bachelor's
    buttons (*Centaurea cyanus*)
Cercis canadensis. See Eastern
    redbud (*Cercis canadensis*)
Certhia americana. See Brown
    creeper (*Certhia americana*)
Cheese, feeding, 114, 127
Chelone glabra. See Turtlehead
    (*Chelone glabra*)
Cherries, birds attracted by, 86
Chestnut-backed chickadee (*Poecile
    rufescens*), 204, **204**

Chickadees, **44**, **63**
    doughnuts and, 113
    feeder height preferred by, 130
    hand-feeding, 153
    peanuts and, 29
    seed-hoarding, 23
    species
        black-capped chickadee, 153,
            202, 202, **202**
        boreal chickadee, 204, **204**
        Carolina chickadee, 203, **203**
        chestnut-backed chickadee, 204,
            204
        mountain chickadee, 203, **203**
    tube feeder use, **40**
Chickweed (*Stellaria media*), 177
Chicory (*Cichorium* spp.), 177
Chilopsis linearis. See Desert willow
    (*Chilopsis linearis*)
China aster (*Callistephus chinensis*),
    162
Chioanthus virginicus. See White
    fringetree (*Chioanthus
    virginicus*)
Chipping sparrow (*Spizella
    passerina*), 258, **258**
Chokecherry (*Prunus virginiana*), 92,
    177
Chollas (*Opuntia* spp.), 96
Christmas fern (*Polystichum
    acrostichoides*), 168
Cicadas, birds attracted by, 108
Cinnamon fern (*Osmunda
    cinnamomea*), 168
Cirsium spp. *See* Thistles (*Cirsium* spp.)
Clark's nutcracker (*Nucifraga
    columbiana*), 240, **240**, 240
Clematis spp.
    C. ligusticifolia (*see* Western white
        clematis)
    C. montana (*see* Anemone clematis)
    C. terniflora (*see* Autumn clematis)
Climbing nightshade (*Solanum
    dulcamara*), 177
Climbing roses (*Rosa* spp.), 167
Clovers, 163
Coccothraustes vespertinus. See
    Evening grosbeak
    (*Coccothraustes vespertinus*)
Cockspur hawthorn (*Crataegus
    crusgalli*), 95
Coconut feeder, **63**
Coffeeberry (*Rhamnus californica*), 92
Colinus virginianus. See Northern
    bobwhite (*Colinus virginianus*)
Columbines (*Aquilegia* spp.), 77, 79,
    165
Common grackle (*Quiscalus quiscula*),
    218, **218**, 219
Common raven (*Corvus corax*)
    pet food and, 116
    profile of, 210, **210**
    Tower Ravens, 210

Common redpoll (*Acanthis flammea,
    Carduelis flammea*), 172, **250**,
    250–51, 251
Compass plant (*Silphium laciniatum*),
    165
Coneflowers, 164
Conifers, 173
Conjunctivitis, mycoplasmal, 151
Containers for seed storage, **42**, 142
Cookies, birds attracted by, 127
Cooper's hawk, 4
Coral bells (*Heuchera* spp.), 79
Coral honeysuckle (*Lonicera
    sempervirens*), 167
Coreopsis (*Coreopsis lanceolata*), 165
Coreopsis tinctoria. See Calliopsis
    (*Coreopsis tinctoria*)
Corn, 33–35
    birds attracted by, 18, 34
    cracked, **18**, 33–34
    growing your own, 34, 35
    privacy screen, 34
    serving, 34–35
    stalks as insect source, 102
    whole, **18**, **34**, 34–35
Cornmeal, birds attracted by, 127
Cornus spp.
    C. canadensis (*see* Bunchberry)
    C. florida (*see* Flowering dogwood)
    C. nuttallii (*see* Pacific dogwood)
    C. racemosa (*see* Gray dogwood)
    C. sericea (*see* Red osier dogwood)
Corvus spp.
    C. brachyrhynchos (*see* American
        crow)
    C. corax (*see* Common raven)
    C. ossifragus (*see* Fish crow)
Cosmos (*Cosmus* spp.), 163
Costa's hummingbird (*Calypte costae*),
    228, **228**
Cotoneasters (*Cotoneaster* spp.), 95, 171
Cottonwoods (*Populus* spp.), 173
Cowbirds, 3, 53, 146
Crabapples (*Malus* spp.), **86**, 95
Crabgrass (*Digitaria* spp.), 169
Crackers, birds attracted by, 127
Cranberries, birds attracted by, 127
Crataegus spp. *See* Hawthorns
    (*Crataegus* spp.)
    C. aestivalis (*see* Mayhaw)
    C. crusgalli (*see* Cockspur
        hawthorn)
    C. douglasii (*see* Black hawthorn)
    C. mollis (*see* Downy hawthorn)
    C. nitida (*see* Glossy hawthorn)
    C. phaenopyrum (*see* Washington
        hawthorn)
Crickets, birds attracted by, 109
Crocosmias (*Crocosmia* spp.), 165
Crop, 5, 23
Crossbills, 172
    red crossbill, **206**, 206–7
    white-winged crossbill, 207, **207**

Crow. *See* American crow (*Corvus brachyrhynchos*); Fish crow (*Corvus ossifragus*)
Cuckoos, 101
Curly dock (*Rumex crispus*), 175, 177
Currant (*Ribes sanguineum*), 77, <u>78</u>, <u>92</u>
Cyanocitta spp.
   C. cristata (*see* Blue jay)
   C. stelleri (*see* Steller's jay)

Dandelion (*Taraxacum officinale*), 177
Dark-eyed junco (*Junco hyemalis*), 233, 233–34, <u>234</u>
Darkling beetle (*Tenebrio molitor*). *See* Mealworms
Deer, dried corn and, 35
Deer-tongue grass (*Panicum clandestinum*), 169
Dendroica coronata. *See* Yellow-rumped warbler (*Dendroica coronata*)
Desert willow (*Chilopsis linearis*), <u>78</u>
Dicentra spp. *See* Bleeding heart (*Dicentra* spp.)
Digitalis spp. *See* Foxgloves (*Digitalis* spp.)
Digitaria spp. *See* Crabgrass (*Digitaria* spp.)
Diospyros spp. *See* Persimmons (*Diospyros* spp.)
Diseases, 151–52
   avian pox, 152
   mycoplasmal conjunctivitis, 151
   West Nile virus, 151–52
Dog food, birds attracted by, <u>127</u>
Dogwoods (*Cornus* spp.), 170, <u>171</u>
Doughnuts, 113, <u>127</u>
Downy hawthorn (*Crataegus mollis*), <u>171</u>
Downy woodpecker (*Picoides pubescens*), **8**, **278**, 278–79, <u>279</u>
Dried fruit, 83
Dryocopus pileatus. *See* Pileated woodpecker (*Dryocopus pileatus*)
Dumetella carolinensis. *See* Gray catbird (*Dumetella carolinensis*)
Dwarf mountain ash (*Sorbus scopulina*), <u>92</u>

Earthworms, 100, 104, 107–8, <u>109</u>
Eastern bluebird (*Sialia sialis*), **98**, **190**, 190–91, <u>191</u>
Eastern redbud (*Cercis canadensis*), <u>78</u>
Eastern red cedar (*Juniperus virginiana*), <u>91</u>, <u>171</u>
Eastern towhee (*Pipilo erythrophthalmus*)
   insect hunting, **103**
   profile of, 273, **273**
   special treats for, <u>273</u>

Echinacea purpurea. *See* Purple coneflower (*Echinacea purpurea*)
Eggs and eggshells, 118–19, <u>127</u>
Elaeagnus spp.
   E. angustifolia (*see* Russian olive)
   E. umbellata (*see* Autumn olive)
Elderberries (*Sambucus* spp.), 88, <u>171</u>
English holly (*Ilex aquifolium*), 95
English ivy (*Hedera helix*), 168
Eremophila alpestris. *See* Horned lark (*Eremophila alpestris*)
Eucephalus spp. *See* Asters (*Eucephalus*, *Eurybia*, and *Symphotrichum* spp.)
Eupatorium purpureum. *See* Joe-pye weed (*Eupatorium purpureum*)
Euphagus cyanocephalus. *See* Brewer's blackbird (*Euphagus cyanocephalus*)
European starlings. *See* Starlings
Eurybia spp. *See* Asters (*Eucephalus*, *Eurybia*, and *Symphotrichum* spp.)
Evening grosbeak (*Coccothraustes vespertinus*)
   profile of, 220, **220**
   seed storage in crop, <u>23</u>
   special treats for, <u>221</u>

Fagus grandifolia. *See* American beech (*Fagus grandifolia*)
Fall feeding tips, 14
Fall webworms, 100–101
Far North, birds of, 182
Fat. *See* Suet
Feeders
   cleaning, 135–39
   coconut, <u>63</u>
   diseased birds at, 151–52
   enjoying the birds at, 153
   for fruit, 84–87, 85, <u>85</u>, **87**
   grouping multiple, 130
   heights, 130, 131–32, 150–51
   hoppers, **41**, 41–42, <u>132</u>
   location, 131
   mealworm, **105**, 107
   mess control beneath, 139–40
   mounting hardware, 133–34, **135**
   for nectar, **69**, 69–71
      accessibility, 69–70
      construction of, 69
      insect problems, 73–74
      location for, 70–71
      materials, 69–70
      mess from, 70–71
      multiple, 71, <u>71</u>
      perches, placing nearby, <u>70</u>
      size, 69
   for orioles, 72
   pests at
      bears, 148–49

      birds, 146–47
      birds of prey, <u>149</u>, 150–51
      cats, 147–48
      raccoons, <u>148</u>
      squirrels, <u>144</u>, <u>145</u>, 145–46
   routine maintenance of, 138–39
   scoops and funnels for, 140–41, **141**
   securing, 132
   for seeds, 38, 40–43
      hoppers, **41**, 41–42
      logs, <u>37</u>
      socks, 40
      tray and platform, 42–43
      tube feeder, **39**, **40**, 40–41
   seeds sprouting in, <u>138</u>
   shopping for, 133–35
      cost, 133
      durability, 133
      ease of hanging or mounting, 133–34
      ease of use for birds, 135
      ease of use for humans, 134–35
      security of contents, 135
   size, <u>132</u>
   squirrel deterring, <u>144</u>, 145–46
   for squirrels, <u>145</u>, 145–46
   for suet, 61–62, <u>63</u>
      coconut feeder, <u>63</u>
      mesh bags, 61
      suet cages, **61**, 61–62
      tray and platform feeders, 62
   temporary, <u>136–37</u>
   tray and platform, 42–43, 62
Feeding station
   adding feeders to, 131
   feeder heights, 130, 131–32, 150–51
   location, 131
   pitfalls, common, 132–33
   varying available foods, 132
   varying styles of feeders, 132
Ferns, <u>168</u>
Fertilizers, 104
Fescues (*Festuca* spp.), 169
Field guide, 3
Field sparrow (*Spizella pusilla*), 260, **260**
Figs, birds attracted by, <u>86</u>
Filberts, birds attracted to, <u>36</u>
Finches
   goldfinch (*see* American goldfinch)
   house (*see* House finch)
   purple, **186**, **214**, 214–15, <u>215</u>
   tube feeders and, 40–41
Firecrackerbush (*Bouvardia ternifolia*), <u>78</u>
Firethorns (*Pyracantha* spp.), 95
Firs (*Abies* spp.), <u>173</u>
Fish crow (*Corvus ossifragus*), 209, **209**
Flax (*Linum* spp.), 31, <u>163</u>
Flickers, ants consumed by, 108–9
Flies, birds attracted by, <u>109</u>

Flowering currant (*Ribes sanguineum*), 92
Flowering dogwood (*Cornus florida*), 90, 170
Flowers. *See also specific plant species*
   annuals, 162–63
   nectar-producing, 75–78, **76**, **77**, 78–79
   perennials, 164, 165
Flying bug eaters, 7
Food scraps. *See* "People foods"
Fouquieria splendens. See Ocotillo (*Fouquieria splendens*)
Four o'clocks (*Mirabilis jalapa*), 79
Foxgloves (*Digitalis* spp.), 79
Fox sparrow (*Passerella iliaca*), 261, **261**
Foxtails (*Setaria* spp.), 169
Fragaria. See Strawberries (*Fragaria* spp.)
Fragrant sage (*Salvia clevelandii*), 78
Fraxinus americana. See White ash (*Fraxinus americana*)
Freezing fruit, 83
Fruit, 81–97
   berries
      bird species attracted by particular berry types, 88
      bramble patches, 89, 93
      digestibility of, 82
      fermented, 94
      marking calendar for availability times, 95
      of native plants, 5
      protecting from birds, 93–94
   bird species attracted by particular fruit types, 86, 127
   color, 97
   digestibility of, 82
   drying, 83
   fermented, 94, 95
   freezing, 83
   plants
      groundcovers and vines, 96, 96–97
      with long-lasting fruits, 95
      trees and shrubs, 90–92, 171
      winter-long fruit-keepers, 97
   preserves, 83–84
   serving for birds
      amount, 82
      Fancy Fruit-Nut Blend (recipe), 118
      feeder types, 84–87, 85, **85**, **87**
      nature's way, 87–89
      "people foods," 117
      on skewers and strings, 117
      timing, 82–83
   spoilage, 82
   stocking up on, 83
Fruit eaters, 7, 82, 86
Funnels, 140–41

*G*aillardia pulchella. *See* Indian blanket (*Gaillardia pulchella*)
Garden balsam (*Impatiens* spp.), 163
Garden cleanup, insects removed by, 103–4
Garden phlox (*Phlox paniculata*), 165
Gaultheria spp.
   G. procumbens (*see* Wintergreen)
   G. shallon (*see* Salal)
Gaylussacia spp. *See* Huckleberries (*Gaylussacia* spp.)
   G. brachycera (*see* Box huckleberry)
Gelsemium sempervirens. See Yellow jessamine (*Gelsemium sempervirens*)
Geographical regions, bird lists for
   California, 186
   Far North, 182
   Midwest, 184
   Northeast, 181
   South, 183
   Southeast, 183
   Southwest, 186
   West, 185
   widespread, 187
Geranium (*Pelargonium*), 76
Gila woodpecker (*Melanerpes uropygialis*), 72, 283, **283**
Gloriosa daisy (*Rudbeckia hirta* 'Gloriosa'), 165
Glossy hawthorn (*Crataegus nitida*), 95
Golden-crowned kinglet (*Regulus satrapa*), 236, **236**
Golden-crowned sparrow (*Zonotrichia atricapilla*), 259, **259**
Goldenrods (*Solidago* spp.), 164, 165, 177
Goldfinch. *See* American goldfinch (*Spinus tristis*)
Grackles
   boat-tailed grackle (*Quiscalus major*), 219, **219**
   common grackle (*Quiscalus quiscula*), 218, **218**, **219**
   food choices
      bread and, 113
      safflower seeds and, 28
      suet and, 53
   water fouling by, 141–42
Grain eaters, 6
Grapes (*Vitis* spp.), 86, 96, 167
Grass areas, decreasing, 157
Grasses, 168–69
Grasshoppers, birds attracted by, 109
Gray catbird (*Dumetella carolinensis*), **80**, 167, **200**, 200–201, **201**
Gray dogwood (*Cornus racemosa*), 171
Gray jay (*Perisoreus canadensis*), 231, **231**, 232
Great lobelia (*Lobelia siphilitica*), 79
Greenbriers (*Smilax* spp.), 96, 167, 177
Green-tailed towhee, 31–32

Grosbeaks
   jewelweed, feeding on, 174
   species
      black-headed grosbeak, 223, **223**
      blue grosbeak, 223, **223**
      evening grosbeak, 23, 220, **220**, 221
      pine grosbeak, 221, **221**
      rose-breasted grosbeak, 222, **222**, **222**
Groundcovers
   bird-worthy, 168, 168–69
   grasses, 168–69
   native fruiting, 96, 96–97
Grouse. *See* Ruffed grouse (*Bonasa umbellus*)
Grubs, 100, 104, 107–8, 109, 160

*H*ackberries (*Celtis* spp.), 90
Hairy manzanita (*Arctostaphylos columbiana*), 96
Hairy woodpecker (*Picoides villosus*), **278**, 278–79, **279**
Hand-feeding, 153
Hardiness Zone Map, USDA, 164, 304
Hawks, 4, **4**, 150, 157
Hawthorns (*Crataegus* spp.), 90
Hazelnuts, birds attracted to, 36
Hedera helix. See English ivy (*Hedera helix*)
Helianthus spp. *See* Annual sunflowers (*Helianthus* spp.); Perennial sunflowers (*Helianthus* spp.)
Hemlocks (*Tsuga* spp.), 173
Hepatic tanager (*Piranga flava*), 263, **263**
Hermit thrush (*Catharus guttatus*), 268, **268**
Heuchera spp. *See* Coral bells (*Heuchera* spp.)
Hibiscus grandiflorus. See Swamp rosemallow (*Hibiscus grandiflorus*)
Hollies (*Ilex* spp.), 88, 170
Honeysuckle (*Lonicera sempervirens*), 96
   coral honeysuckle, 167
   trumpet honeysuckle, 75, 79
Hooded oriole (*Iterus cucullatus*), 246, **246**
Hopper feeders, **41**, 41–42, 132
Hormones, 11, 15
Horned lark (*Eremophila alpestris*)
   profile is, 237, **237**
   special treats for, 237
Hostas, 79
House finch (*Carpodacus mexicanus*), **178**
   eye disease, 213
   fruit feeding, 117
   profile of, **212**, 212–13
   tube feeders and, 40–41

House sparrow
    bread and, 113
    earthworm stealing by, 107
    at feeders, 147
    positive aspects of, 121
Housing, 152
Huckleberries (*Gaylussacia* spp.), 94,
    168
Hummingbirds
    aggressiveness of, 71, 71
    attraction to color red, 68, 75, 76, 77
    diet of, 66
    fascination with, 225
    nectar drinking, **64**, 65–71, 67, **74**,
        75–77, **76**, **77**
    number present, 71, 72
    sap feeding, 79
    species
        Allen's hummingbird, 226, **226**
        Anna's hummingbird, **77**, **187**,
            226, **226**
        broad-billed hummingbird, **74**
        broad-tailed hummingbird, 227,
            227
        calliope hummingbird, 227, **227**
        Costa's hummingbird, 228, **228**
        ruby-throated hummingbird, **64**,
            76, 102, **184**, **224**, 224–25
        rufous hummingbird, 228, **228**
Hylocichla mustelina. See Wood
        thrush (*Hylocichla mustelina*)

Ilex spp. *See* Hollies (*Ilex* spp.)
    I. aquifolium (*see* English holly)
    I. decidua (*see* Possumhaw)
    I. opaca (*see* American holly)
    I. verticillata (*see* Winterberry
        holly)
    I. vomitoria (*see* Yaupon holly)
Impatiens (*Impatiens* spp.), 163
    I. capensis (*see* Jewelweed)
Indian blanket (*Gaillardia pulchella*),
    165
Indian grass (*Sorghastrum* spp.), 169
Indigo bunting (*Passerina cyanea*),
    196, **196**, **196**
Insecticides, 104, 158
Insects, 99–109
    ants, **108**, 108–9
    bird species that eat insects, **100**,
        100–101, 108–9
    mealworms, **105**, 105–7, 106
    nectar feeder problems and,
        73–74
    plants for, 102, 102–3, 158
    promoting in your yard
        decreased chemical use, 104
        delayed garden cleanup, 103–4
        native plant use, 102–3
        reasons for, 101–2
        seed stock infestation, 140
Interrupted fern (*Osmunda claytonia*),
    168

Intoxication from fermented fruit, 94,
    95
Ipomoea coccinea. See Morning glory
    (*Ipomoea coccinea*)
Ipomoea x *multifida. See* Cardinal
    creeper (*Ipomoea* x *multifida*)
Iterus spp.
    I. bullockii (*see* Bullock's oriole)
    I. cucullatus (*see* Hooded oriole)
    I. galbula (*see* Baltimore oriole)
    I. spurius (*see* Orchard oriole)
Ixoreus naevius. See Varied thrush
    (*Ixoreus naevius*)

Japanese beetle, 160
Jays
    aggressiveness at feeders, 146
    diverting away from feeders, 120,
        146–47
    food choices
        bread, 113
        cooked pasta and rice, 115
        corn, 34
        pet food, 116, 116
    species
        blue jay, 28, 29, 116, **229**, 229–30,
            230
        gray jay, 231, **231**, 232
        Steller's jay, 230, **230**
        Western scrub-jay, **59**, **110**, 232,
            232
Jelly, 83–84, 86
Jewelweed (*Impatiens capensis*), 174,
    177
Joe-pye weed (*Eupatorium
    purpureum*), 164, 165
Junco (*Junco hyemalis*)
    dark-eyed junco, **233**, 233–34
    Oregon junco, 234, **234**
Juneberries (*Amelanchier* spp.), 88
Juniper (*Juniperus* spp.), 88, 170
Juniper titmouse (*Baeolophus
    ridgwayi, Baeolophus griseus*),
    271, **271**
Juniperus, 88, 170
    J. scopulorum (*see* Rocky Mountain
        juniper)
    J. virginiana (*see* Eastern red cedar;
        Eastern red cedar [*Juniperus
        virginiana*])

Kestrels, 149
Kinglets
    golden-crowned kinglet, 236, **236**
    ruby-crowned kinglet, 235, **235**, 236
Kitchen castoffs. *See* "People foods"
Knotweed (*Polygonum* spp.), 177

Landscape. *See* Plants
Lard, 48
Larix occidentalis. See Western larch
    (*Larix occidentalis*)
Lawn, decreasing amount of, 157

Lazuli bunting (*Passerina amoena*),
    197, **197**
Lespedeza spp. *See* Bush clover
    (*Lespedeza* spp.)
Licorice plant, for hummingbird
    attraction, 77
Lilies (*Lilium* spp.), 79
Linden viburnum (*Viburnum
    dilatatum*), 95
Lindera benzoin. See Spicebush
    (*Lindera benzoin*)
Linum spp. *See* Flax (*Linum* spp.)
    L. perenne (*see* Blue flax)
Liriodendron tulipifera. See Tulip tree
    (*Liriodendron tulipifera*)
Liriope (*Liriope*), 165, 168
Little bluestem (*Schizachyrium
    scoparium*), 169
Lobelia spp.
    L. cardinalis (*see* Cardinal flower)
    L. siphilitica (*see* Great lobelia)
Lolium multiforum. See Ryegrass,
    annual (*Lolium multiforum*)
Lonicera sempervirens. See
        Honeysuckle (*Lonicera
        sempervirens*)
Lotus corniculatus. See Bird's-foot
    trefoil (*Lotus corniculatus*)
Love-lies-bleeding (*Amaranthus
    caudatus*), 162
Loxia spp.
    L. curvirostra (*see* Red crossbill)
    L. leucoptera (*see* White-winged
        crossbill)
Lupines (*Lupinus* spp.), 165

Magnolia grandiflora. *See*
        Southern magnolia (*Magnolia
        grandiflora*)
Magpies, 115, 117, 238, 238, **238**
Mahonia aquifolium. See Oregon
        grape holly (*Mahonia
        aquifolium*)
Maidenhair fern (*Adiantum pedatum*),
    168
Malus fusca. See Pacific crabapple
    (*Malus fusca*)
Maples (*Acer* spp.), 170, 173
Marigolds (*Tagetes* spp.), 163
Mayapple (*Podophyllum peltatum*),
    168
Mayhaw (*Crataegus aestivalis*), 90
Mealworms, **105**
    birds attracted by, 107
    bluebirds and, **105**, 105–7, 106
    feeder, **105**, 107
    raising, 105–7
Meat, feeding, 116
Melanerpes spp.
    M. carolinus (*see* Red-bellied
        woodpecker)
    M. erythrocephalus (*see* Red-
        headed woodpecker)

Melanerpes spp. *(cont.)*
  M. formicivorus (*see* Acorn
    woodpecker)
  M. uropygialis (*see* Gila
    woodpecker)
Melon seeds, birds attracted by, <u>127</u>
Melospiza melodia. See Song sparrow
  (*Melospiza melodia*)
Mertensia virginica. See Virginia
  bluebells (*Mertensia virginica*)
Mesquites (*Prosopis* spp.), <u>173</u>
Metabolism of birds, 5, 18
Mexican sunflower (*Tithonia
  rotundifolia*), <u>79</u>, <u>102</u>, <u>163</u>
Midwest, birds of, 184
Migration, 10
Milk jug feeder, **136**, <u>136</u>
Milkweed (*Asclepias* spp.), <u>79</u>
Millet
  appearance of, **28**
  bird species attracted by, <u>18</u>,
    28–29
  growing your own, 29, 169
  red, in seed mixes, 31
Milo
  appearance, 32, **32**
  birds attracted by, <u>18</u>
  growing your own, 32–33, 169
  in seed mixes, 21, 31, <u>31</u>, 32, 37
Mimosa tree (*Albizia julibrissin*), 76
Mimus polyglottos. See Northern
  mockingbird (*Mimus
  polyglottos*)
Mirabilis jalapa. See Four o'clocks
  (*Mirabilis jalapa*)
Mitchella repens. See Partridgeberry
  (*Mitchella repens*)
Mockingbird, 146, **175**. *See also*
  Northern mockingbird
  (*Mimus polyglottos*)
Mock orange (*Philadelphus* spp.), <u>78</u>
Mold, in nectar feeders, <u>73</u>, 74, <u>75</u>
Monarda spp. *See* Bee balm (*Monarda*
  spp.)
Morning glory (*Ipomoea coccinea*), 76,
  <u>167</u>
Morus spp. *See* Mulberries (*Morus*
  spp.)
  M. rubra (*see* Red mulberry)
Mosquitoes, birds attracted by, <u>109</u>
Moths, birds attracted by, <u>109</u>
Mountain ash (*Sorbus americana*), <u>92</u>,
  95
Mountain bluebird (*Sialia
  currucoides*), 193, **193**
Mountain chickadee (*Poecile gambeli*),
  203, **203**
Mountain ninebark (*Physocarpus
  monogynus*), <u>91</u>
Mourning dove (*Zenaida macroura*)
  profile of, 211, **211**
  special treats for, <u>211</u>
  summer feeding, <u>15</u>

Mulberries (*Morus* spp.), <u>88</u>, <u>89</u>, 94,
  177
Mullein (*Verbascum thapsus*), 175, 177
Mycoplasmal conjunctivitis, 151
Myrica pensylvanica. See Bayberry
  (*Myrica pensylvanica*)

Nannyberry (*Viburnum lentago*),
  <u>171</u>
Nectar, 67–79
  additives in, 68
  bird species attracted to, <u>7</u>, <u>67</u>, 72
  commercial products, 68
  feeders, **69**, 69–71
    accessibility, 69–70
    cleaning, <u>73</u>, 74–75, <u>75</u>
    construction of, 69
    insect problems, 73–74
    location for, 70–71
    materials, 69–70
    mess from, 70–71
    multiple, 71, <u>71</u>
    perches, placing nearby, <u>70</u>
    size, 69
  homemade, 67–68, <u>68</u>
  plants, 75–78, **76**, **77**, <u>78–79</u>
  red coloring in, 68
  sugar percentage in, 67
  sugar type in, 67, <u>68</u>
Nectar drinkers, <u>7</u>, <u>67</u>, 72
Nesting birds
  badgering, <u>13</u>
  feeding of nestlings, <u>12</u>, 12–13, **98**,
    101
  number of broods, 15
  nutrition for, 11
Nestlings, <u>12</u>, 12–13, **98**, **101**, 158
Nests
  author's experience with robins,
    151
  birdhouses, 152
  boxes, **150**
New Mexico locust (*Robinia
  neomexicana*), <u>78</u>
Nootka rose (*Rosa nutkana*), <u>92</u>
North, birds of, 182
Northeast, birds of, 181
Northern bayberry. *See* Bayberry
  (*Myrica pensylvanica*)
Northern bobwhite (*Colinus
  virginianus*), **194**, 194–95, <u>195</u>
Northern cardinal (*Cardinalis
  cardinalis*), 41, **128**, **178**, **182**
  food choices, 2
    corn, <u>34</u>
    fruit, **117**
    safflower seeds, 27, **28**
  ground feeding, 130–31
  profile of, **198**, 198–99
  special treats for, <u>199</u>
Northern mockingbird (*Mimus
  polyglottos*)
  insects fed to nestlings, **101**

profile of, 239, **239**
  special treats for, <u>239</u>
Nucifraga columbiana. See Clark's
  nutcracker (*Nucifraga
  columbiana*)
Nut butters, 118
Nut eaters, <u>6</u>, 35, <u>36</u>
Nuthatches
  corn and, 34
  seed-hoarding by, <u>23</u>
  species
    brown-headed nuthatch, 242,
      242
    pygmy nuthatch, 242, **242**
    red-breasted nuthatch, 53, 241,
      <u>241</u>, **241**
    white-breasted nuthatch, <u>23</u>, **187**,
      243, <u>243</u>, **243**
  suet and, **44**
Nutrition for nesting birds, 11
Nuts
  birds attracted by, <u>6</u>, 35, <u>36</u>
  Fancy Fruit-Nut Blend (recipe), <u>118</u>
  growing your own, 36
  "people foods," 118, <u>119</u>
  salted, 29, 118
  spoilage of, 35–36
  winter serving of, 35
Nyjer/niger ("thistle"), <u>19</u>, **25**, 25–27,
  <u>26</u>
Nyssa sylvatica. See Black gum (*Nyssa
  sylvatica*)

Oaks (*Quercus* spp.), 170, <u>173</u>
Oak titmouse (*Baeolophus inornatus*),
  271, **271**
Obedient plant (*Physostegia
  virginiana*), <u>79</u>
Ocotillo (*Fouquieria splendens*), <u>78</u>
Oenothera spp. *See* Sundrops
  (*Oenothera* spp.)
Omnivores, <u>7</u>
Opuntia spp. *See* Chollas (*Opuntia*
  spp.)
Oranges, birds attracted by, <u>86</u>, 117
Orchard oriole (*Iterus spurius*), 246,
  246
Oregon grape holly (*Mahonia
  aquifolium*), <u>91</u>, <u>171</u>
Oregon junco (*Junco hyemalis, Oregon
  subspecies*), 234, **234**
Orioles
  feeders for, 72
  food choices
    fruit, 84, 86, 117
    nectar, 65, <u>67</u>, 72
  fruit feeders for, 84, 86
  species
    Baltimore oriole, 244, **244**, <u>245</u>
    Bullock's oriole, **72**, 84, 245,
      245
    hooded oriole, 246, **246**
    orchard oriole, 246, **246**

Osmunda spp.
 O. cinnamomea (*see* Cinnamon fern)
 O. claytonia (*see* Interrupted fern)
Owl, fake, <u>134</u>

Pachysandra procumbens. *See*
 Allegheny spurge
 (*Pachysandra procumbens*)
Pacific crabapple (*Malus fusca*), *91*
Pacific dogwood (*Cornus nuttallii*),
 <u>90</u>, 170
Painted bunting (*Passerina ciris*), **183**,
 197, **197**
Panicum spp.
 P. clandestinum (*see* Deer-tongue
  grass)
 P. virgatum (*see* Switchgrass)
Parthenocissus
 P. quinquefolia (*see* Virginia
  creeper)
 P. tricuspidata (*see* Boston ivy)
Partridgeberry (*Mitchella repens*), *168*
Passerella iliaca. See Fox sparrow
 (*Passerella iliaca*)
Passerina spp.
 P. amoena (*see* Lazuli bunting)
 P. caerulea (*see* Blue grosbeak)
 P. ciris (*see* Painted bunting)
 P. cyanea (*see* Indigo bunting)
Pasta, feeding, 115, <u>127</u>
Peaches, birds attracted by, <u>86</u>
Peanut butter
 birds attracted by, <u>127</u>
 spreading, 50–53
Peanuts
 appearance of, **29**
 birds attracted by, <u>19</u>, 29
 growing your own, 30
 salted, 29
 tube feeder for, <u>39</u>
Pears, birds attracted by, <u>86</u>
Pecans, birds attracted to, <u>36</u>
Pelargonium. See Geranium
 (*Pelargonium*)
Penstemons, <u>79</u>
"People foods," 111–27
 baked goods, 112, <u>113</u>, 113–14
 bird species attracted by, 112, <u>127</u>
 breads, <u>113</u>, 113–14
 cheese, 114
 cupboard clean-outs, 114, <u>115</u>
 as distraction for bird bullies, <u>120</u>
 eggs and eggshells, 118–19
 fruit, 117, **117**
 how to serve, 119–20
 meat, 116
 nuts, 118, <u>119</u>
 pasta and rice, cooked, 115
 pet food, <u>116</u>, 116–17
 processed foods, 112
 recipes
  Basic Bird-Friendly Quick
   Bread, 126

Easy Suet-Feeder Mix-'N'-
  Match, 125
 Fancy Fruit-Nut Blend, <u>118</u>
 Homemade Seed Bells, 122–23
 Pinecone Goodies, 124–25
 spoilage of, 120
 for "urban" birds, 120–21
 value in bird's diet, 112
 vegetables, 116
Perennials, for nectar, <u>79</u>
Perennial sunflowers (*Helianthus*
 spp.), <u>165</u>
Perisoreus canadensis. See Gray jay
 (*Perisoreus canadensis*)
Periwinkle (*Vinca minor*), 168
Persimmons (*Diospyros* spp.), <u>86</u>, <u>91</u>
Pesticides, 104, 158
Pests, at feeders
 bears, 148–49
 birds, 146–47
 birds of prey, <u>149</u>, 150–51
 cats, 147–48
 raccoons, <u>148</u>
 squirrels, <u>144</u>, <u>145</u>, 145–46
Pet food, <u>116</u>, 116–17, 127
Phaseolus coccineus. See Scarlet
 runner beans (*Phaseolus
 coccineus*)
Phasianus colchicus. See Ring-necked
 pheasant (*Phasianus colchicus*)
Pheasant. *See* Ring-necked pheasant
 (*Phasianus colchicus*)
Pheucticus spp.
 P. ludovicianus (*see* Rose-breasted
  grosbeak)
 P. melanocephalus (*see* Black-
  headed grosbeak)
Philadelphus spp. *See* Mock orange
 (*Philadelphus* spp.)
Phlox paniculata. See Garden phlox
 (*Phlox paniculata*)
Phragmites (*Phragmites*), 174, 177
Physocarpus monogynus. See
 Mountain ninebark
 (*Physocarpus monogynus*)
Physostegia virginiana. See Obedient
 plant (*Physostegia virginiana*)
Phytolacca americana. See Pokeweed
 (*Phytolacca americana*)
Pica hudsonia. See Black-billed
 magpie (*Pica hudsonia*)
Picea spp. *See* Spurces (*Picea* spp.)
Picoides spp.
 P. pubescens (*see* Downy
  woodpecker)
 P. villosus (*see* Hairy woodpecker)
Pigeons, 120–21
Pigweed (*Amaranthus* spp.), 177
Pileated woodpecker (*Dryocopus
 pileatus*)
 ants and, 109
 author's experience with, <u>280</u>
 profile of, 280, **280**

Pine (*Pinus* spp.), 170, <u>173</u>
Pinecone, placing food in, 124–25
Pine grosbeak (*Pinicola enucleator*),
 221, **221**
Pine siskin (*Spinus pinus, Carduelis
 pinus*)
 nyjer/niger seed, 27
 profile of, 255, **255**
 special treats for, <u>255</u>
Pinicola enucleator. See Pine grosbeak
 (*Pinicola enucleator*)
Pink azalea (*Rhododendron
 periclymenoides*), <u>78</u>
Pipilo spp.
 P. crissalis (*see* California
  towhee)
 P. erythrophthalmus (*see* Eastern
  towhee)
 P. maculatus (*see* Spotted towhee)
Piranga spp.
 P. flava (*see* Hepatic tanager)
 P. ludoviciana (*see* Western
  tanager)
 P. olivacea (*see* Scarlet tanager)
 P. rubra (*see* Summer tanager)
Plants, 155–77. *See also specific plant
 species*
 annuals, <u>162–63</u>
 backyard habitat designation and
  certification programs, 157
 choosing bird-friendly, 158–60
 fruit-bearing, 87–97
  berries, 88, <u>89</u>, 89–95
  groundcovers and vines, 96,
   96–97
  with long-lasting fruits, 95
  safe locations for, 95
  trees and shrubs, <u>90</u>–92, <u>171</u>
  winter-long fruit-keepers, 97
 groundcovers
  bird-worthy, <u>168</u>, 168–69
  grasses, 168–69
  native fruiting, 96, 96–97
 imperfect, accepting, 158
 for insects, <u>102</u>, 102–3, 158
 invasive, <u>159</u>
 investing in habitat, 156–57
 native, 4–5, <u>159</u>, 159–60
 nectar-producing, 75–78, **76**, **77**,
  <u>78</u>–79
 perennials, 164, <u>165</u>
 pesticide use, 104, 158
 planning for growth, <u>161</u>
 plant communities, 156–57
 seed, growing your own
  corn, <u>34</u>, 35
  millet, 29
  milo, 32–33
  from mixed seed, 32
  nuts, 36
  peanuts, 30
  safflower, 28
  sunflower, 24–25

Plants (cont.)
  shopping for, 161–66
  shrubs
    choosing for birds, 170–72
    fruiting, 90–92, 171
    for nectar, 78
  spring planting, 11
  trees
    choosing for birds, 170–73
    native fruiting, 90–92
    for nectar, 78
    for seeds, 172–73, 173
  USDA Hardiness Zone Map, 164, 304
  vines
    bird-worthy, 166–67, 167–68
    native fruiting, 96, 96–97
    for nectar, 79
  weeds
    allowing for bird-worthy, 174–76
    grasses, 169
    list of bird-attracting, 177
    for seeds, 176–77
Plastic jugs, feeders from, 136, 136–37, 137
Platform feeders
  for seeds, 42–43
  for suet, 62
Podophyllum peltatum. See Mayapple (Podophyllum peltatum)
Poecile spp.
  P. atricapillus (see Black-capped chickadee)
  P. carolinensis (see Carolina chickadee)
  P. gambeli (see Mountain chickadee)
  P. hudsonica (see Boreal chickadee)
  P. rufescens (see Chestnut-backed chickadee)
Poison ivy and poison oak, 96–97, 177
Pokeweed (Phytolacca americana), 174, 176, 177
Polygonum spp. See Knotweed (Polygonum spp.)
Polystichum acrostichoides. See Christmas fern (Polystichum acrostichoides)
Populus spp. See Cottonwoods (Populus spp.)
Porcelain berry (Ampelopsis brevipedunculata), 166
Possumhaw (Ilex decidua), 171
Poultry (chicken) scratch, birds attracted by, 19
Pox, avian, 152
Prairie dropseed (Sporobolus heterolepsis), 169
Project Feederwatch, 180
Prosopis spp. See Mesquites (Prosopis spp.)
Prunus spp.
  P. besseyi (see Western sandcherry)

P. caroliniana (see Carolina cherry laurel)
  P. virginiana (see Chokecherry)
Pumpkin seeds, birds attracted by, 19, 127
Purple coneflower (Echinacea purpurea), 165
Purple finch (Carpodacus purpureus), 186
  profile of, 214, 214–15
  special treats for, 215
Purple martin, 13
Pygmy nuthatch (Sitta pygmacea), 242, 242
Pyracantha spp. See Firethorns (Pyracantha spp.)
Pyrrhuloxia (Cardinalis sinuatus), 199, 199

Quail. See California quail (Callipepla californica)
Quiscalus major. See Boat-tailed grackle (Quiscalus major)
Quiscalus quiscula. See Common grackle (Quiscalus quiscula)

Raccoons, 117, 148
Ragweed (Ambrosia spp.), 175
Raisins, birds attracted by, 127
Ranunculus spp. See Buttercups (Ranunculus spp.)
Rapeseed (canola)
  birds attracted by, 19
  in seed mixes, 31
Raptors, 3–4, 4, 149, 150–51
Raspberries, birds attracted by, 88
Rattan vine (Berchemia scandens), 166
Raven. See Common raven (Corvus corax)
Recipes
  for homemade suet, 53–60
    Easy Spreadable Suet-and-Cereal, 56
    Easy Suet-Feeder Mix-'N'-Match, 125
    Fruity Suet Smorgasbord, 58
    Fun and Festive Suet Shapes, 60
    Martha Sargent's Suet Recipe, 55
    Rudy's Basic Budget Suet, 57
    Simple Suet-Peanut Butter Bird Snack, 59
    Southern Summer "Suet" Treat, 54
  "people foods"
    Basic Bird-Friendly Quick Bread, 126
    Easy Suet-Feeder Mix-'N'-Match, 125
    Fancy Fruit-Nut Blend, 118
    Homemade Seed Bells, 122–23
    Pinecone Goodies, 124–25
Red-bellied woodpecker (Melanerpes carolinus), 281, 281, 281

Red-breasted nuthatch (Sitta canadensis)
  profile of, 241, 241
  special treats for, 241
  suet feeding, 53
Red buckeye (Aesculus pavia), 76, 78, 90
Red chokecherry (Aronia arbutifolia), 95
Red crossbill (Loxia curvirostra), 206, 206–7, 207
Red flowering currant (Ribes sanguineum), 78
Red-headed woodpecker (Melanerpes erythrocephalus), 282, 282
Red millet, in seed mixes, 31
Red mulberry (Morus rubra), 91
Red osier dogwood (Cornus sericea), 90, 171
Redpoll. See Common redpoll (Acanthis flammea, Carduelis flammea)
Red-winged blackbird (Agelaius phoeniceus), 178, 178, 178
Regulus spp.
  R. calendula (see Ruby-crowned kinglet)
  R. satrapa (see Golden-crowned kinglet)
Rhamnus spp. See Buckthorns (Rhamnus spp.)
  R. californica (see Coffeeberry)
  R. caroliniana (see Carolina buckthorn)
Rhododendron periclymenoides. See Pink azalea (Rhododendron periclymenoides)
Rhus spp. See Sumacs (Rhus spp.)
  R. thyphina (see Skunkbush sumac [Rhus thyphina])
  R. trilobata (see Staghorn sumac [Rhus trilobata])
Ribes spp.
  R. nigrum (see Black currant)
  R. sanguineum (see Currant)
Rice, 33, 115
Ring-necked pheasant (Phasianus colchicus), 249, 249
Robin. See American robin (Turdus migratorius)
Robinia neomexicana. See New Mexico locust (Robinia neomexicana)
Rock doves, 120–21
Rocky Mountain juniper (Juniperus scopulorum), 91
Rosa spp. See Climbing roses (Rosa spp.)
  R. nutkana (see Nootka rose)
Rose-breasted grosbeak (Pheucticus ludovicianus), 222, 222, 222
Rubus spp. See Brambles (Rubus spp.)
Ruby-crowned kinglet (Regulus calendula), 235, 235, 236

Ruby-throated hummingbird
(*Archilochus colubris*), **184**
insect consumption by, <u>102</u>
nectar feeding, **64**, **76**
profile of, **224**, 224–25
Rudbeckia spp.
R. hirta (*see* Black-eyed Susan)
R. hirta 'Gloriosa' (*see* Gloriosa
daisy)
Ruffed grouse (*Bonasa umbellus*), 249,
249
Rufous hummingbird (*Selasphorus
rufus*), 228, **228**
Rufous-sided towhee, 31
Rumex crispus. See Curly dock
(*Rumex crispus*)
Russian olive (*Elaeagnus
angustifolia*), <u>159</u>
Ryegrass, annual (*Lolium multiforum*),
169

Safflower seeds, **27**, 27–28
birds attracted by, <u>19</u>, **28**
growing your own, 28
Salal (*Gaultheria shallon*), 91
Salvia spp., <u>79</u>, <u>165</u>
S. clevelandii (*see* Fragrant sage)
Sambucus spp. *See* Elderberries
(*Sambucus* spp.)
S. mexicana (*see* Blue elderberry)
Sapsuckers
sap feeding, 79
yellow-bellied sapsucker
(*Sphyrapicus varius*), 254, <u>254</u>,
254
Scarlet runner beans (*Phaseolus
coccineus*), 76
Scarlet tanager (*Piranga olivacea*),
264, <u>264</u>, **264**
Schizachyrium scoparium. See Little
bluestem (*Schizachyrium
scoparium*)
Scoops, 140–41, **141**
Screens, over windows, <u>134</u>
Scrub-jay, Western (*Aphelocoma
californica*), **59**, **110**, **231**, 232
Seasonal feeding, 8–9
fall feeding tips, 14
spring feeding tips, 10–11
summer feeding tips, 14
winter feeding tips, 9
Seed eaters, <u>6</u>, <u>18–19</u>, <u>20</u>
Seeds, 17–43. *See also specific seed types*
bird species attracted by particular
seed types, <u>18–19</u>
caches, <u>23</u>
feeder types, 38, 40–43
hoppers, **41**, 41–42
socks, 40
tray and platform, 42–43
tube feeder, **39**, **40**, 40–41
Homemade Seed Bells (recipe),
122–23

mixes
creating your own mix, 21–22, 31
disadvantages of, 21, 30–31
filler seeds in, 21, **31**, 37
growing your own, 32
labels, 21, <u>31</u>
mess-free, 37–38
seeds to avoid in, 21, 31, <u>31</u>
shopping for, 21–22, **31**, 37–38
plants for, 162–64
corn, <u>34</u>, 35
millet, 29
milo, 32–33
for mixed seed, 32
safflower, 28
sunflower, 24–25
trees, 172–73, <u>173</u>
weeds, 176–77
serving strategies, 38
shopping for, 19–22
labels, 21, <u>31</u>
mixes, 21–22, **31**
online sellers, 21
preseason sales, 21
where to buy seed, 20–21
spoilage of, 100
sprouting in feeders, <u>138</u>
storage containers for, **42**, 140
types
bird species attracted by
particular, <u>18–19</u>
canary seed, 33
corn, 33–35, **34**, <u>34</u>
milo, **32**, 32–33
nuts, 35–36, <u>36</u>
nyjer/niger, **25**, 25–27, <u>26</u>
peanuts, **29**, 29–30
safflower, **27**, 27–28, <u>28</u>
sunflower, **22**, 22–25, <u>24</u>
white millet, **28**, 28–29
Seed socks, 41
Selasphorus spp.
S. platycercus (*see* Broad-tailed
hummingbird)
S. rufus (*see* Rufous hummingbird)
S. sasin (*see* Allen's hummingbird)
Serviceberries (*Amelanchier* spp.), **88**,
<u>90</u>, 170, <u>171</u>
Setaria spp. *See* Foxtails (*Setaria*
spp.)
Shadbush, birds attracted by, <u>88</u>
Shorebirds, <u>13</u>
Shrubs
choosing for birds, 170–72
fruiting, <u>90–92</u>, <u>171</u>
for nectar, <u>78</u>
Sialia spp.
S. currucoides (*see* Mountain
bluebird)
S. mexicana (*see* Western bluebird)
S. sialis (*see* Eastern bluebird)
Silphium laciniatum. See Compass
plant (*Silphium laciniatum*)

Sitta spp.
S. canadensis (*see* Red-breasted
nuthatch)
S. carolinensis (*see* White-breasted
nuthatch)
S. pusilla (*see* Brown-headed
nuthatch)
S. pygmaea (*see* Pygmy nuthatch)
Skunkbush sumac (*Rhus typhina*), <u>92</u>
Smartweed (*Polygonum* spp.), 177
Smilax spp. *See* Greenbriers;
Greenbriers (*Smilax* spp.)
Snowberries (*Symphoricarpos* spp.),
<u>88</u>, 95, <u>161</u>, <u>171</u>
Soaptree yucca (*Yucca elata*), <u>78</u>
Socks, seed, 41
Solanum dulcamara. See Climbing
nightshade (*Solanum
dulcamara*)
Solidago spp. *See* Goldenrods
(*Solidago* spp.)
Song sparrow (*Melospiza melodia*),
258, **258**
Sorbus spp.
S. americana (*see* Mountain ash)
S. scopulina (*see* Dwarf mountain
ash)
Sorghastrum spp. *See* Indian grass
(*Sorghastrum* spp.)
South, birds of, 183
Southeast, birds of, 183
Southern magnolia (*Magnolia
grandiflora*), <u>91</u>
Southwest, birds of, 186
Sparrows. *See also specific sparrow
species*
food choice, 2
roosting in Boston ivy, 167
special treats for, <u>261</u>
species
American tree sparrow, 260, **260**
chipping sparrow, 258, **258**
field sparrow, 260, **260**
fox sparrow, 261, **261**
golden-crowned sparrow, 259,
259
house sparrow, 107, 113, 121, 147
song sparrow, 258, **258**
white-crowned sparrow, 259, **259**
white-throated sparrow, 256,
256–57
Sphyrapicus varius. See Yellow-bellied
sapsucker (*Sphyrapicus varius*)
Spicebush (*Lindera benzoin*), <u>88</u>, <u>89</u>, <u>91</u>
Spiders, 109, <u>109</u>
Spinus spp.
S. pinus (*see* Pine siskin)
S. tristis (*see* American goldfinch)
Spiny hackberry (*Celtis
ehrenbergiana*), <u>90</u>
Spizella spp.
S. arborea (*see* American tree
sparrow)

Spizella spp.
  S. passerina (*see* Chipping sparrow)
  S. pusilla (*see* Field sparrow)
Sporobolus heterolepsis. See Prairie
    dropseed (*Sporobolus
    heterolepsis*)
Spotted towhee (*Pipilo
    maculatus*), 31–32, 274, **274**
Spreading suet or peanut butter,
    50–53
Spring
  decision to feed during, 8
  feeding tips, 10–11
Spruces (*Picea* spp.), 173
Squash seeds, birds attracted by, 19,
    127
Squirrels
  deterring, 144, 145–46
  feeders for, 145, 145–46
  foods eaten by
    corn, 34–35
    nuts, 36, 118, 119
    peanuts, 39
    safflower seeds, 27–28
    suet, 48, 50
  nest raiding by, 146
Staghorn sumac (*Rhus trilobata*), 92
Starlings
  diverting away from feeders, 120
  earthworm stealing, 107
  at feeders, 3, 27, 87, 146
  food choices
    bread, 113
    cooked pasta and rice, 115
    suet, 52, 53, 63, 146
  positive aspects of, 121
Stellaria media. See Chickweed
    (*Stellaria media*)
Steller's jay (*Cyanocitta stelleri*), 230,
    230
Stellula calliope. See Calliope
    hummingbird (*Stellula calliope*)
Storage containers for seeds, 42, 142
Strawberries (*Fragaria* spp.)
  berries
    birds attracted by, 86
    protecting from birds, 87
  plants, 96, 168
Suet
  balls from butchers, 49
  birds attracted by, 6, 10, 46, 51, 53
  caloric density of, 46
  forms of fat
    bacon grease and meat
      drippings, 48
    fat trimmings and suet from
      butchers, 46–47
    lard, 48
    rendered suet cakes, 47, 47–48,
      52
    vegetable shortening, 48
  labels, 49–50
  mammals attracted by, 47

  recipes for homemade, 53–60
    Easy Spreadable Suet-and-
      Cereal, 56
    Fruity Suet Smorgasbord, 58
    Fun and Festive Suet Shapes, 60
    Martha Sargent's Suet Recipe,
      55
    Rudy's Basic Budget Suet, 57
    Simple Suet-Peanut Butter Bird
      Snack, 59
    Southern Summer "Suet" Treat,
      54
    stir-ins for, 59
  rendering it yourself, 50
  serving away for seed feeders, 57
  serving suggestions, 61–62
    coconut feeder, 63
    mesh bags, 61
    suet cages, 61, 61–62
    tray and platform feeders, 62
  shopping for, 48–50
  spreading, 50–52
  summer use of, 52–53
  year-round, benefits of, 51
Suet cages
  bagels in, 113
  for fruit feeding, 86–87
  types, 61, 61–62
Suet eaters, 6, 10, 46, 51, 53
Sumacs (*Rhus* spp.), 88, 95
Summer feeding tips, 14
Summer tanager (*Piranga rubra*), 262,
    262, **262**
Sundrops (*Oenothera* spp.), 79
Sunflowers, 161
Sunflower seeds, 22–25
  allelopathic compounds in, 24
  birds attracted by, 19
  black-oiled, 19, 22, 22–23
  growing your own, 24–25
  hulled seeds, 24, 25
  in seed mixes, 30–31
  striped, 19, 22, 23–24
Sunset hyssop (*Agastache rupestris*),
    79
Swamp rosemallow (*Hibiscus
    grandiflorus*), 78
Switchgrass (*Panicum virgatum*), 169
Symphoricarpos spp. *See* Snowberries
    (*Symphoricarpos* spp.)
Symphotrichum spp. *See*
    Asters (*Eucephalus, Eurybia,*
    and *Symphotrichum* spp.)

*T*agetes spp. *See* Marigolds
    (*Tagetes* spp.)
Tanagers
  hepatic tanager, 263, **263**
  scarlet tanager, 264, 264, **264**
  summer tanager, 262, 262, **262**
  Western tanager, 263, **263**
Taraxacum officinale. See Dandelion
    (*Taraxacum officinale*)

Tea viburnum (*Viburnum setigerum*),
    170
Temporary feeders, 136, 136–37, **137**
Tenebrio molitor. See Mealworms
Tent caterpillars, 100–101
Termites, birds attracted by, 109
Thimbleberries, birds attracted by, 88
Thistles (*Cirsium* spp.), 175, 177
Thrashers
  brown thrasher, **265**, 265–66, 266
  California thrasher, 266, **266**
Thrushes
  hermit thrush, 268, **268**
  special treats for, 269
  varied thrush, 268, **268**
  wood thrush, 267, **267**, 267
Thryothorus ludovicianus. See
    Carolina wren (*Thryothorus
    ludovicianus*)
Tickseed sunflower (*Bidens aristosa*),
    162
Tilia americana. See Basswood (*Tilia
    americana*)
Time of day, feeding differences and, 5
Tithonia rotundifolia. See Mexican
    sunflower (*Tithonia
    rotundifolia*)
Titmice
  feeder height preferred by, 130
  peanuts and, 29
  seed-hoarding, 23
  species
    black-crested titmouse, 272, **272**
    bridled titmouse, 272, **272**
    juniper titmouse, 271, **271**
    oak titmouse, 271, **271**
    tufted titmouse, 41, 181, 270,
      270, **270**
Tovara virginiana. See Virginia
    knotweed (*Tovara virginiana*)
Towhees
  California towhee, 274, **274**
  Eastern towhee, 103, 273, 273, **273**
  green-tailed towhee, 31–32
  rufous-sided towhee, 31
  spotted towhee, 31–32, 274, **274**
Toxostoma spp.
  T. redivivum (*see* California
    thrasher)
  T. rufum (*see* Brown thrasher)
Tray feeders
  for seed, 42–43
  for suet, 62
Trees
  choosing for birds, 170–73
  native fruiting, 90–92
  for nectar, 78
  for seeds, 172–73, 173
Tree sap, 79
Trumpet creeper (*Campsis radicans*),
    79, 166
Trumpet honeysuckle (*Lonicera
    sempervirens*), 75, 79

Tsuga spp. *See* Hemlocks (*Tsuga* spp.)
Tube feeder, <u>39</u>, **40**, 40–41
Tufted titmouse (*Baeolophus bicolor*), **41**, **181**, 270, <u>270</u>, **270**
Tulip tree (*Liriodendron tulipifera*), <u>78</u>
Turdus migratorius. See American robin (*Turdus migratorius*)
Turkey (*Meleagris gallopavo*)
  profile of, 275, **275**
  special treats for, <u>275</u>
  Virginia knotweed, feeding on, 174
Turtlehead (*Chelone glabra*), <u>79</u>
Typha latifolia. See Cattail (*Typha latifolia*)

Urban" birds, feeding, 120–21
USDA Hardiness Zone Map, <u>164</u>, 304

Vaccinium spp. *See* Blueberries (*Vaccinium* spp.)
Varied thrush (*Ixoreus naevius*), 268, **268**
Veery (*Catharus fuscescens*), 269, **269**
Vegetables, feeding, 116
Vegetable shortening, 48
Verbascum thapsus. See Mullein (*Verbascum thapsus*)
Viburnum (*Viburnum* spp.), <u>88</u>, <u>92</u>, 170
  V. dentatum (*see* Arrowwood)
  V. dilatatum (*see* Linden viburnum)
  V. lentago (*see* Nannyberry)
  V. setigerum (*see* Tea viburnum)
  V. trilobum (*see* American cranberry bush)
Vinca minor. See Periwinkle (*Vinca minor*)
Vines
  bird-worthy, <u>166–67</u>, 167–68
  native fruiting, <u>96</u>, 96–97
  for nectar, <u>79</u>
Violets (*Viola* spp.), <u>165</u>
Virginia bluebells (*Mertensia virginica*), <u>79</u>
Virginia creeper (*Parthenocissus quinquefolia*), <u>88</u>, 96, <u>96</u>, <u>164</u>, <u>167</u>, 168
Virginia knotweed (*Tovara virginiana*), 174
Vitis spp. *See* Grapes (*Vitis* spp.)

Walnuts, birds attracted to, <u>36</u>
Washington hawthorn (*Crataegus phaenopyrum*), 95
Wasps
  birds attracted by, <u>109</u>
  nectar feeders and, 73
Water
  birdbaths, 142, <u>143</u>, 143–44
  birds attracted by, 142, <u>143</u>
  providing, 141–42
  sound of running, 144
  winter access to, 9
Watermelon, birds attracted by, <u>86</u>, 117

Waxwing
  Bohemian, **154**, **169**
  cedar waxwing (*Bombycilla cedrorum*), <u>94</u>, 277, <u>277</u>, **277**
Weeds
  allowing for bird-worthy, 174–76
  grasses, 169
  list of bird-attracting, 177
  for seeds, 176–77
Weevils, birds attracted by, <u>109</u>
Weigela (*Weigela florida*), <u>78</u>
West, birds of, 185
Western bluebird (*Sialia mexicana*), **192**, 192–93, <u>193</u>
Western larch (*Larix occidentalis*), <u>173</u>
Western sandcherry (*Prunus besseyi*), <u>91</u>
Western scrub-jay (*Aphelocoma californica*), 59, **110**, 232, **232**
Western tanager (*Piranga ludoviciana*), 263, **263**
Western white clematis (*Clematis ligusticifolia*), <u>166</u>
West Nile virus, 151–52
Wheat
  birds attracted by, <u>19</u>
  in seed mixes, <u>31</u>, 37
Wheatberries, <u>31</u>, 37
White ash (*Fraxinus americana*), <u>173</u>
White-breasted nuthatch (*Sitta carolinensis*), **187**
  profile of, 243, **243**
  seed-hoarding, <u>23</u>
  special treats for, <u>243</u>
White-crowned sparrow (*Zonotrichia leucophrys*), 259, **259**
White fringetree (*Chionanthus virginicus*), **171**
White millet seed
  appearance of, **28**
  bird species attracted by, <u>18</u>, 28–29
  growing your own, 29
  in seed mixes, 31
White-throated sparrow (*Zonotrichia albicollis*), **256**, 256–57
White-winged crossbill (*Loxia leucoptera*), 207, **207**
Wild turkey. *See* Turkey (*Meleagris gallopavo*)
Window decals, <u>134</u>
Windows, bird deaths from, <u>134</u>
Wineberries, birds attracted by, <u>88</u>
Winterberry holly (*Ilex verticillata*), 95, <u>171</u>
Winter feeding tips, 9
Wintergreen (*Gaultheria procumbens*), <u>168</u>
Wood borers, birds attracted by, <u>109</u>
Woodpeckers
  food choices
    corn, 34
    peanuts, 29

  sap feeding, 79
  suet, <u>10</u>, 51, <u>51</u>, **62**
  fruit feeders for, 87
  seed-hoarding, <u>23</u>
  special treats for, <u>283</u>
  species
    acorn woodpecker, 282, **282**
    downy woodpecker, **8**, **278**, 278–79, <u>279</u>
    Gila woodpecker, **72**, 283, **283**
    hairy woodpecker, **278**, 278–79, <u>279</u>
    pileated woodpecker, 109, 280, **280**, <u>280</u>
    red-bellied woodpecker, 281, <u>281</u>, **281**
    red-headed woodpecker, 282, **282**
Wood thrush (*Hylocichla mustelina*), 267, <u>267</u>, **267**
Wrens
  Cactus wren, 285, <u>285</u>, **285**
  Carolina wren, 284, <u>284</u>, **284**
  roosting in Boston ivy, 167

Xanthocephalus xanthocephalus. *See* Yellow-headed blackbird (*Xanthocephalus xanthocephalus*)

Yarrows (*Achillea* spp.), <u>165</u>
Yaupon holly (*Ilex vomitoria*), <u>91</u>
Year-round feeding, 8–9
Yellow-bellied sapsucker (*Sphyrapicus varius*), 254, <u>254</u>, **254**
Yellow-headed blackbird (*Xanthocephalus xanthocephalus*), 189, **189**
Yellow jessamine (*Gelsemium sempervirens*), <u>79</u>
Yellow-rumped warbler (*Dendroica coronata*)
  poison ivy berries and, 97
  profile of, 276, **276**
  special treats for, <u>276</u>
Yellow-shafted flicker, 108
Young birds. *See* Nestlings
Yucca (*Yucca* spp.), <u>165</u>
Yucca elata. See Soaptree yucca (*Yucca elata*)

Zenaida macroura. *See* Mourning dove (*Zenaida macroura*)
Zinnias (*Zinnia* spp.), <u>163</u>
Zonotrichia spp.
  Z. albicollis (*see* White-throated sparrow)
  Z. atricapilla (*see* Golden-crowned sparrow)
  Z. leucophrys (*see* White-crowned sparrow)

USDA Plant Hardiness Zone Map

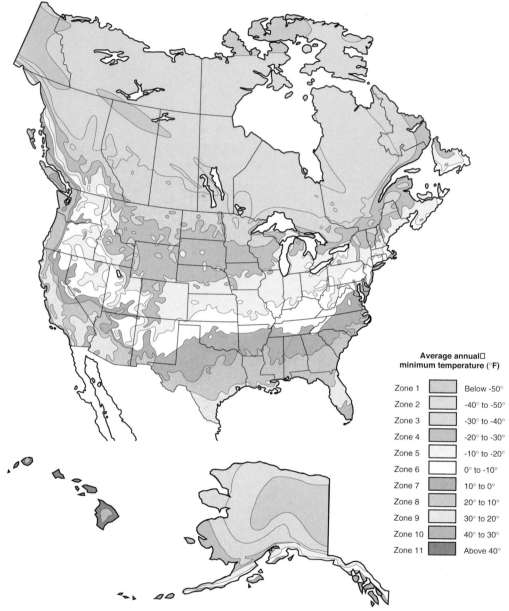

Average annual minimum temperature (°F)

Zone 1	Below -50°
Zone 2	-40° to -50°
Zone 3	-30° to -40°
Zone 4	-20° to -30°
Zone 5	-10° to -20°
Zone 6	0° to -10°
Zone 7	10° to 0°
Zone 8	20° to 10°
Zone 9	30° to 20°
Zone 10	40° to 30°
Zone 11	Above 40°

Revised in 1990 to reflect changes in climate, this map is now recognized as the best estimator of minimum temperatures available. Look at the map to find your area, then match its pattern to the key on the right. When you've found your pattern, the key will tell you what hardiness zone you live in. Remember that the map is a general guide; your particular conditions may vary.